HUNTING THE BISMARCK

MIROSŁAW ZBIGNIEW SKWIOT AND
ELŻBIETA TERESA PRUSINOWSKA

HUNTING THE BISMARCK

The Crowood Press

First published in 2004 by
AJ-Press, Gdansk, Poland

English edition published in 2006 by
The Crowood Press Ltd
Ramsbury, Marlborough
Wiltshire SN8 2HR

www.crowood.com

British Library Cataloguing-in-Publication Data
A catalogue record for this book is available from the British Library.

ISBN 1 86126 819 X
EAN 978 1 86126 819 8

Author's acknowledgements
We express our especial thanks to Mr Döringhoff of the Bundesarchiv/Militärarchiv in Freiburg for his help in obtaining archival sources of information on Operation *Rheinübung*.

English edition typeset by D & N Publishing, Lambourn Woodlands, Hungerford, Berkshire.

Printed and bound in Great Britain by Biddles Ltd, King's Lynn, Norfolk.

Contents

Comparative Table of Ranks

Kriegsmarine	*Royal Navy*
Grossadmiral	Admiral of the Fleet
Generaladmiral	Admiral (Fleet Commander)
Kapitän zur See	Captain
Fregattenkapitän	'Senior Commander'*
Korvettenkapitän	Commander
Kapitänleutnant	Lieutenant Commander
Oberleutnant sur Zee	Lieutenant
Leutnant zur See	Ensign
Oberbootsmaan	Warrant Officer
Obermachinist	Warrant Officer (Machinist)
Bootsmannsmaat	Petty Officer
Matrosenhauptgefreiter	Able Seaman
Machinengefreiter	Seaman Apprentice (Machinist)

NB Suffix '(Ing)' = Engineer

* No direct RN equivalent.

Introduction

How important the threat of the German battleship *Bismarck* was to the British is perhaps best shown by the statement delivered in the House of Commons by Prime Minister Winston Churchill in August 1940. He stated that, based on the most recent intelligence reports, the *Bismarck* had not yet been fully fitted out and made operational. Therefore she could not be deployed in the Atlantic as soon as the Germans would have liked. However, when she and her sister-ship *Tirpitz* entered service, the Germans would be very likely to gain a considerable naval advantage. Churchill's fears were shared by the RAF, which decided to carry out regular bombing raids on the German battleships *Scharnhorst* and *Gneisenau* at Kiel, *Bismarck* at Hamburg and *Tirpitz* at Wilhelmshaven, beginning in mid-August. Still, the *Bismarck* was the most vital target. A few months' delay in her entering service or leaving port would maintain the existing equilibrium of power between the Royal Navy and the Kriegsmarine, as long as Japan did not join the war. If Japan did join the Axis, the British would have to send a strong battleship force to the Far East, which would reduce their power in the Atlantic and the North Sea. Sending any warship away was out of the question. The only alternatives were either to speed up shipbuilding and fitting-out new vessels or to eliminate the enemy. The latter option seemed better and more feasible, as the British intelligence had estimated that the *Tirpitz* would be launched some three months after the *Bismarck*. This short period would allow a new battleship, the *Prince of Wales*, to be put into service, thus partly restoring the balance, for even though the older battleships *Nelson* and *Rodney* had a more powerful main battery than the *Bismarck*, their top speed of only 21 knots made them inferior to the latter in battle; the faster *Bismarck* could simply escape them at will. For this reason, they were not considered as effective opponents to the *Bismarck* or *Tirpitz*.

The time thus gained would let the British send the only battleship which could challenge the *Bismarck* – the *King George V* – to operate in the Mediterranean, to help support the nearly exhausted defenders of Malta. Until the next *King George V* class battleship, the *Prince of Wales*, entered service, the British had to maintain a large force of capital ships at Scapa Flow in the Orkney Islands. Their basic mission was to prevent the *Bismarck* from breaking out into the North Atlantic. The *Prince of Wales* was to be commissioned in the second half of March 1941. Until then, the *Bismarck*'s movements had to be closely watched. When a third battleship, the *Duke of York*, would be ready and a fourth, the *Anson*, shortly afterward, they would relieve most of the vessels assembled at Scapa Flow, allowing them to be sent to the Far East to

The battleship Bismarck *as seen in September 1940 in the Bay of Kiel. As can be seen, the fitting-out of the warship had not yet been completed, which would require another six months.*

Photo by Schäffer, via M. Skwiot

Via CAW

The Bismarck*'s launching ceremony took place on 14 February 1939, at the Blohm & Voss shipyard in Hamburg. As was the case with previous launchings, this event was also attended by numerous guests, among whom were high-ranking officers, politicians, shipyard workers and citizens of Hamburg.*
The Bismarck *is shown here a moment after she was christened. The battleship's hull is sliding down the No. 9 slipway into the dock.*

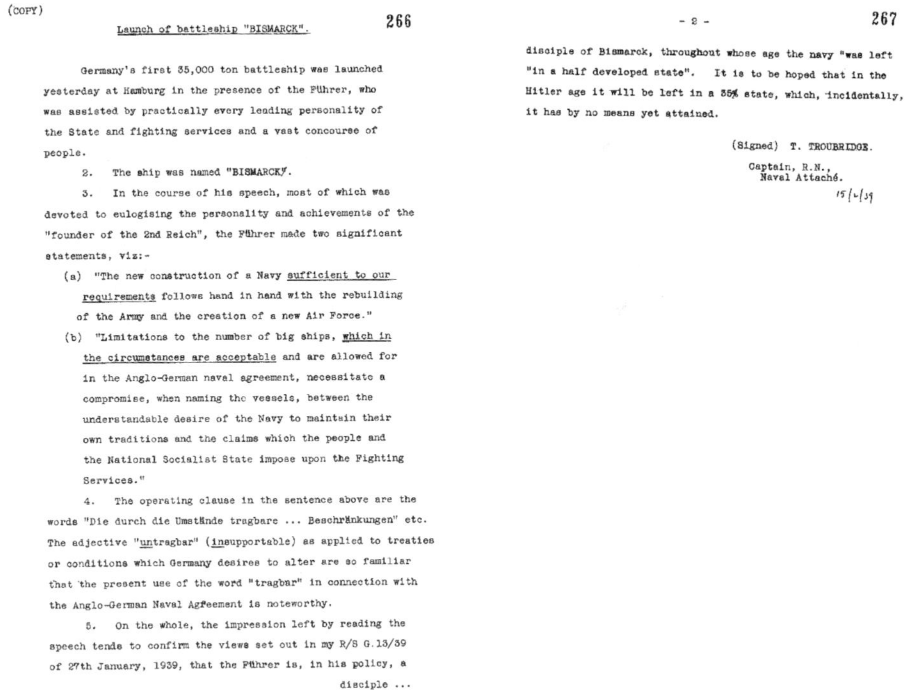

(COPY)

266

Launch of battleship "BISMARCK".

Germany's first 35,000 ton battleship was launched yesterday at Hamburg in the presence of the Führer, who was assisted by practically every leading personality of the State and fighting services and a vast concourse of people.

2. The ship was named "BISMARCK".

3. In the course of his speech, most of which was devoted to eulogising the personality and achievements of the "founder of the 2nd Reich", the Führer made two significant statements, viz:-

(a) "The new construction of a Navy sufficient to our requirements follows hand in hand with the rebuilding of the Army and the creation of a new Air Force."

(b) "Limitations to the number of big ships, which in the circumstances are acceptable and are allowed for in the Anglo-German naval agreement, necessitate a compromise, when naming the vessels, between the understandable desire of the Navy to maintain their own traditions and the claims which the people and the National Socialist State impose upon the Fighting Services."

4. The operating clause in the sentence above are the words "Die durch die Umstände tragbare ... Beschränkungen" etc. The adjective "untragbar" (insupportable) as applied to treaties or conditions which Germany desires to alter are so familiar that the present use of the word "tragbar" in connection with the Anglo-German Naval Agreement is noteworthy.

5. On the whole, the impression left by reading the speech tends to confirm the views set out in my R/S G.13/39 of 27th January, 1939, that the Führer is, in his policy, a

disciple ...

- 2 -

267

disciple of Bismarck, throughout whose age the navy "was left "in a half developed state". It is to be hoped that in the Hitler age it will be left in a 35% state, which, incidentally, it has by no means yet attained.

(Signed) T. TROUBRIDGE.

Captain, R.N.,
Naval Attaché.

15/4/39

A report on the launch of the Bismarck *by Captain Troubridge.*

Via A. Jarski

protect the threatened British possessions there. The British supposed that the *Bismarck* and *Tirpitz* would be completed toward the end of January 1941 at the earliest. It was also assumed that both ships would not begin operations for some time after that. RAF Bomber Command was determined to take the chance and put the *Bismarck* and the *Tirpitz* out of the game at all costs before they saw combat. A list was made of the most important strategic targets, which included German shipyards and naval bases at Hamburg, Wilhelmshaven, etc.

A very important British success was the cracking of the German Enigma code, allowing their cryptologists to read enemy messages. The first code they deciphered was the Luftwaffe's, but when cipher machines, code books and rotors were captured in May 1941, they very quickly broke the code used by the Kriegsmarine. This allowed for the destruction of the German seaborne resupply system for surface raiders and submarines. Most of the support vessels involved in Operation *Rheinübung* ('Rhine Exercise') were quickly either sunk or captured. The first victim was the tanker *Gonzeheim*, intercepted and sunk on 4 June by the battleships *Nelson* and *Rodney*. On the same day, the heavy cruiser *London* sank the tanker *Esso Hamburg*. Soon afterward, more supply vessels were captured and sunk: on 12 June, the *Friedrich Breme* was intercepted by the *Sheffield*; three days later the *Lothringen* was taken by the *Dunedin*. The *Kota Pennang* managed to escape her pursuers in June; however, it was not for long – she was intercepted in the Indian Ocean in October by the cruiser *Kenya*. The destruction of the supply system put a stop to further operations. With very helpful American reconnaissance of the Atlantic by Catalina flying boats, it was practically impossible for the Germans to operate freely in the area.

The *Bismarck*'s career, particularly her fight to the last, has remained an important chapter in the history of Germany and Second World War naval operations. It still survives in the

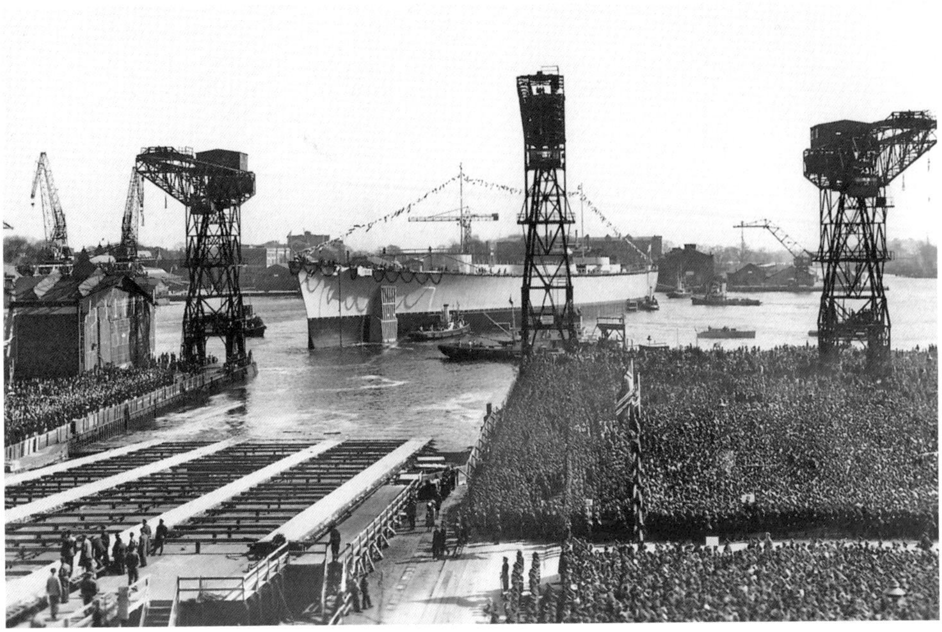

The hull of the Bismarck's *sister-ship* Tirpitz, *launched on 1 April 1939 from the No. 2 slipway of the Kriegsmarine Werft shipyard in Wilhelmshaven.*

Photo by Schäffer, via S. Breyer

Via S. Breyer

The Bismarck *at the fitting-out pier of the Blohm & Voss yard, photographed while completing fitting-out in August 1940.*

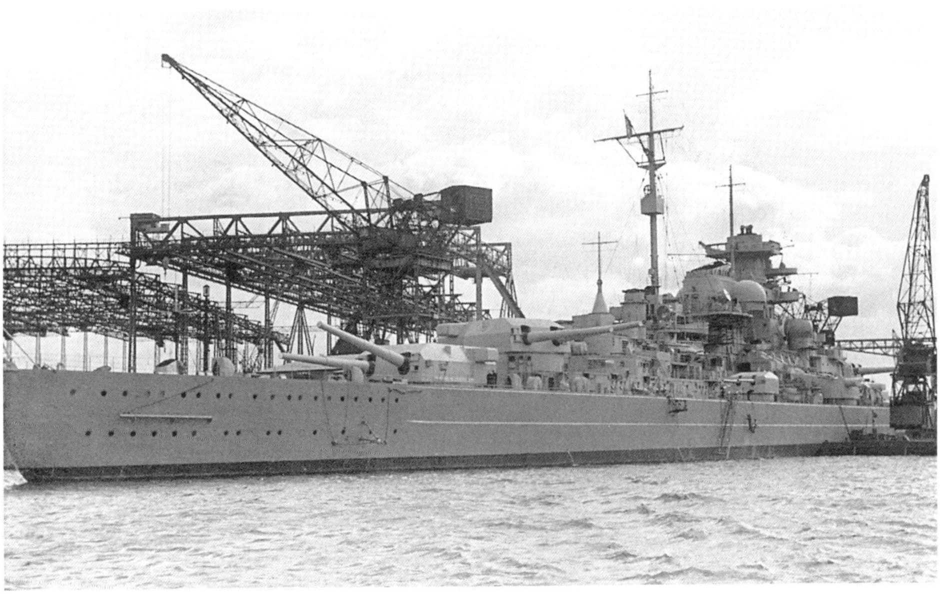

The battleship King George V *launched on 21 February 1939.*

Via CAW

Via S. Breyer

The forward superstructure of the Tirpitz *whilst being fitted-out in the winter of 1940/41.*

The fitting-out of the Tirpitz *was closely watched by the British, who were intent on delaying her commissioning. They carried out repeated air raids on Wilhelmshaven and the battleship anchored there. In order to make it more difficult for British reconnaissance to accurately assess the progress of her fitting-out, the ship was camouflaged. It was a very unusual camouflage indeed: applied to the deck and port side were images of buildings and a road matched in colour to the surroundings of the vessel. The photograph shows the early stage of repainting the ship to the standard scheme.*

Photo by Schäffer, via S. Breyer

The battleship Tirpitz *anchored off the lee side of Haakøy Island in Norway, just before Operation* Catechism, *which finally put her out of action.*

Via IWM

memory of many people, particularly those who participated in her battle in May 1941. Today – many years later, when top-secret documents regarding this operation have been disclosed, and when emotions and bias are gone – we can take one more look at the entire operation. It can be unhesitatingly said that the *Bismarck*'s crew honorably lived up to the maxim of the man after whom the ship was named, the Iron Chancellor Otto von Bismarck: *Partiae inserviendo consumor* ('Everything I did, I did for the Motherland'). Viewed in this light, the history of her sister battleship *Tirpitz* appears less interesting, she having spent most of the time in Norwegian fjords. It was there that she was finally defeated by aircraft, which dropped tons of bombs on her. Having continually served without leave for several years, the ship's crew were reluctant to continue fighting for Germany at the end of the war; there were cases of crewmen hiding inside the ship instead of standing to their posts.

Both sides had their weaknesses and failures that have not been mentioned for many years. We have tried to bring some of them to the reader's attention without passing comment on them. We have presented the plain facts for everyone to judge for themselves. We are aware that this subject has not yet been exhausted and much can be added. We leave that for later – perhaps a second, extended edition of *Hunting the Bismarck.*

Gdansk, 16 December 2003.

Via CAW

The battleship King George V *departing Chesapeake Bay on 24 January 1941. Her first mission had been to deliver the new British Ambassador, Lord Halifax, to the USA.*

The *Bismarck*

Bismarck's first crew began work in mid-April 1940, with engineer officers and a few dozen petty officers and enlisted men aboard. Two months later they were joined by gunnery personnel. They were the first to become familiar with the ship and its equipment. As usual, the petty officers were the busiest; with technical manuals in hand, burrowing away in the machinery, armament, pipes and valves, they were preparing a detailed training programme for the first crew. It was not an easy task, as the ship was still being fitted-out, and the 'provisional' crew had to make do with cramped living quarters aboard two depot ships, the *Oceana* and *General Artigas*. The men began an intensive course of study of the battleship, her powerplant and armament. They examined the ship in small groups, eagerly looking into individual sections, holds and rooms; they climbed the tallest masts and bridges, whereas at the lowest level they examined the tanks and compartments of her double bottom. The specialist subjects were supplemented by obligatory classes in general battleship service. Although these last were some of the most boring topics, they could not be neglected.

The first period of service on the battleship was spent in gaining knowledge of the entire ship, her machinery, armament, fire control systems and all the many other things vital for the proper functioning of a warship. The seamen studied combat and damage-control routines. These exercises began quite early and focused mainly on the procedure for quickly taking their assigned positions. As it was wartime, anti-aircraft drills were of equal importance. Particular emphasis was placed on constant repetition of the drills, as the crew had to become faster and more precise, and learn to carry out their assigned tasks almost automatically.

Commissioning

On 24 August 1940, the *Bismarck* was moored at the outfitting pier of the Blohm & Voss shipyard. The entire crew was on deck, assembled by divisions for the ship's commissioning ceremony. The officers made sure the ranks were correctly drawn up, and reported their readiness to the battleship's Executive Officer, Fregattenkapitän Hans Oels. Soon a white motorboat arrived with the ship's commanding officer aboard. All watched it slowly come alongside and tie up to a rope ladder at the starboard side. The Honour Guard presented arms, salutes were given, and the battleship's first commander, Kapitän zur See Ernst Lindemann, came aboard. Oels announced that the battleship's crew was ready for the hoisting of the flag. The commander walked in front of the crew and moved toward a dais on the bridge. In his short speech, he appealed to the

The fitting-out of the forward superstructure of the Bismarck *at the beginning of 1940. The picture shows 'Anton' and 'Bruno' 380mm turrets while fitting-out was being completed. In the foreground, the ship's capstans are covered with tarpaulins.*

From the Blohm & Voss archives, via Jörg Schmiedeskamp

crewmen to make the *Bismarck* fully operational in the shortest possible time. He expressed his gratitude to the shipyard workers for their devoted work during the building and fitting-out. When he finished, the German battle flag was raised at the stern and the commander's pennant hoisted at the mast.

The British closely monitored how the building of both battleships proceeded. They decided to attempt to delay the ships' entering service, and the only means of doing this was by air raids. The first of these took place when the *Bismarck* was in the Blohm & Voss yard. Two days after her commissioning, in the late evening of

26 August 1940, the ship's guns threw up a wall of fire: a total of fifty-two 37mm and 400 20mm shells were fired at the attacking aircraft but no hits were observed. The weather over the next two days worsened, hindering raids on the battleship. A very dark night and low fog provided the ship with good protection. Three air raid alerts had been issued for Hamburg by the end of the month, but it was only on 31 August that the ship again opened fire on the enemy with her 37mm guns, not scoring any hits. Early September saw preparations of the *Bismarck* to leave the Blohm & Voss yard; there were also more air raid alerts on the nights of the 1st, 3rd and 4th, but only on the 8th and 10th did British aircraft approach to within 1,500–2,500m (1,600–2,750 yards) of the ship, within range of her AA guns. As before, none of the attackers were hit. Attacks on the harbour and the battleship continued on the 11th, but without result for either side.

At 16:00 on 14 September, the *Bismarck* left her moorings for the first time and headed for Brunsbüttel Roads at the entrance to the Kiel Canal. At 16:58 on the 15th, just prior to her arrival, she collided with the tug *Atlantik*, but the disparity in the ships' sizes meant the battleship suffered no damage and she anchored in the roadstead at about 19:00. The evening that followed was not peaceful: there was another air raid but again no enemy aircraft were seen to be hit. The next day the *Bismarck* entered the Canal. Taking two days to transit the narrow passage, she moored at Scheerahafen in Kiel on the late evening of 17 September. This change of bases had been closely watched by the British, who had been hoping to score a hit; an air raid alert had been issued during the journey along

Via S. Breyer

The starboard bow of the Bismarck *as photographed in the summer of 1940 during the final stages of fitting-out at the Blohm & Voss shipyard. The picture provides a good view of the ventilation shafts on the starboard side of 'Bruno' barbette. In heavy seas, they were swamped by the waves. In order to prevent water entering them, they were modified so that the inlets were directed toward the stern and raised a little.*

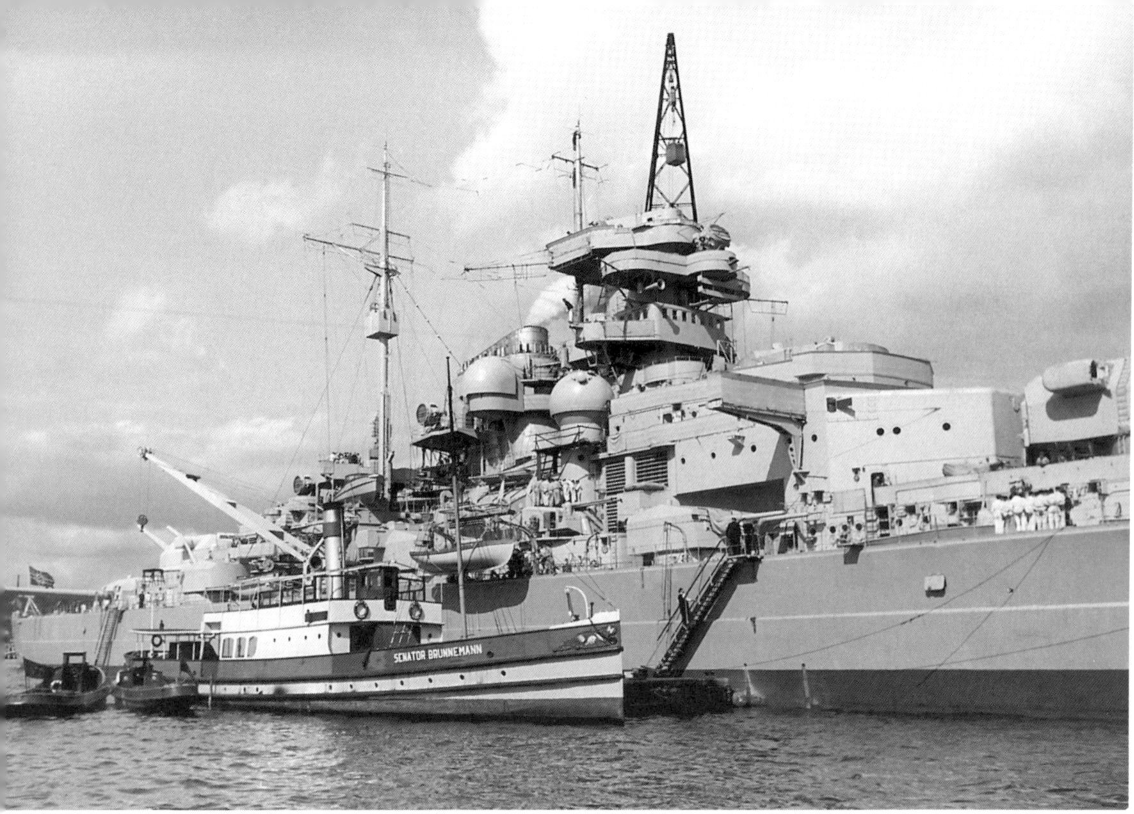

The Bismarck *completing fitting-out at the Blohm & Voss shipyard in August 1940. Some of the crew had already been on board since mid-April. These were mainly engineering officers, petty officers and sixty-five ratings. Two months later, they were joined by a sixty-strong gunnery crew. As fitting-out was still in progress, the* Bismarck's *'temporary' crew were not quartered aboard her but on two depot ships: the* Oceana *and the* General Artigas.

From the Blohm & Voss archives, via Jörg Schmiedeskamp

Via S. Breyer

The completing of the Bismarck *was sometimes filmed for propaganda purposes.*

Kapitän zur See Ernst Lindemann coming aboard for the Bismarck*'s commissioning ceremony on 24 August 1940.*

Via S. Breyer

Via CAW

Kapitän zur See Ernst Lindemann inspecting the crew.

The first days of September were spent preparing the battleship to leave the Blohm & Voss shipyard. Only on 15 September did the Bismarck *depart the shipyard, watched by numerous citizens of Hamburg, and head up the Elbe River. The photograph was taken at about 14:20, as the ship was casting off from the pier.*

Via M. Skwiot

Photo by Urbahns, via M. Skwiot

The Bismarck *steaming along the Elbe assisted by tugboats on 15 September 1940. Unfortunately, the battleship began this voyage with a collision with the tug* Atlantik, *which took place at 16:58.*

The Bismarck *headed for the Kiel Canal on the afternoon of 15 September 1940.*

Photo by Urbahns, via S. Breyer

Via S. Breyer

In the evening, the battleship reached Brunsbüttel Roads, where she dropped anchor at 19:20. However, that night was not peaceful, with an air raid alert issued in town and on the ship. It was only on the next day that the Bismarck *entered the Kiel Canal. After two days of sailing through the narrow passage, she moored at Scheerahafen in Kiel on the late evening of 17 September.*

The Bismarck *in the Bay of Kiel.*

From the Blohm & Voss archives, via Jörg Schmiedeskamp

Photo by Schäffer, via M. Skwiot

The Bismarck *anchored at the A12 buoy in the Heikendorf roadstead off Kiel. This photograph was taken sometime between 25 and 27 September 1940. Two seaplanes were already aboard the ship, and one can be seen on the catapult. They were coded T3+IH (serial no. 0052) and T3+AK (serial no. 0110).*

The Bismarck *in the Bay of Kiel* en route *to her base at Gotenhafen.*

Photo by Urbahns, via M. Skwiot

The Bismarck *at Kiel, heading for Gotenhafen. As can be seen, the battleship does not yet have her aft 105mm anti-aircraft guns mounted, nor the forward fire-control position for the main battery.*

Photo by Schäfer, from the Blohm & Voss archives, via Jörg Schmiedeskamp

Photo by Schäffer, from the Blohm & Voss archives, via Jörg Schmiedeskamp

The gunnery trials of the main and anti-aircraft batteries caused damage to parts of the superstructure, the ventilation system, and the main hangar gate. This damage could not be repaired at Gotenhafen, and her outfitting was still incomplete, so she had to return to the Blohm & Voss shipyard in Hamburg. She departed Gotenhafen on 5 December 1940, and headed for Kiel. On 7 December, the Bismarck *entered the Kiel Canal to moor at the shipyard pier in Hamburg two days later. This photograph was taken on passing through the Brunsbüttel sluice* en route *to Hamburg.*

While at Gotenhafen, the Bismarck *underwent intensive sea trials and combat training from early October, including full-speed tests, measuring fuel consumption, manoeuvring, and manual control. This photograph, taken in the second half of November 1940, shows that the aft 105mm guns had now been fitted.*

Via CAW

the Canal around noon. The next week was quite uneventful, and the crew were busy calibrating the armament.

Toward the end of the month, on the 28th, the battleship, escorted by *Sperrbrecher 13* (a *Sperrbrecher* was a converted merchant ship designed to clear mines ahead of other ships), moved to Arkona and then further into the Baltic, to her base at Gotenhafen (now Gdynia in Poland). Here, beginning in early October, the *Bismarck* underwent intensive sea trials and combat training. Navigation and high-speed trials were conducted along with measurements of fuel consumption. These tests proved that the ship handled well and was extremely responsive to rudder movements. The only difficulty arose with navigational stability when testing manoeuvring by means of propeller rotation control. Also during these trials, the manual control at speeds below 20 knots was readjusted because it required the strength of no less than thirty-two men to control the rudders. In the first half of October 1940, the captain made regular inspections of all departments. He was satisfied with the development of his crew's combat skills. Normally, this training would have taken about two years, but since there was a war on, the *Bismarck* could not wait that long.

In the meantime, the British had suspended further air raids until the ship reappeared in native German ports, because Gotenhafen was at the extreme range of their bombers. To their satisfaction, this absence was not long because, having finished sea trials, the battleship had to return to Blohm & Voss in Hamburg. The second wave of attacks began after she had returned from the Baltic, with a formation of thirty-one Wellington bombers attacking Hamburg and the warship on the night of 21/22 October 1940.

The heavy cruiser Prinz Eugen *undergoing sea trials in the Baltic Sea. As there are no fire control positions yet, the ship can only carry out speed tests.*

Via A. Jarski

The heavy cruiser Prinz Eugen *at Kiel, ready for commissioning. The ceremony took place on 1 August 1940.*

Via A. Jarski

Prior to her commissioning, the Tirpitz *had to be docked to have her hull below the waterline cleaned and painted. In this photograph, tugboats are helping her transfer from the Wilhelmshaven shipyard's fitting-out area to a floating dry dock.*

Via S. Breyer

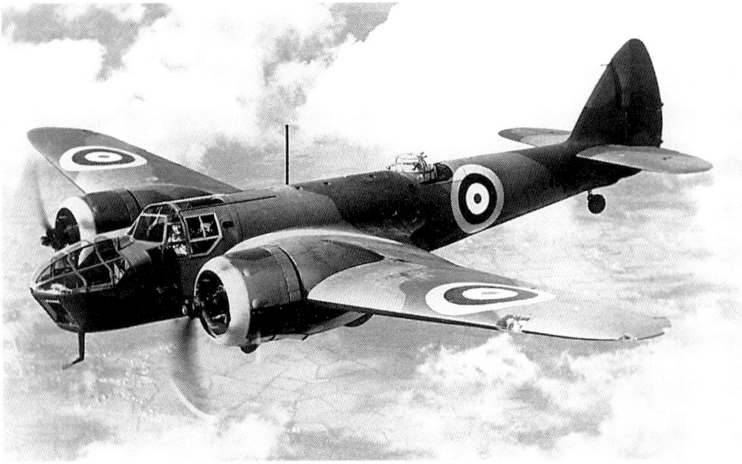

Via MAP

A Bristol Blenheim Mk IV.

Via MAP

A Handley Page Hampden bomber.

A Lockheed Hudson reconnaissance bomber.

Via MAP

Raids continued but had no effect apart from disrupting work at the shipyard to some extent.

November saw the *Bismarck* continuing her gunnery trials. Between 4 and 18 November, new 105mm anti-aircraft guns were mounted aft. At almost the same time, from the 14th to the 21st, the ship received 10m (33ft) range-finders. One was placed above the foretop, the other above the aft fire control position. Only then was it possible to conduct shooting trials with broadside salvoes, which was done from 25 to 27 November. The initial stage of battery trials, machine tests, calibration and co-ordination of fire control equipment ended in November. The problems revealed by the tests were, among others, strong vibrations at high speeds, inaccuracies in fire-control equipment, flooding of the ventilation shafts in the 'Bruno' turret barbette (*Bismarck*'s four 380mm turrets were named, from bow to stern, 'Anton', 'Bruno', 'Cäsar' and 'Dora') and both large machine-room ventilation shafts in the forward conning tower. Firing both the main and anti-aircraft batteries also affected parts of the conning towers, ventilation equipment and the main hangar door. These problems were too serious to be dealt with at Gotenhafen. On top of that, the fitting-out of the ship had not yet been completed. Therefore the battleship was sent back to Blohm & Voss in Hamburg. She set out from Gotenhafen on 5 December, heading for Kiel. At Ruegen Island she was joined by *Sperrbrecher 6*. Undisturbed in her westward passage, she safely entered the Kiel Canal on 7 December and moored at a shipyard pier in Hamburg two days later. From 10 to 22 December, shipyard workers and weapons specialists were correcting the defects, so most of the ships' crew were given leave for Christmas.

Freezing conditions gripped most of Europe in December 1940, and the Gulf of Gdansk and the Kiel Canal froze, forcing the *Bismarck* to remain at Hamburg. She stayed there for New

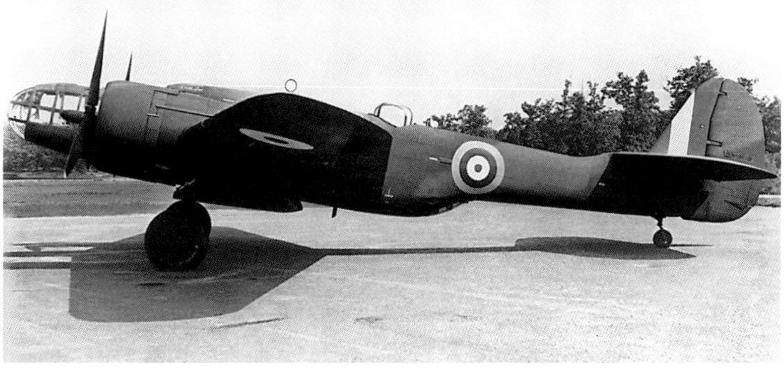

Via MAP

A Martin Maryland bomber.

An Armstrong Whitworth Whitley Mk V bomber of No. 102 Sqn RAF.

Via MAP

Year's Day and on until mid-January 1941. The continuing bad weather, especially the heavy frosts, were delaying the repairs of the battleship. Only on 24 January were all the scheduled jobs completed. Still, the frozen waters prevented any trials. Ready to move to another base, the ship was unfortunate: a steamer carrying ore through the Kiel Canal sank, thus blocking the entire canal to traffic. The removal of the wreckage was a slow job, and the thick ice did not help. The first realistic date when the *Bismarck* could be moved was 5 February. However, owing to the continuing ice cover and boiler damage due to low temperatures, the operation was postponed. The boiler damage was repaired by 16 February, but the Canal was still blocked by wreckage and ice, and the ship's redeployment was then set for 5 March.

❦

Operation *Berlin*

Gaining experience

The first attempt at Operation *Berlin*, the forerunner to Operation *Rheinübung*, began on 28 December 1940. Admiral Lütjens, commander of the fleet, departed Kiel aboard the flagship *Gneisenau* along with her sister-ship *Scharnhorst* and escorts that were to protect the group from enemy submarines and mines laid between the coasts of Norway, Denmark and Germany. The main purpose of the operation was to attack British convoys in the Atlantic, easy targets for the German battleships, as most were at that time escorted by small warships. The passage began in already very bad weather which worsened hourly. Strong winds and heavy waves sweeping over the deck caused some slight damage and completely prevented both optical and radar equipment from working. On top of that, the weather forecasts were not optimistic and warned about worse to come, which eventually made Admiral Lütjens give up the attempt to break through into the Atlantic. The ships took shelter in Korsofjord. The storm damage to the *Gneisenau* and *Scharnhorst* was serious enough for the authorities of Group North to order that the operation be cancelled and both vessels return to Germany. After minor repairs in Norwegian waters both ships headed for Germany. On 2 January 1941, the *Gneisenau* entered Kiel, where she underwent repairs, while the *Scharnhorst* dropped anchor in Neufahrwasser roadstead (now Nowy Port, a district of Gdansk).

Lütjens' second attempt began on the afternoon of 22 January 1941. Despite thick ice along the way, the ships safely made it into the Norwegian Sea without having to call at Norway. Owing to this move the German vessels were missed by British air reconnaissance, which regularly operated over the Norwegian coast. The weather forecasts the fleet was receiving predicted bad weather off Iceland, which was favourable for the German ships' passage, but the attempt of 27 January to pass between Iceland and the Faeroe Islands failed due to their being sighted by the British cruiser *Naiad*. The latter notified Admiral Tovey, commander of the British Home Fleet, about them, and capital ships were dispatched to intercept them. Admiral Lütjens was well aware that his battleships had been discovered by the enemy. He ordered a change of course, heading north for Jan Mayen Island to wait there a few days and try to make the passage once more but this time via the Denmark Strait. The lively exchange of radio signals between the British warships and air forces was being systematically intercepted and decoded. This kept the admiral informed about the wide-ranging search for his battleships.

British warships searching for the German battleships Scharnhorst *and* Gneisenau. *The photograph was taken from the battlecruiser* Hood.

Via M. Krzyżan

On 4 February the Germans sailed past Iceland, and by the next day were already safe in the waters of the North Atlantic, off Cape Farewell. They refuelled from the tanker *Schlettstadt* and commenced raiding operations. Their first target was Convoy HX 106 but the attack was a complete failure. After this misfortune, Admiral Lütjens returned to Cape Farewell to top up his ships' tanks. Lütjens' other adversaries in the operation were weather conditions and low temperatures. Rolling up to 50 degrees, the warships sustained damage to longitudinals, brackets and the connections between the deck and the barbettes. Small 1- or 2mm (0.4 or 0.8in) fissures were opened in the connection between the deck and B turret through which water flooded into the ship. Water flooding the decks and conning towers put most of the anti-aircraft guns out of action, whereas the low temperatures caused the fire control equipment on both battleships to malfunction. Bad luck haunted Lütjens until 22 February, when smoke and masts were spotted on the horizon. It turned out that two merchant vessels had come their way. Having no escort, they proved easy prey and were quickly sunk. After this successful event, an Arado floatplane was catapulted from the *Gneisenau* to reconnoitre the surrounding area, as the Germans were hoping for more targets. Lütjens was right – more ships were soon found. By evening, the German flotilla had sunk a total of five vessels.

Nearly a month passed before the next success. On 15 March 1941, they managed to sink six lone ships sailing completely unescorted off the American coast. The evening that followed proved to abound in victims, a total of ten having been sunk by the end of the day! The Germans' winning streak was broken by the battleship *Rodney*, part of the escort of Convoy HX 114, coming upon the German flagship. However, no clash with the *Gneisenau* resulted, as the faster German ship sailed from under her nose at the last moment, leaving her far behind. A later British attempt to set up an ambush and intercept the German flotilla as it was returning to Germany or France failed. The ships safely made Brest, entering port on the early morning

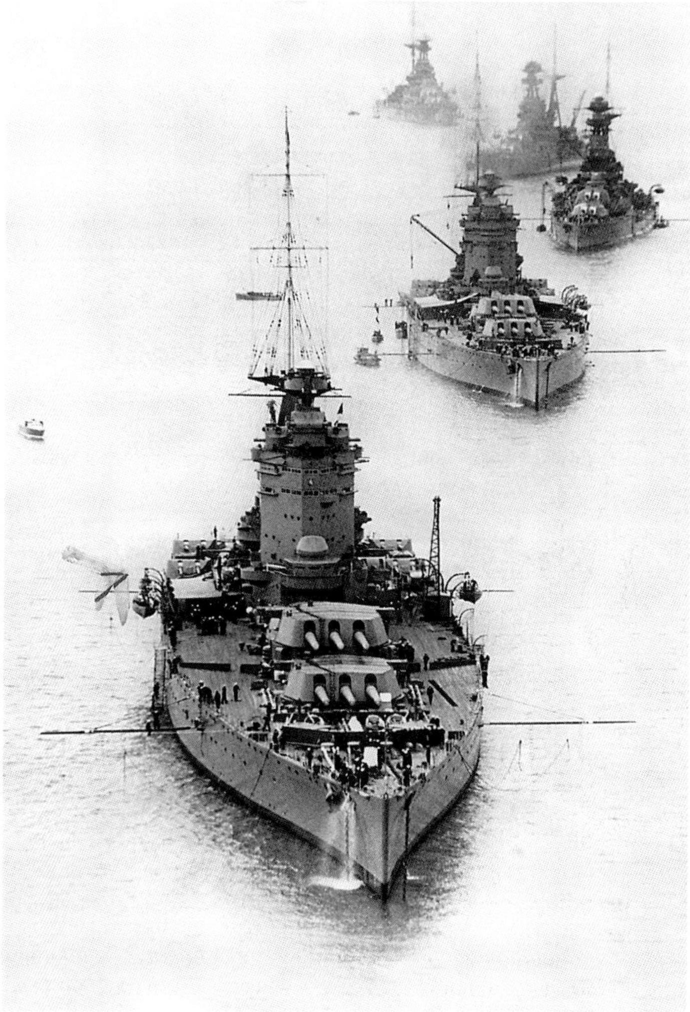

British battleships at anchor. The Nelson class battleships in the foreground had to concentrate at Scapa Flow in order to prevent German battleships from breaking out into the Atlantic Ocean.

Via CAW

The battleship Scharnhorst *in Wilhelmshaven in the summer of 1939 after completion of her refit, which took place at the Kriegsmarine Werft. The refit included the fitting of the new 'Atlantic' bow, replacement of the funnel cowling and the installation of a new tripod mast aft of the aircraft hangar. The refit, carried out between June and August 1939, was to prepare the ship for raiding activity in the Atlantic.*

Via M. Skwiot

of 22 March 1941. This operation was a reasonable success for the Germans, the battleships sinking twenty-two ships totalling some 115,622 tons in their 59-day cruise.

However, the most important thing gained was experience, which would help Admiral Lütjens plan further and more wide-ranging raiding cruises. Operation *Berlin* had shown that heavy surface ships required air reconnaissance and more information on every convoy to be attacked. German intelligence intercepted messages and signals from Allied merchant ships and warships and decoded them at once. The information on their routes and scheduled convoys was forwarded to the Naval War Staff (*Seekriegsleitung*, abbreviated SKL), and from there on to the U-boat and surface naval flotillas currently operating in a given zone

The battleship Gneisenau *in Kiel Bay photographed in May 1939, just after her refit at the Deutsche Werke shipyard. It included the rebuilding of the bow hawse-holes and replacement of the existing radio mast, previously mounted on the rangefinder.*

Photo by Urbahas, via M. Skwiot

Via S. Breyer

The monotony of searching for enemy convoys was from time to time interrupted by an encounter with a supply vessel or a submarine. In the picture, the Admiral Scheer *is seen as photographed from the* U-boat U-66. *Such meetings were usually very short and concerned refuelling and delivery of provisions, and a very important event in the everyday lives of all sailors – long-awaited letters from home, which were delivered by supply ships.*

The pocket battleship Admiral Scheer *as seen from* U-66.

Via ADM

Via IWM

The heavy cruiser Admiral Hipper *entering Brest after a raiding cruise in the Atlantic.*

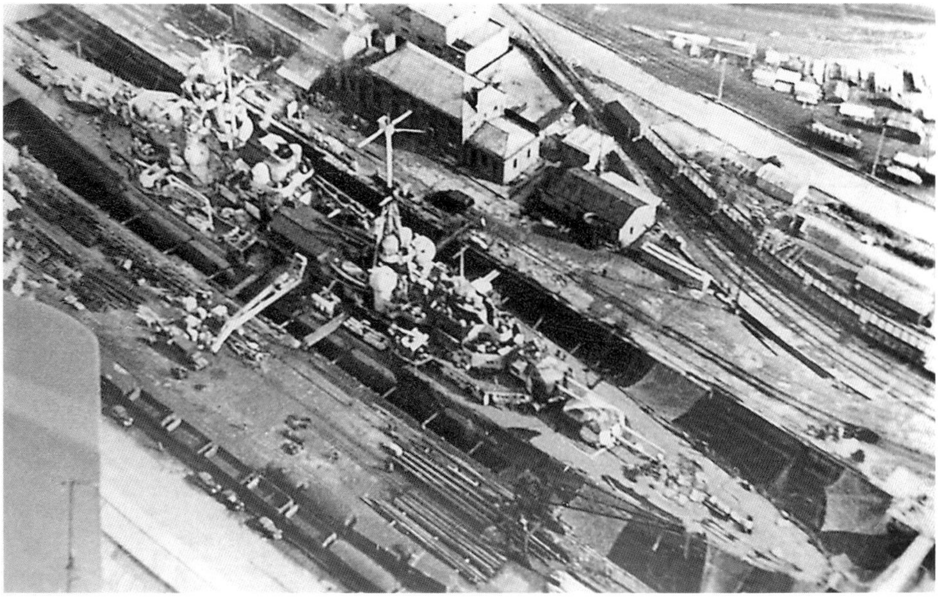

On return from her raiding cruise, the Admiral Hipper *had to enter dock to undergo repairs. Her seaplanes carried out regular exercises throughout that period. This photograph, with the cruiser in dock, was taken during such an exercise.*

Via A. Jarski

Via M. Skwiot

Another view of the Admiral Hipper *in dock. This one was taken from the pier.*

The Kriegsmarine adapted small auxiliary vessels for weather patrol duties in the Denmark Strait.

Via T. Klimczyk

They were to send information about the current weather conditions as well as detailed reports concerning the shifting boundary of the floating ice. In order to navigate, valid data on the width of the ice-free passage was needed.

Via CAW

Via CAW

Apart from that, these vessels also reported on mines laid by the British navy and on enemy naval patrols.

The battleship Gneisenau *in the Hjeltefjord, off Bergen, while making the first attempt to begin Operation Berlin. On 30 December 1940, this operation was called off owing to the damage that the ship had sustained; together with her sister-ship Scharnhorst, the Gneisenau returned to the Baltic.*

Via CAW

providing the basis for the commander on the spot to formulate his plan of attack. Reconnaissance by ship-borne seaplanes had proved very helpful because they provided accurate real-time reports on the attacked convoy, its escort and the courses of individual ships (by this means, even after a convoy had scattered, the individual ships could, in theory at least, all be tracked down and sunk). Apart from this, it was indispensable to employ special patrol vessels,

Photo by Dr. Wehlau, via A. Jarski

The Scharnhorst's *forward superstructure (April 1940 off Wilhelmshaven). The battleship is carrying characteristic markings to facilitate her rapid identification so that German aircraft did not mistake her for an enemy vessel. These included national flags painted on the bow and stern decks, and specific colours, different from the rest of the ship, applied to the tops of the main and secondary battery turrets.*

The battleships Gneisenau *and* Scharnhorst *in Trondheim roadstead in the summer of 1940. This harbour was a good starting point for operations in the Norwegian Sea and the North Atlantic.*

Via CAW

The Gneisenau *as seen from her sister-ship* Scharnhorst *while on their longest raiding voyage – Operation* Berlin, *commenced on 28 January 1941.*

Via M. Skwiot

so-called '*Spähschiffe*', to report on ships, convoys and reconnaissance aircraft present in the sea zone they were assigned to.

Before another operation commanded by Lütjens began, two freighters, the *Gonzeheim* and the *Kota Pennang*, were chosen to be appropriately equipped and adapted for long service at sea (at least four months) as support ships for the surface raiders. They could accommodate naval personnel and could take up to 300 prisoners from captured or sunk enemy merchant ships. The *Gonzeheim* left Stettin on 11 April *en route* to Holland, when she was diverted to the Wilton shipyard in Schiedam. The adaptation of the ship took about two weeks. In order to participate in Operation *Rheinübung*, both vessels

Via M. Skwiot

During Operation Berlin *the commander of the force, Admiral Lütjens, had several U-boats directly under him, which were supposed to be co-operating with the surface vessels. This photograph shows the* Gneisenau *as seen from* U-124 *in mid-Atlantic on 6 March 1941.*

Encounters with German submarines were always a welcome event for both parties. Every such occasion was a nice change from the monotony of searching for the enemy. The U-boat could refuel and receive fresh supplies, while those of the battleship's crew who were not on duty had an opportunity to talk for a while with the real 'sea wolves'. Such meetings were rare, though, and did not last very long. Such, too, was the case in this picture – on receiving information, the submarine quickly submerged. Shown here is the moment of the farewell to U-124.

Via S. Breyer

Via CAW

The Gneisenau *in a stormy Atlantic during Operation* Berlin. *This photograph was taken from her sister-ship.*

The battleship in search of British convoys during Operation Berlin.

Via CAW

The Gneisenau *in the stormy waters of the Atlantic. This view of her between the waves was also taken from her sister* Scharnhorst, *and, like the previous photographs, the radar antenna has been removed by the censor.*

Via CAW

Via CAW

One of the few views of the battleship taken during Operation Berlin *which show the stern painted a different colour than the rest of the hull – the other side was probably painted the same. For identification by German aircraft, the tops of the main and secondary battery turrets were painted yellow.*

The Gneisenau *mooring at a pier at Brest on 22 March 1941. Operation* Berlin *lasted for fifty-nine days without interruption and resulted in both warships sinking or capturing ships totalling 115,622 tons. On entering the base, the battleship immediately underwent repairs and modernization, which was to take about three months. For the British forces, this was a unique opportunity to put the battleship out of commission.*

Via S. Breyer

had to be ready by 26 April. They sailed under the German flag but were commanded by officers assigned from the *Gneisenau*.

Weather patrol ships were of vital importance. Returning to Germany in March 1941, the heavy cruisers *Admiral Scheer* and *Admiral Hipper*

Photo CAW

PoWs from sunk British ships disembark from Scharnhorst, *moored at Brest, France.*

found such ships patrolling the Denmark Strait. Their duty was to provide information on current weather conditions and detailed reports about the shifting of the floating ice boundaries; data on clear passage were indispensable for navigation in the Strait. Additionally, these ships reported on minefields and British naval patrols. But the Commander of Group North, Admiral Carls, believed that weather patrol ships would be at too much risk operating there. He insisted that submarines be used for this purpose. In the end, the deployment of the small trawler *Sachsen* into that area was decided on; the loss of a small trawler would be less costly than that of a large specialist weather patrol vessel. When there, the *Sachsen* could send direct, real-time reports on the weather to Lütjens' flotilla as it headed for the strait. The *Sachsen* left Trondheim on 16 March 16 and immediately steered for her assigned patrol area, some 555km (300 nautical miles) east of the Langanes Peninsula. Another ship dispatched for a similar purpose was the small trawler *Coburg*, which was stationed in the Davis Strait off Resolution Island, between Canada and Greenland. The *Sachsen*, so far patrolling the Danish passage, was to be replaced by the *Coburg*, advancing in her direction. A message that the latter later received from Group North ordered her to leave the Davis Strait and head for the Denmark Strait.

Another extensive report on the weather and ice conditions in the Denmark Strait came from air reconnaissance carried out on 27 March by Luftwaffe aircraft based at Trondheim. However, the greatest amount of detail was provided by the *Coburg* as she returned to Germany via the Denmark Strait. The activity of both these small vessels is worthy of note. The information they passed to the German staff was of great value, just as it was for the enemy: when decoded, it revealed to them with a high degree of probability what surface and submarine operations the SKL was planning. The British regularly intercepted and deciphered messages, trying to locate the source and then catch the enemy in an ambush they set up. Only when destroyed or captured could the German vessels be prevented from sending their seemingly unimportant, but in fact vital, meteorological information. At the turn of March 1941 the trawlers *Hohmmann* and *Sachsen* were operating off Iceland, carrying out meteorological duties; the latter was later replaced by the *Ostmark*.

Weather patrols could also be performed by long-range aircraft such as the Fw 200 Condor. They could provide the most up-to-date information about the weather in the strait. However, their operations could be hampered by the very weather they were to report on, and sometimes they would not be able to take off at all because of it. Also, their weather data were not very reliable; they recorded conditions at only certain altitudes, not at sea level, which they could estimate only in good visibility. This was a great inconvenience for the SKL, which had to rely on uncertain weather forecasts from air patrols.

Preparing for the Operation

The *Bismarck*

On 6 March, the *Bismarck* left the Blohm & Voss yard and steamed down the Elbe, dropping anchor in the Brunsbüttel Roads about noon. She was accompanied by a tanker and two *Sperrbrechen* which anchored in the roadstead alongside the battleship, thus forming protection against possible torpedo attack. On her way to Brunsbüttel, an air escort had been provided by three fighters. Next day the *Bismarck* entered the Kiel Canal, reaching the Kiel roadstead on 8 March. She remained there for several days, having the light anti-aircraft battery calibrated. Under the supervision of her Administrative Officer, Korvettenkapitän Rudolf Hartkopf, the *Bismarck* took on all necessary provisions. Ammunition for the main and the anti-aircraft armament was also loaded, and on the 15th, two of her designed complement of four seaplanes were taken aboard. Next day, the ship left Kiel, heading east for Gotenhafen. As the western Baltic was still icebound, the group was led by an ice-breaker, followed by the old battleship *Schlesien*, with *Sperrbrecher 36* and the *Bismarck* astern of her. The ships dropped anchor in the roadstead of Gotenhafen on the afternoon of 17 March. There she began to prepare for operations.

The days that followed were spent in intensive full-speed trials, measuring fuel consumption and range, and testing echo-location equipment (GHG and NHG) fitted in the bows. The devices sent out single impulses which were reflected by obstacles in their way, allowing their precise distance and location to be plotted. The hydro-phone operators also practised recognition of the sounds emitted by various types of ships. How-ever, most of this time was taken up with practice shoots with the main and secondary batteries. The ship's commander, Ernst Lindemann, expected high performance and strict discipline from the gun crews, and trials and practice shoots were conducted by both day and night.

On 19 March, the *Bismarck*'s commander received new secret information from Kapitän zur See Topp, captain of the *Tirpitz*, saying that the SKL were planning to deploy the *Bismarck* on her first mission within the next three or four weeks, which was earlier than initially assumed. At this stage, the ship could not be made operational before the end of April. Considering what he had learnt, Lindemann rapidly cut the anti-aircraft training programmes for the battleship provided by the *Artillerieversuchskommando* (Gunnery Testing Command). He organized the training in such a way as to finish it on 2 April 1941. A highly-skilled gunnery officer himself, he decided to supervise this training personally. This period served to

Cleaning the main gun barrels aboard the Prinz Eugen *– not one of the sailors' favourite jobs.*

Via M. Skwiot

increase discipline among the anti-aircraft crews, vital for the new ship facing her first action. As scheduled, the gunnery trials were finished at the beginning of April. In the meantime, the *Bismarck* had practised shooting at both surface and aerial targets, as well as shoots with the heavy and secondary batteries at towed targets. The ship practised submarine searches with the 24th *Unterseebootsflottille*, while refuelling at sea was practised with the tanker *Bromberg*. The battleship had begun exercises with her searchlights, which consisted of aiming at targets or, as the seamen would call it in their naval slang, 'catching' a target on its first entering the light beam, and subsequent identification of the illuminated object at night. Strong emphasis was put on keeping the beam on the target as the battleship steamed along at low and medium speeds.

The delays in both finishing work on the *Bismarck* and the *Tirpitz*'s commissioning on 25 February 1941, put off the date of both battleships beginning operations as planned by the SKL. Unfortunately for the *Tirpitz*, there were delays in deliveries of equipment and problems with the engines, and it was not until April that the ship underwent her first sea trials, the results being unsatisfactory owing to problems with the starboard turbine assembly. On top of that, the Berlin-based Kreiselgeräte GmbH was late in supplying the anti-aircraft fire control positions, further delaying the ship from reaching combat readiness. Finally, the lack of rangefinders excluded the ship from any naval operations at least until the middle of the year. Thus, in the first quarter of 1941, the SKL could only operate three of the expected four vessels. The *Scharnhorst* and the *Gneisenau* spent eight weeks in the waters of the central and North Atlantic raiding Allied shipping in Operation *Berlin* (*see* Chapter 2). When the warships arrived at Brest on 22 March 1941, they both needed immediate repairs and improvements as well as installation of additional equipment. But the German battleships were to be markedly unfortunate:

Via M. Skwiot

The forward main turrets of the Prinz Eugen *were named 'Graz' and 'Brunnau'. This is one of the few colour photographs showing the tops of the turrets as being painted carmine during the cruiser's sea trials in the Baltic.*

The superstructure of the Prinz Eugen, *photographed in March 1941. Note the lack of SL-8 anti-aircraft fire control positions. They had not been installed aboard by the time of her departure on the operation.*

Via AJ-Press

upon receipt of an intelligence report on 27 March, RAF Coastal Command dispatched a reconnaissance patrol that quickly located the warships at Brest. A preventative air raid was mounted against them immediately. Failing to score hits on the first day, the British continued bombing the next day, hoping to eventually put both vessels out of commission. Fortune soon smiled on the British, whom French agents had informed that the German warships would remain at Brest for at least three months because of the necessary repairs and improvements. This chance was not missed, and regular 'carpet-bombing' attacks commenced against the docked German warships. The advantage was that the aircraft had a relatively short distance to travel, thus allowing them to carry more bombs in place of fuel. In any event, the base at Brest was already on the RAF's list of German military installations to be regularly attacked.

Early April saw the first of a series of heavy raids on the dry docks in which both warships sheltered. As before, no direct hits were observed. But when one bomb, which fortunately for the Germans failed to explode, fell into one of the docks, the *Gneisenau* was moved to a mooring at a buoy in the Rade Abri roadstead, about 400m (450 yards) from the dry dock. This change of location resulted in the

The Prinz Eugen*'s crew applying camouflage to their vessel while she was at Kiel.*

Photo by Lagemann, via AJ-Press

British scheduling a torpedo attack on the battleship and preventative mining of the roadstead. Carried out on 6 April, this attack left the *Gneisenau* hit on the starboard side at sections IV and V. Another heavy raid was carried out by forty-seven aircraft on the night of 10/11 April 1941, and it was another success for the British. The *Gneisenau* took four direct bomb hits, which ruled her out of the operation scheduled for April. Inspecting the ship on 14 April, Admiral Lütjens estimated that the work would take at least four more months. The *Scharnhorst*, too, required urgent repairs and, as a result, would be out of service until the end of June. In this way, the strike force organized by the SKL had been reduced to just one warship. There still was the heavy cruiser *Prinz Eugen* 'in reserve', which, like the *Bismarck*, was undergoing final sea trials and could be employed for the planned operation. The plan of operations for spring 1941 in the North Atlantic had assumed the participation of four major surface units: the *Bismarck* and *Tirpitz* (based in German ports) and the *Scharnhorst* and the *Gneisenau* (based at Brest). According to the plan, both groups were to have assembled in the Atlantic so as to form a powerful task force, an invincible one, in fact. The *Bismarck* and the *Tirpitz* were to have concentrated on attacking escort ships, while the *Gneisenau* and the *Scharnhorst* would have attacked and sunk all the merchant ships in a convoy. However, the British raids on the German bases thwarted these plans, successfully putting two of the battleships out of the game. With no other options open, it was decided that the battleship *Bismarck* would operate in company with the newly-commissioned heavy cruiser *Prinz Eugen*.

Enigma

A vital factor in the course of Operation *Rheinübung* was radio communication between German warships in the Atlantic and their headquarters. Such messages were also valuable for the enemy; on decoding them, they could deduce with a high degree of accuracy what surface and underwater operations the SKL was planning. The navy used a cipher machine named Enigma, but their version differed slightly from the army and Luftwaffe versions, which the British codebreaking centre 'Ultra' at Bletchley Park had been reading for some time. The history of this unit dated back to before the war, when the French and the British had received a Polish-built copy of a machine modelled on the German Enigma from Polish intelligence. Polish intelligence and their co-operating mathematicians had worked out part of the encoding system. They successfully decoded Luftwaffe messages until the end of 1940. The only problem was to crack the naval key, M-3. It soon turned out that the early months of 1941 were a time of great success for the British in this area. On 3 and 4 March 1941, seven German transports were sunk during a British attack on the Lofoten Islands, but the

Gunnery drill with the forward turrets of the Prinz Eugen *– the results were very good – was one of the most important skills to learn prior to setting out on operations.*

Photo by Lagemann, via CAW

greatest achievement was the capturing of an Enigma machine from the armed German trawler *Krebs*; the boarding party from the destroyer *Somali* also captured a current abridged setting sheet with message keys.

Two months later, on 7 May, a weather patrol trawler, the *München*, was intercepted to the south of Jan Mayen Island by a group of British destroyers and cruisers. A boarding party was able to recover the Enigma before the ship sank. Two days later, off Greenland, the British managed to capture another complete Enigma with codes and documents used for communication between U-boats and headquarters. The German submarine *U-110* was ferociously attacked by convoy escorts, severely damaged and obliged to surface. The boat's commander, Kapitänleutnant Fritz Lemp, ordered the men to abandon ship and leave her to sink. However, the British managed to get on board before she went down and take the Enigma from the radio room. The commander, who was in the water with the other survivors, saw that the U-boat was sinking too slowly, and decided to swim back to the boat and destroy the cipher machine. But on seeing this, the British shot him dead before he could reach the submarine. This particular Enigma and the documents obtained earlier by the British allowed them to break the code and accurately decipher German signals from the period preceding Operation *Rheinübung*.

Operation *Rheinübung*

On 2 April, Captain Lindemann of the *Bismarck* received an operational order (B.Nr.1.Skl. I Op. 410/41 Gkdos Chefs.) concerning the battleship's participation in an operation planned by the SKL. Basically, the document laid out tactical guidelines for future naval operations carried out by Kriegsmarine surface vessels. The operations carried out by such ships during the winter of 1940/1941 had been satisfactory, according to the SKL. Even though the *Scharnhorst* and the *Gneisenau* had only sunk twenty-two merchant ships, their appearance in the North Atlantic had obliged the British to concentrate a greater number of capital ships in the operational area of both German battleships. This in turn badly affected the entire system of convoy protection. From that moment on, every Allied convoy had to be accompanied by at least one capital ship – a battleship or a battlecruiser. The German response came soon. The Kriegsmarine decided to introduce newly-commissioned surface vessels into the North Atlantic as soon as possible. Item Two of the document announced a new campaign to be launched in the summer of 1941 and codenamed Operation *Barbarossa* (the invasion of the Soviet Union). Some of the surface fleet, therefore, would be involved in support of this offensive and thus would not be available for deployment in the North Atlantic. It was impossible at this stage of

Photo by Busch, via AJ-Press

The Prinz Eugen *moored at a pier at Kiel preparing for the operation. Details of the starboard side of the superstructure are clearly visible. Note again the lack of anti-aircraft fire control positions.*

Maintenance on the port torpedo launcher of the Prinz Eugen.
Via AJ-Press

the war for the Kriegsmarine to gain surface supremacy in the North Atlantic, principally because of the small number of capital ships they had (and many of these were under repair or incomplete), meaning they were unable to wrest control of the main sea lanes from the numerically superior British Home Fleet. However, like the Germans, the British were too in need of more capital ships. With the German battleships having appeared in the Atlantic, they had to have at least one battleship and one aircraft carrier in readiness at Gibraltar, a further drain on their already limited resources in the Mediterranean.

Item Three was the most important for Operation *Rheinübung*, as it provided instructions regarding the operations of the *Bismarck*, the *Gneisenau* and the heavy cruiser *Prinz Eugen*. The *Bismarck* and the *Prinz Eugen* were to begin the operation in early April, at the time of the nearest new moon. The *Gneisenau* would be by then still undergoing repairs and outfitting, but on their completion she was to leave Brest and join the *Bismarck* near the Azores, taking a long curving route. The *Prinz Eugen* was assumed to spend most of the time operating with the *Bismarck*, or the *Bismarck* and the *Gneisenau*. The warships were to cover the area north of the

The Tirpitz *during machinery trials in the Baltic, March 1941. The battleship is still without the forward fire control position and the 10m (33ft) rangefinder, which was not fitted in the foretop until May.*

Via S. Breyer

Equator. The rest of the order contained detailed instructions for the relevant warships and supply vessels. However, the most vital point of the order was that the main objective of the operation was to destroy enemy merchant shipping, and warships where to be engaged only if the further pursuit of the main aim of Operation *Rheinübung* was not jeopardized.

In company with the *Prinz Eugen*

At the end of March the *Prinz Eugen* left dock at Kiel, where she had had additional equipment installed on the admiral's bridge. On 8 April, she sailed to Gotenhafen to prepare for the coming operation. In the calm waters of the Bay of Gdansk, at the measured mile marker of Neukrug (Pilawa), the *Prinz Eugen* ran full-speed trials. It was then that the SKL established the first viable date for the operational deployment of both ships – late April. The tactical command of the group was to be taken by Admiral Günther Lütjens. He in turn was directly controlled by the SKL in Berlin, Group North in Wilhelmshaven and Group West in Paris.

On 13 April, the *Bismarck* left Gotenhafen for Kiel, where she stayed for a few days to replenish ammunition supplies and for minor repairs to the engine room. The main turbine was too loud, and the noises had to be reduced. Furthermore, high speeds were causing dangerous vibrations affecting the operation of the directors for the main battery. During this voyage, the *Bismarck* carried out combat exercises – simulating an attack on a convoy escort composed of battleships. The *Bismarck* 'received' two hits during this process, and damage that could have been sustained in real combat was also simulated: a rapid power failure in the ammunition feed systems of all the guns, explosions in various sections of the ship, and a fire which wreathed the entire ship in smoke. There were several simulated problems at various sections which served to test the damage control parties' procedures and the performance of the entire young crew. The individual teams reported to the first damage control officer in the command post at section XIV. In this way, the ship's commanding officers would quickly learn about all the damage she had sustained.

Order 100/41 A 1

An annex to the SKL order 100/41 A1 that Lütjens received on 22 April 1941 chiefly envisaged the destruction of the greatest number of enemy merchantmen sailing for Britain. The experience of the *Scharnhorst* and *Gneisenau* had shown that despite the possession of detailed information on their routes, convoys were difficult to locate. Therefore it was decided to attack ships sailing alone, which would be located by the raiders' own catapult-launched seaplanes. The rest of the document outlined the procedures that the *Bismarck* and the *Prinz Eugen* had to follow when attacking a convoy. The experience so far gained had revealed that single capital ships – battleships or battlecruisers – had been used as escorts for convoys. It was logical to assume that this would still be the case. If so, Group West envisaged the *Bismarck* engaging the escorting battleship so as to increase the *Prinz Eugen*'s chance of success in fighting the rest of the escorts or the merchant ships of the convoy. The first thing in an attack on a convoy was to immobilize as many ships as possible and then begin to sink them. There should be no rescue efforts, as this might place the German ships in danger. If need be, the smallest ship of the British convoy should be spared and ordered to take care of survivors. Particular emphasis was put on lone ships, of which fast motor ships and refrigerated cargo vessels were of the greatest importance to the Germans. They were to be manned by prize crews and sailed to French harbours whether or not they carried any cargo, and the conditions they had to meet *en route* to French harbours were specified in detail. Detailed instructions were also provided in case the enemy attacked the ships in attempts to retake them. The operational order from the Fleet Chief dispatched the *Bismarck* and the *Prinz Eugen* to the North Atlantic to carry out an operation codenamed *Rheinübung* (Rhine Exercise).

Damage to the *Prinz Eugen*

Because of the weather in the Denmark Strait, Operation *Rheinübung* was to be launched by the end of May 1941 at the latest. The Arctic latitudes during this period were in semi-darkness instead of the darkness of perpetual night, and allowing safer passage through the Strait, where small icebergs broken off Greenland could prove a serious obstacle. The short ice-free period of about a month should have been taken advantage of. But this was not to be.

On 22 April, with her trials completed, the *Prinz Eugen* left Gotenhafen for Kiel escorted by the *Sperrbrecher Rothenburg*. In the late afternoon, after they turned for the Bay of Kiel, there was an underwater explosion in the wake of the escorts, about 20–30m (22–33 yards) ahead of the cruiser off the starboard bow. The blast wave shook the entire ship and she rapidly lost steam and all power. Manual control was applied at

Via CAW

The Commander-in-Chief of the Kriegsmarine, Grossadmiral Erich Raeder.

The Tirpitz *during her first gunnery exercises in May 1941.*

Photo by Drüppel, via S. Breyer

once, and the starboard engine was quickly repaired. However, the bow gyro-compass and the degaussing gear were temporarily put out of action. Twenty minutes later, the ship's engineer, Kapitänleutnant Graser, reported from the centre turbine room that all turbines would be working within the next twenty minutes. The damaged *Prinz Eugen* then slowly sailed to the Deutsche Werke shipyard in Kiel. On entering dock, she underwent detailed examination and repairs. The blast had split open fuel tanks, fractured the mounting of one turbine, and affected the propellers and shafts. It had also knocked out the electronics of the fire-control system. The exact cause of the explosion is unknown, but it was most probably caused by a mine, which RAF aircraft regularly dropped in the area. The cruiser had to remain in dock until 2 May, and transferred to Gotenhafen nine days later.

After the *Prinz Eugen* was damaged, the plans for Operation *Rheinübung* had to be changed. There were three options: the first was for the *Bismarck* to set out on her own during the next new moon; the second was to postpone departure until the subsequent new moon, as both could then sail together; the third, dis-regarding the phase of the moon, was only to delay the departure of the cruiser and dispatch her as soon as her repairs were completed. The commander of Group North, Generaladmiral Carls, was inclined toward the first option, while the SKL was for the third. On the morning of 25 April 1941, the *Bismarck* was given the order to leave Gotenhafen on the evening of 28 April, along with the *Prinz Eugen*. The pair was to be escorted in their passage to the arctic waters by the 6th Destroyer Flotilla. But that afternoon Lindemann received another message from Fleet Command, postponing the operation by at least twelve days owing to the *Prinz Eugen*'s hull damage.

In the meantime, on 26 April, Admirals Lütjens and Raeder met in Berlin to discuss the operation. The problems with the *Prinz Eugen* issue gave them an occasion to reorganize the task force for South Atlantic operations. Lütjens saw no reason to change the established complement of ships, considering the *Bismarck* and the *Prinz Eugen* a well-matched team; with the cruiser soon to be available, the operation could wait until the next new moon. The deployment of the *Bismarck* alone seemed too risky. Lütjens recommended waiting until the *Scharnhorst* was operational or, best of all, until the *Tirpitz* was commissioned. However, the *Scharnhorst*'s engines were still out of service, while the *Tirpitz* had not yet been completed and fitted-out. Thus, there was no vessel to replace the *Prinz Eugen* for the time being. In the course of the discussion, Lütjens fully agreed with Raeder that a strong force of warships had to be deployed against the enemy. Only a strong and well-matched team could challenge British warships. Besides, he was aware that it was not the wisest thing to argue with the official standpoint of the SKL, as that might lead to a premature end of one's naval career.

Adolf Hitler at Gotenhafen

On 28 April, Lindemann notified the Naval High Command, Group North, Group West, and the Fleet Command that the *Bismarck* was fully prepared and equipped for the scheduled operation. On 1 May, Admiral Lütjens received a telephone call from Adolf Hitler's Naval Adjutant, von Puttkamer, informing him of the Führer's decision to personally inspect the *Bismarck* and the *Tirpitz* at Gotenhafen on 5 May. The ships were carefully prepared for this visit. When the day came, the *Bismarck* was at anchor in the Gotenhafen roadstead, where the fleet tender *Hela* brought the visitors to the battleship. Adolf Hitler came on board the *Bismarck* with Generalfeldmarschall Wilhelm

Via M. Skwiot

The Tirpitz *during a break in sea trials,* en route *to Kiel Bay. The photo was taken in the first half of July 1941.*

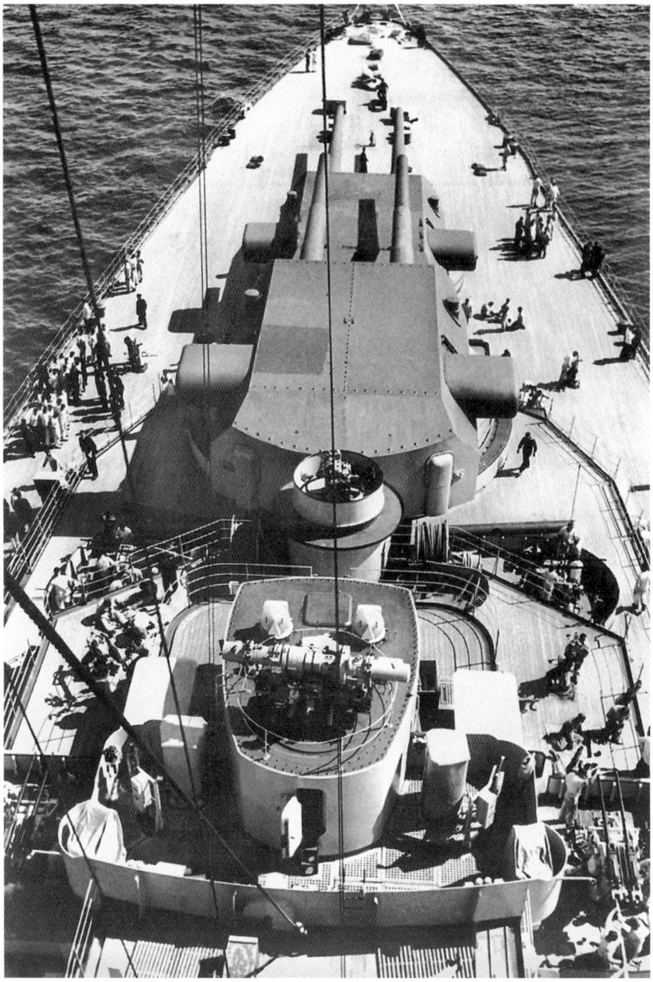

The Tirpitz*'s stern photographed from the main mast. In the foreground, an EM II rangefinder installed on the aft fire control position; in the background, main turrets 'C' and 'D'. The photo was taken in June 1941, during a break in sea trials in the Baltic.*

Via M. Skwiot

Via M. Skwiot

Admiral Günther Lütjens inspecting the crew of the Prinz Eugen *in May 1941 at Gotenhafen.*

The light cruiser Leipzig *helped in the preparations of the* Bismarck *and the* Prinz Eugen *for Operation* Rheinübung.

Via A. Jarski

Ready for the mission, the cruiser leaves Kiel for Gotenhafen.

Via M. Skwiot

Via CAW

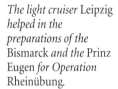

When the Bismarck *was ready for action, her sister* Tirpitz *was still conducting gunnery trials, shown here.*

The battleship being inspected by Admiral Raeder.

Via CAW

Keitel, von Puttkamer, his Air Adjutant von Below, and others. The guests were shown around the ship by Admiral Lütjens himself, in a detailed inspection that took about four hours. Hitler spent some time in the after control position, where he received a thorough explanation of the equipment installed there. The visit ended in a short conference in the Admiral's quarters. Admiral Lütjens informed the group about the positive results of the South Atlantic mission by the *Scharnhorst* and the *Gneisenau.* He was very optimistic about the operations to be carried out by the *Bismarck* class vessels. On Hitler's comment that a fight with numerous British warships might be a great risk for the German vessels, Lütjens replied that the *Bismarck* was at the moment superior to any British warship, and that she would certainly emerge victorious from an engagement with other battleships. He openly admitted, though, that the torpedo planes of the British aircraft carriers were a serious threat to the ship that could not be ignored. Hitler listened to the report in silence, but with an anxiety inside. The Führer was afraid to lose such a state-of-the-art battleship as the *Bismarck* was at the time. After this meeting, the guests were served dinner and a short discussion between Hitler and the senior officers followed about the current situation and the possibility of the United States entering the war. The Führer's negative attitude to the *Bismarck*'s deployment to the Atlantic alarmed Admiral Raeder and the SKL. They were worried that the Führer might cancel the *Bismarck*'s mission and therefore endeavoured to keep her departure a secret as long as they could, and so it was only on 22 May that Hitler was informed about the departure of the *Bismarck* and *Prinz Eugen.*

Final trials in the Baltic

On 12 May, the Fleet Staff, some sixty-five strong, came aboard the *Bismarck*, and conducted familiarization exercises with the crew. Admiral Günther Lütjens was Fleet Commander, and his Chief of Staff was Kapitän zur

See H. Netzbandt. Besides them, there were three staff officers, an engineer, a physician (surgeon), intelligence officers (B-Dienst) and a few young officers and petty officers. On 13 May, the intercom announced to the crew a planned inspection and drills on board under the Fleet Staff's command. Before noon, the staff led practical exercises and very closely inspected the ship's internal communications system linking the various command posts. The results were satisfactory, and the staff left the *Bismarck* in the afternoon to return to Gotenhafen on board the *Hela*. On the same day Admiral Lütjens ordered additional refuelling exercises with the *Prinz Eugen*. He wanted this procedure to be performed perfectly. These exercises comprised passing the fuel-oil hose from the *Bismarck*'s bow to the cruiser and transferring to her fuel from the battleship's tanks. Such a situation arising in battle conditions was undesirable but had to be practised just in case. After the cruiser had refuelled, the *Bismarck* was supposed to immediately begin her own refuelling from the tanker.

Next day saw war games with the participation of the light cruiser *Leipzig*. A simulation of aerial combat was arranged in the Bay of Gdansk, with the *Bismarck*'s seaplanes being attacked by 'enemy' aircraft. With half of the exercise over, one of the Bismarck's seaplane-hoisting cranes broke down, 'putting a premature end to its service on board the ship'. The damage was severe enough for it to need proper repairs, and the battleship returned to the Gotenhafen roadstead. The crane incident was reported to the commanders with the conclusion that the ship

IWM

The battleships Gneisenau *(above) and* Scharnhorst *in dry dock at Brest as photographed by British aerial reconnaissance in December 1941. Both warships are covered with camouflage nets and tarpaulins.*

The Prinz Eugen *in May 1941, during final trials in the Baltic.*

Photo by Drüppel, via A. Jarski

would not be fully operational for some time. The Executive Officer, Fregattenkapitän Hans Oels, and the Electrical Engineer, Korvettenkapitän Wilhelm Freytag, discussed the problem in the briefing room. They both knew it would not be easy to complete the repair within a short time. The complete change of oil in the crane's hydraulic system was very difficult. Mechanics from the Demag crane factory were quickly brought to the ship and immediately set to work. Group North was not happy to receive yet another message from Lindemann announcing a delay. The time necessary for the repairs, and thus the delay to the operation, was estimated to be about three days.

Finally, on 16 May, Group North was informed of both ships' full readiness to commence Operation *Rheinübung* on 18 May. The Fleet

This photograph of the Bismarck *was taken from the* Prinz Eugen *in May 1941 as both ships teamed up to conduct sea trials in the Baltic Sea. These exercises were to co-ordinate the command of both ships with Admiral Lütjens' staff.*

Photo by Lagemann, via M. Skwiot

Command ordered that the ships enter the Great Belt on the night of 19/20 May 1941. Group North asked the Luftwaffe for a weather patrol to determine the limits of floating ice in the Denmark Strait on 19 May. The Admiral Commanding, Norwegian Sea, ordered that the tankers *Weissenburg* and *Heide* sail with 7,000cu m of fuel each and provisions for a month, and arrive in their assigned zones on 22 May at the latest. The *Heide* was a reserve vessel to the *Weissenburg*. The tanker *Wollin* was then stationed off the central stretch of the Norwegian coast. At the same time, the fleet tankers *Ermland* (with 9,366cu m of heating oil for the boilers) and *Spichern* (with 8,000cu m of heating oil and 3,000cu m of diesel oil) sailed from harbours in western France. They, too, steamed to their assigned positions. Additionally, five other tankers were assigned to Operation *Rheinübung*: the *Belchen*, operating in square AJ 26; the *Lothringen* in AJ 27; the *Esso Hamburg* in CD 32; the *Breme* in DF 96; and the *Weissenburg* off Jan Mayen Island.

The Prinz Eugen *practising taking the* Bismarck *in tow on 13 May 1941, during exercises preliminary to Operation* Rheinübung. *The same afternoon, Lütjens also ordered the* Bismarck *to practise refuelling with the* Prinz Eugen, *a procedure the Admiral wanted both crews to be expert in.*

IWM

Bibliothek für Zeitgeschichte

The Bismarck *as seen from the foredeck of the* Prinz Eugen. *This photograph was taken during a joint exercise in the Baltic in May 1941.*

The Bismarck *during sea trials in the Baltic. This photograph is one of the few in which it is noticeable that the top of 'Anton' turret A is a different colour from the other turrets, probably carmine but this is not certain.*

Via M. Skwiot

One of the more famous photographs of the Bismarck *taken from the* Prinz Eugen. *Until recently, it had been assumed that it shows the beginning of Operation* Rheinübung, *but this is not the case. The German warships took up cruising formation only after they had passed Rügen Island, positioning themselves quite far one behind the other (about 1.5km/1 mile). In this photograph, the distance between them is a only few cables.*

Via M. Skwiot

Via AJ-Press

Adolf Hitler decided to personally inspect the Bismarck *and the* Tirpitz *at Gotenhafen. This photograph, taken on 5 May 1941, shows the tender* Hela *delivering the guests to the* Bismarck. *They were shown around the battleship by Admiral Lütjens. The detailed inspection of the ship took almost four hours.*

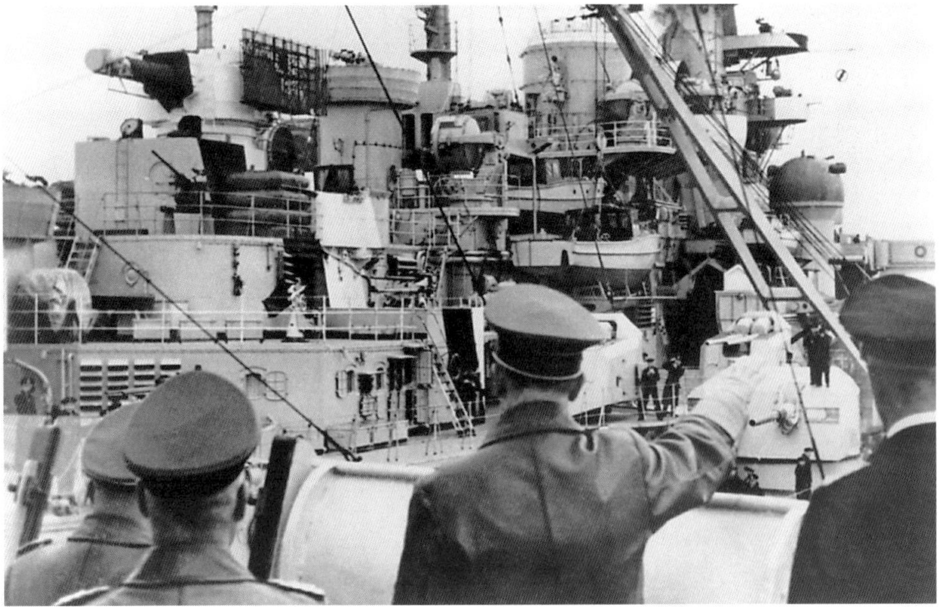

After visiting the Bismarck, *Hitler visited the* Tirpitz, *moored at the Dworzec Morski (boat terminal) pier at Gotenhafen.*

Via S. Breyer

The aft turrets of the Prinz Eugen *carried striped camouflage. This photograph was taken while she was at Gotenhafen.*

Photo by Busch, via AJ-Press

The Prinz Eugen *setting out from Gotenhafen for more practice at sea.*

Photo by Busch, via AJ-Press

Via M. Skwiot

Admiral Lütjens inspecting the crew of the Prinz Eugen *in May 1941 at Gotenhafen. This convinced him that the ship's crew were ready for operations despite the ship not being completely fitted out.*

Via M. Skwiot

Admiral Lütjens inspecting the crew of the Prinz Eugen *in May 1941 at Gotenhafen.*

One of several German tankers assigned to Operation Rheinübung *departs for her operational area.*

Via CAW

Via AJ-Press

The commander of Operation Rheinübung – *Admiral Günther Lütjens.*

Via AJ-Press

Kapitän zur See Ernst Lindemann, captain of the Bismarck.

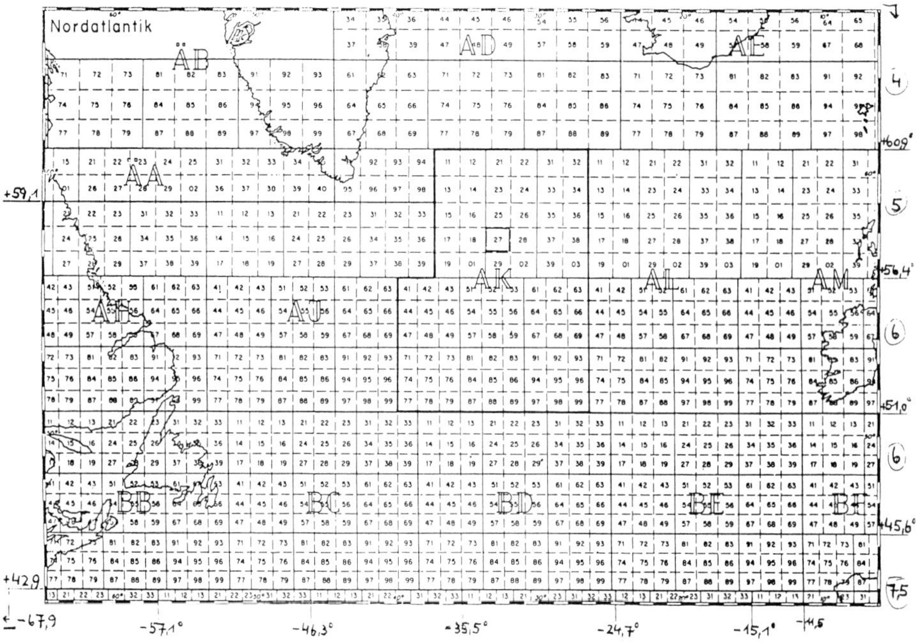

Grid squares in the North Atlantic.

Operation *Rheinübung* Begins

Preparations

From the afternoon of 17 May, no-one was permitted to leave either ship and preparations for refuelling were made. First of all, the tanks had to be cleaned of sediment and refilled. On 18 May, at a conference aboard the *Bismarck*, Lütjens revealed to Lindemann and Brinkmann the last details of the operation. The Admiral was planning to lead the group to the Norwegian Sea and on to the Denmark Strait between Iceland and Greenland to eventually enter the Atlantic. They agreed that, weather permitting, the group would first refuel in Norwegian fjords without meeting the tanker *Weissenburg*. That location would give them three possible options for breaking out into the ocean. The Luftwaffe was to make a detailed reconnaissance of Scapa Flow and provide cover to the group during the passage. From the beginning Admiral Lütjens favoured the route via the Denmark Strait because he had taken it successfully aboard the *Gneisenau* in his previous operation. The floating ice boundary in this passage could help the German ships hide from enemy radar and aerial reconnaissance, while the Germans could make use of their own radar and take advantage of their ships' speed. The arctic mist should cover the vessels in their quick dash through the strait. It was assumed that any enemy cruisers and auxiliary cruisers they encountered would be attacked by the German force. The dash would have to be made in complete radio silence. The existing camouflage schemes of the ships were to be retained until they had been identified by the enemy; they would then be changed to make future identification more difficult. Prize crews would be drawn first from the tankers' crews, not the warships'. When finally in the Atlantic, the warships would take fuel, ammunition and provisions from supply vessels present in their appropriate operational squares. The individual ships of the group were to assemble on 19 May off Rügen Island.

Around noon on 18 May, the *Bismarck* left her berth at Gotenhafen. The band on board played the traditional tune always heard when a ship set out on a long journey. However, this was not in fact to be the exact beginning of the operation. The ship dropped anchor in the roadstead in order to refuel – the tanks had to be full. The procedure was expected to finish about midnight, but the rubber refuelling hose was torn open during the process, and a compartment was flooded with fuel. The refuelling was halted and cleaning of the affected area began. After the broken hose was examined, it was decided not to repair it in order to avoid delaying her departure any longer and the refuelling was abandoned, so the *Bismarck*

The Prinz Eugen *in the roadstead of Gotenhafen in May 1941, several days before the operation began.*

Via W. Rusiniak

sailed 200 tons below her full fuel capacity of 8,924 tons.

At 11:12, the *Prinz Eugen* had been towed out into the bay. The tugs helped her to raise steam. But, steaming along in the shallow and muddy waters of the bay, her condenser became blocked, and this problem had to be rectified immediately, which took a few hours of hard work. In the evening, the *Prinz Eugen* was the first of the two ships to weigh anchor and set out on her journey. She joined the *Bismarck* next day.

Commencing the operation

On the night of 18/19 May 1941, at 02:00, the *Bismarck* weighed anchor and began her westward cruise, to the Great Belt. In the open sea the crew was briefed about their first operation. Morale was high. After months of preparations and regular trials, the first sortie had begun. The passage to the west was in overcast and moderate wind and seas. At 11:25 off Rügen Island she was joined by the *Prinz Eugen* and an escort consisting of the destroyers Z 23 and *Eckold*, and *Sperrbrechern 13* and *31*. Leaving Rügen, they

Via W. Rusiniak

The Prinz Eugen *anchored in the roadstead of Gotenhafen.*

Bismarck *as seen from* Prinz Eugen*'s deck.*

From P. Schmalenbacha collection

formed up off Arkona and began a voyage along the green route, and later took the red one toward the Great Belt. About 22:30, the squadron was joined by the destroyer *Hans Lody* (red point 05) with the commander of the 6th Destroyer Flotilla, Fregattenkapitän Alfred Schultze-Hinrichs, on board. The whole group headed north for the Great Belt and the Kattegat. The destroyer *Galster*, also intended to escort the group, did not participate due to machinery trouble. In order to make it more difficult for the enemy to discover the German ships sailing through the Danish straits, Group North halted all other traffic in the straits on the night of 19/20 May.

Unfortunately for the Germans, 20 May was a very clear and sunny day. The coast of Sweden and a multitude of Swedish and Danish fishing boats working in that area were clearly visible. It was also a great opportunity for British reconnaissance aircraft to fly patrols. It was almost impossible in this case to keep the sailing secret. British intelligence officers at the embassies in Stockholm and Helsinki reported

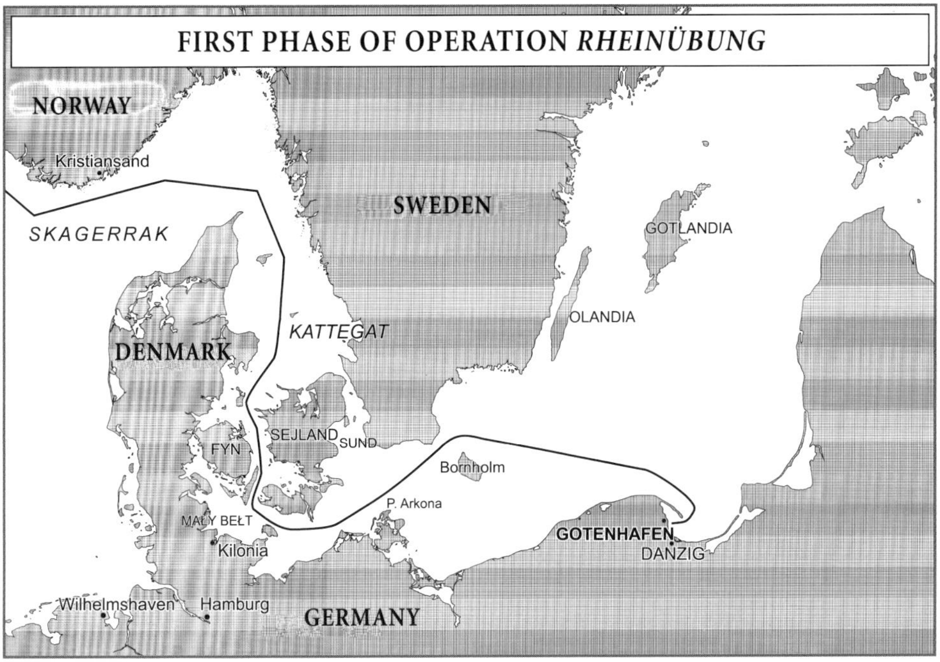

British battleships on patrol in the North Sea. In the foreground – the Revenge*; behind her – Queen Elizabeth class ships.*

Via CAW

all German operations in these waters. Since 15 March 1941, the British naval attaché in Stockholm had been informing the Admiralty in London about the preparations by German warships for a passage through the Great Belt. About noon, the ships had left the Great Belt behind. The Luftwaffe kept an eye on them throughout the entire passage, patrolling the skies above the flotilla. So far, no word of the German operation had reached British intelligence. The only witnesses were the boats fishing in these waters. But there were a lot of them out there, and Lütjens had no doubt the British would soon be informed of his ships. Then, the German squadron was sighted by the Swedish aircraft-carrying cruiser *Gotland*, which reported that it consisted of three *Leberecht Maas* class destroyers, one battlecruiser and one very large ship (this was the *Bismarck*). They were moving north, with ten to twelve aircraft overhead. The encounter took place about 22km (12 nautical miles) off the city of Vinga (west of Göteborg). The *Gotland* was sailing along the Swedish coast to starboard conducting gunnery exercises. Captain Ågren, the cruiser's commander, immediately reported the sighting to the senior naval officer in Göteborg and the information was forwarded to headquarters in Stockholm. Later, the *Gotland* reported once again, informing that the two German battleships and three *Maas* class destroyers had passed Nya Varvet about 13:00. On receiving this message, the British naval attaché to the embassy in Stockholm, Captain Henry Denham, informed London of the German sortie, giving the complement, course and speed of the squadron.

In the meantime, the *Gotland* had increased speed, staying on a course parallel to that of the Germans as far as the limit of Swedish territorial waters. On the *Bismarck*, Admiral Lütjens informed Group North about the *Gotland* passing nearby at 13:00. He assumed that their ships would be reported to the British. In reply, the commander of Group North, Generaladmiral Carls, reminded him of Sweden's neutrality and said that it was of no importance anyway, as the enemy had been constantly observing all passages of German ships through the Baltic straits and their presence could not have been kept a secret for much longer. Admiral Carls was not surprised by Lütjens' message because both he and the SKL knew that on 25 January the British naval attaché in Stockholm had reported the fact of the *Gneisenau* and the *Scharnhorst* having passed through the Belt to the Admiralty. He had been expecting that the passage of the other ships would likewise be reported.

After 13:30, the warships were joined by the 5th Minesweeper Flotilla under Kapitänleutnant Rudolf Lell. The minesweepers were to clear the way through minefields left by the British off Norway. The entire group slowed down to match the minesweepers' speed. Three mines were detonated, and some merchantmen waiting nearby took the opportunity to enter the now-cleared passage after the *Bismarck* and the *Prinz Eugen*.

The battlecruiser Renown *was one of the many warships watching the passage into the Atlantic. She participated in the hunt for the* Bismarck.

Via CAW

The Swedish cruiser Gotland *was the first warship to encounter the* Bismarck *and the* Prinz Eugen *as they passed the coast of Sweden.*

Via CAW

Photo by Busch, via AJ-Press

An escorting destroyer in the wake of the cruiser Prinz Eugen.

The German squadron approaching the Norwegian coast. The ship ahead of the Prinz Eugen *is the* Bismarck.

Via AJ-Press

The Bismarck *on the morning of 21 May 1941, as she was seen from astern entering the Korsfjord. Shortly afterward, the ship passed through the southern entrance and headed toward Bergen, eventually dropping anchor at the entrance to the Fjörangerfjord.*

From the Prinz Eugen *archives*

They were sighted by the British and mistakenly counted as part of Lütjens' force. Messages received by the British Admiralty reported merchant ships, which resulted in confusion about the 'real' purpose of the German ships.

About 15:45, the *Gotland* reported that the German vessels had passed out of sight to the north-west. The cruiser turned back at Marstand, leaving the Germans behind. Admiral Lütjens knew that now the *Gotland* had sighted them, in a few hours the Admiralty would be informed about their numbers and the intended route. Soon, the destroyer *Hans Lody* issued an air alert. The *Bismarck* was informed of the presence of British reconnaissance aircraft. It was the only encounter with British aircraft until entering Grimstadfjord. The *Bismarck* and the *Prinz Eugen* with their destroyer escorts steamed steering 300 degrees zigzagging at 17 knots. This speed allowed them to completely avoid British submarines hunting in these waters. In the evening, between 21:11 and 22:00, the Germans took the southern passage through the Kristiansand minefield. They were now making 27 knots, the 5th Minesweeper Flotilla having turned back to base. For all that time half of the batteries on each of the warships was at readiness. Passing the Kattegat and the Skagerrak, the destroyers arranged in an anti-submarine formation, with the *Hans Lody* leading, the *Eckold* to port, and

The German warships entering the Bergen fjord. In the lead, in the cover of light fog, is the Bismarck. *In order to make it more difficult for British reconnaissance to identify the German warships, the swastikas painted on the bow and stern were covered with tarpaulins. This photo of the* Prinz Eugen, *taken from her bridge, shows the tarpaulin covering the Nazi markings.*

Photo by F.O. Busch, from the Prinz Eugen *archives*

the *Z 23* to starboard. Aerial cover was provided by two He 115 seaplanes and six Bf 110 twin-engined fighters. On coming closer to the Norwegian coast, the group turned west.

As the German warships approached the south-west tip of Norway, the Swedish processed the information of their cruise. On the afternoon of 20 May, Captain Egon Tarnberg of Swedish Intelligence telephoned the 'C' department of the Main Army Headquarters in Stockholm, saying that two large German warships and a few auxiliary vessels had passed toward the Kattegat on that day, and then headed north toward the Skagerrak under air cover. He also delivered this message to the British embassy, which in turn radioed the Admiralty in London saying about two large warships escorted by three destroyers, five ships and ten or twelve aircraft had been sighted about 15:00 moving north-west. On the British side, the operational division of the Admiralty informed Coastal Command's HQ about the receipt of the message from the naval attaché in Stockholm. No. 18 Group, Coastal Command, was ordered to carry out immediate reconnaissance between Trondheim and Naze at dawn on 21 May. German Intelligence intercepted this order and on decoding it they found out that the British were looking for two large vessels and three destroyers.

The message sent to the *Bismarck* at 00:41 was good news because it was clear that the British had not yet located the German group. Shortly afterward, the ship received another report regarding the photo-reconnaissance of the Scapa Flow base at 12:50 on 20 May, which had shown one aircraft carrier, three battleships (one being the *Hood*), six light cruisers, two submarines, four destroyers, six freighters, two tankers and thirty-three small ships in port.

Entering Grimstadfjord

Lütjens' group continued the voyage north at full alert in the morning. The horizon was being watched more closely, and a larger sea area was being scanned, because British submarines were known to be patrolling in these waters. At 06:40, B-Dienst on the *Prinz Eugen*, supervised by Kapitänleutnant Hans Henning von Schultz, received and decoded a British signal about the search for the German group. Five minutes later a similar signal from the Naval High Command (Oberkommando der Kriegsmarine – OKM). was received on the *Bismarck* reporting a search for two battleships and three destroyers headed north. Then, at 07:06, while entering the Korsofjord, they were spotted by four RAF Blenheims of 254 Sqn. The first to see them was the pilot of aircraft 'H'. The *Bismarck*'s lookouts saw the aircraft formation but were unable to identify their nationality due to their distance and the blinding sunlight. Three minutes later, the *Bismarck* sailed into the Korsofjord. After passing the southern entrance, she headed for Bergen to eventually drop anchor at 09:00 at the entry to the Fjörangerfjord. The *Prinz Eugen* and the destroyers steamed further north, toward Kalvanes Bay. Steamships in the fjord anchored around the cruiser to serve as protection owing to the lack of anti-torpedo nets. In order to hamper the identification of the warships by British air reconnaissance, the swastikas painted on the deck at the bow and stern were covered with tarpaulins. Soon after, the tanker *Wollin* began pumping fuel into the *Bismarck*'s tanks. The *Bismarck*'s tanks had a much greater capacity than those of the *Prinz Eugen*, and since the cruiser had used up much of her fuel to cover the distance travelled, she was the first to be refuelled.

At 11:15, the ship received a message from Fleet Command with orders for 21 and 22 May. They were to continue heading north, keep the anti-aircraft and secondary batteries in readiness, and change the existing camouflage scheme to uniform light grey while in and departing the Korsofjord. When refuelling, they had already begun to change the striped camouflage to light grey on Lütjens' orders, a colour with matched the conditions in the Denmark Strait. As the white and dark grey stripes on both sides of the ship were painted over, a pair of Messerschmitt Bf 109 fighters patrolled the skies.

About 13:00, a single reconnaissance Spitfire flown by Michael Suckling appeared overhead. He was coming to the end of his sortie when he noticed the German warships anchored below. He took a number of photographs from which the British inferred that they were dealing with the battleship *Bismarck* and an Admiral Hipper class battlecruiser (i.e. *Prinz Eugen*). Judging by previous sorties by German warships, they assumed that this one was also aimed at breaking out into the North Atlantic. An air raid on Bergen and the ships anchored there was immediately ordered to prevent or at least delay their departure from the Norwegian fjords.

Meanwhile, Admiral Lütjens realized that his presence at Bergen had been discovered by the reconnaissance Spitfire. He decided that the *Bismarck* would not now refuel from the same tanker as the *Prinz Eugen* had done. He was aware that British bombers would arrive within hours, and he had already learned from his Intelligence Officer, Korvettenkapitän Werner Reichard, that his squadron was being hunted by the British. Reichard handed a message to him from headquarters in Germany which said that all RAF aircraft had been instructed to be on the alert for two German

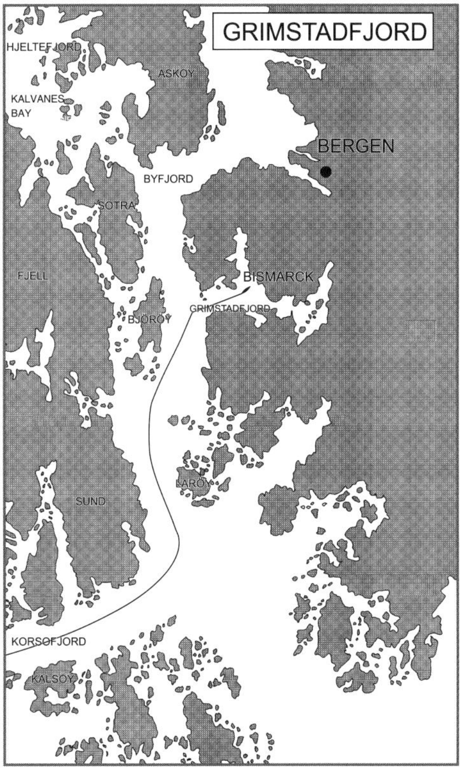

The Bismarck *entering the Grimstadfjord on 21 May 1941, photographed from the* Prinz Eugen.

Via AJ-Press

battleships and three destroyers which were reportedly moving north.

At 19:00, Admiral Lütjens ordered the squadron's departure from Norway. Half an hour later the *Bismarck* weighed anchor and sailed north to join the *Prinz Eugen* and the three destroyers outside Kalvanes Bay. The escort aircraft having turned back about 20:00 at the entrance to the Hjeltefjord, the group started north for Schasen at 17 knots. The ships took up a defensive formation, with *Sperrbrecher 13* leading, then the *Bismarck* and the *Prinz Eugen*, the *Sperrbrecher 31*, and the destroyers in the rear.

In the afternoon, a formation of six Whitley bombers of 612 Sqn RAF, ten Hudsons of 222 Sqn and two from 269 Sqn took off from British airfields to attack the German warships at Bergen. The weather over the fjords was very bad, and only two of the Hudsons succeeded in bombing the fjords and the anchored ships. The RAF prepared a force of thirty Hampdens of 42 Sqn, armed Beauforts at Wick with torpedoes, and alerted seven Albacores of 828 Sqn Fleet Air Arm, but bad weather in Britain grounded the aircraft and also prevented any reconnaissance sorties, with an overcast of 10/10 at 30m (100ft) altitude. The weather in the North Atlantic

Via Dr A. Price

A reconnaissance Spitfire PR ID.

The Bismarck *on 21 May in the Korsfjord. This picture was taken by the reconnaissance Spitfire flown by Michael Suckling.*

Via A. Jarski and IWM

J.G.D./TM

SECRET
22nd May, 1941.

APPENDIX 'A' OF INTERPRETATION REPORT NO. 1490.

SORTIE NO. N/183

LOCALITY:- BERGEN AND ADJACENT FJORDS – HERLØ

Photo Nos.

SHIPPING: DETAIL.

HJELTE FJORD

AT 60° 25' 16" N. 05° 01' 20" E.
1 8" Cruiser 'Hipper Class.
1 Destroyer 385'
4 'M' Class minesweepers.
3 M/V 400/450'
1 " 350/400'
1 " 250/300'
1 coaster 150/200'
2 tugs. — 634 – 635

OFF TORSKEN:
1 M/V 300/350' with gun mounted on bow proceeding N.
2 small craft (1 proceeding N. and the other S.) — 916. 613

OFF MANGEN:
2 coasters each escorted by a small vessel and all proceeding N. — 611

GRIMSTAD FJORD

AT 19' 4?" N. 05° 14' 48" E.
Battleship of BISMARK Class.
2 M/V 450/500'
2 " 400/450' (1 arriving)
1 " 350/400'

2 coasters 150/200' – 1 at Jetty and 1 leaving the Fjord. Both are possibly Flak ships. — 964 – 967

BERGEN

	Present.	Change since 10.5.41 (N/176)
PUDDEFJORD:	1 tanker 300/350' 1 M/V 400/450' 1 " 300/350' 2 " 250/300' 4 " 200/250' 3 coasters under 200'.	Departures – 1 M/V 400/450' 1 " 350/400' [illegible] " 300/350' 1 " 250/300' 1 " 200/250' Arrivals – 1 tanker 300/350' 1 M/V 400/450' 4 " 200/250' 2 coasters. — 944
LAKESTAAG:	1 T/B Garm Class. 1 T/B Lom Class. 2 M/V 450/500' (1 in floating dock) 1 M/V 400/450' 3 " 300/350' (1 probably a tanker) 2 " 250/300' 3 " 200/250' 1 coaster 150/200'	Departures – 1 M/V 350/400' 1 " 200/250' Arrivals – 1 " 350/400'

APPENDIX 'A' TO INTERPRETATION REPORT NO. 1490. 22nd May, 1941.

– 2 –

Photo Nos.

	Present	Change	Photo Nos.
COALING WHARF OF THE BERGEN STEAMSHIP CO:	1 coaster.	1 M/V 400/450' has left. 1 coaster has arrived.	944
SOLHEJMSVIK & NAVAL QUAY:	1 S/M 140' 2 Snogg Class T/B's 1 sailing vessel 250' 1 M/V 200/250' (building). 1 " 250/300' 2 " 200/250' 5 coasters. About 10 small steamers.	Arrivals – 1 S/M 140'. (may have been present 10.5.41). 1 M/V 250/300' Departures – 1 M/V 200/250'	945
DOKSJAER:	1 T/B Lom Class. 5 small steamers 100/150' Some small craft.	Departures 1 M/V 250/300' 1 " 200/250' Some change in small craft.	
NOSTET:	Few small steamers and a number of small craft.	No change.	
VAAGEN:	2 M/V 250/300' 2 " 200/250' 6 coasters 150/200' 8 steamers 100/150' Many small craft.	Arrivals – 2 M/V 250/300' 1 " 200/250' 1 coaster. Departures – 1 training hulk. 1 M/V 250/300' 1 " 200/250'	
SKOLTEGRUND MOLE:	2 M/V 400/450' 1 " 250/300' 1 coaster Small craft.	Arrivals – 2 M/V 400/450' 1 " 250/300' Departures – 1 M/V 250/300'	944
SKUTEVIK:	The Stella Polaris.	No change.	642
PORT SANDVIK:	2 M/V 350/400' 1 " 300/350' 1 " 250/300'	Departures – 1 M/V 400/450' 1 " 300/350' Arrivals – 1 M/V 300/350' 2 " 350/400'	642
BREDINK BAY:	1 M/V 250/300'	Departures – 1 M/V 250/300' Arrivals – 1 M/V 250/300'	

Distribution:-

	Reports.	Prints.
C.A.S.	1	0
Intelligence C.C.	2	0
Plans C.C.	1	0
Bomber Command	1	0
Admiralty	2	1
A.I.3 (c)	1	0
M.I.14 (d)	1	1
A.I.1 (c)	1	0
G.S.I. G.H.Q.	1	0
F.O.2 (b)	2	2
Capt. Pim (Room 035a War Office)	1	0
No.1. P.R.U. Benson	1	0
P.I.S. Benson	2	0
No.18 Group	1	0
P.I.S. Wick	3	0
O.C. No.1. P.R.U. Wick	1	0
A.I.9	1	0
A.I.3 (d)	2	0

J.G.D. Clark

J.G.D. CLARK, P/O.
INTERPRETATION OFFICER,
R.A.F. STATION, MEDMENHAM.

T.O.O. 1800 hrs. (22. 5. 41)

A report on the analysis of the aerial photographs taken during the reconnaissance sortie over Bergen on 21 May 1941.

Via A. Jarski

J.G.D./DLW

SECRET

22nd. May 1941

INTERPRETATION REPORT NO. 1490

Photographs taken by No. 1 P.R.U. on 21.5.41.
Interpretation by C.I.U. on 22.5.41.

SORTIE N/183

Contact Scale: 1/16,000 (F.L.20").
Mean time of photography: 13.10 hours.
Flying Height: 27,000'.
Quality of photography: Good: Medium Scale.

LOCALITY: BERGEN & ADJACENT FJORDS – HERLØ.

BERGEN and adjacent FJORDS. — Photo Nos

SHIPPING

A Battleship of the BISMARK class and a HIPPER class Cruiser have arrived in Fjords in the neighbourhood of BERGEN since 10.5.41 when the port was last covered.

These are accompanied by one GERMAN Destroyer (385') and four 'M' class minesweepers.

The BISMARK class Battleship which is at anchor in the GRIMSTAD FJORD is accompanied by four M/V's (two 450/500', one 400/450', and one 350/400'). These are anchored down the centre of the FJORD and one of them has her engines turning slowly, but there is no evidence to show whether or not she is newly arrived. There is no deck cargo on the M/V's and they carry no conspicuous armaments.

The HIPPER class Cruiser is at anchor on the West side of the HJELTE FJORD accompanied by a Destroyer 385', four 'M' class minesweepers and 5 M/V's (three 400/450', one 300/350', and one 250/300'). These M/V's again have no deck cargo and only one is definitely armed.

There are no indications of any unusual activity either among the vessels accompanying the naval units or among the shipping in BERGEN itself, and the photographic evidence does not suggest a shipborne expedition.

The position of the battleship is — 964-967
60° 19' 48" N.
05° 14' 48" E.

and that of the cruiser — 634-635
60° 25' 16" N.
05° 01' 20" E.

At the time of photography neither was protected by booms.

A visual report states that these vessels were seen on course N. off MARSTRAND at 15.00 hours on 20.5.41 and it is therefore evident that they cannot have been long in the Port; the photographs appear to bear this out, since accompanying vessels are still in some cases in movement. This HIPPER class Cruiser was last seen on photographs in KIEL on 3.5.41 and was reported as having departed by 18.5.41 (Sortie H/964).

A small tanker type vessel is lying alongside the Destroyer and an M/V 450/500' is being manoeuvred by tugs into a position alongside the Cruiser. This, coupled with the fact that few shore facilities exist in the Fjords in which the vessels are lying, gives the impression that the presence of the M/V's is connected with refuelling and revictualling.

SECRET

INTERPRETATION REPORT NO. 1490 (CONTD) — Photo No

BERGEN and adjacent FJORDS (CONTD)

A further M/V 400/450' is seen entering GRIMSTAD FJORD from the S. at the time of photography. No tankers accompany the Battleship; however, oil might be obtained from the mediumsized tank situated on the S. side of the FJORD. A small jetty leads from this, alongside which lies a vessel 150/200', possibly a flakship.

In BERGEN itself one coastal S/M is seen at the naval base. This was thought to have departed on the previous Sortie N/176, but may have been present obscured by cloud. The only new arrival amongst the naval units is an ex-Norwegian T/B of the 'LOM' class at the DOKSJAER.

Nine small motor boats (70') are moored in two tiers alongside an M/V 250/300' which is a new arrival in PUDDE FJORD. These appear similar to those which arrived on the "OSNABRUCK" and which have been seen in BERGEN for sometime. The photographs give no clue as to their purpose.

Since 10.5.41 Sortie N/176 (Report No. 1457) the total tonnage of merchant shipping has remained at its normal level and, as usual, there has been a considerable turnover, approximately 17 M/V's having departed and 18 arrived; a total of 34 M/V's over 200', an increase of one, is now present. No especial activity is noted bearing on the presence of the Warships in the adjacent Fjords. — 642 944 945

BERGEN

SHIPPING TOTAL

This total does not include the shipping in HJELTE FJORD and GRIMSTAD FJORD.

(a)	NAVAL	Active:	1 T/B GARM class 2 T/B's LOM class. 2 T/B's SNOGG class.
(b)	SUBMARINES	Active:	1 S/M 140'
(c)	NON NAVAL (OVER 200')	Active:	1 tanker 300/350' 2 M/V's 450/500' 4 M/V's 400/450' 3 M/V's 350/400' 4 M/V's 300/350' 10 M/V's 250/300' 11 M/V's 200/250'
		Building:	1 M/V 200/250'
(d)	NON NAVAL (UNDER 200')		16 coasters. Usual number of small craft.

SHIPPING DETAIL (SEE APPENDIX A)

HERLØ

SHIPPING

The M/V 225', which has been present for some considerable time anchored between the Island of JAKOBSØ and HERLØ, is no longer present. A few small craft are seen in the harbour. — 920

AERODROME: HERDLA (HERLØ)

19 aircraft are present, the largest number ever seen on the aerodrome:-
1 Ju. 52
7 medium aircraft.
11 small aircraft. — 920

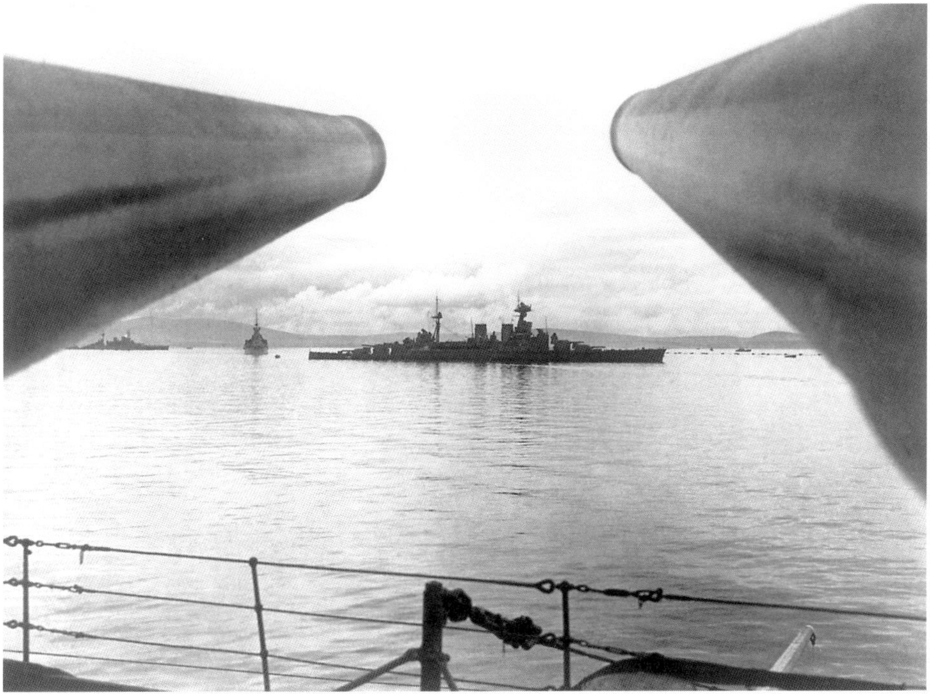

The battlecruiser Hood *at Scapa Flow in March 1941, photographed from the* Renown. *On the left is the battlecruiser* Repulse.

Via IWM

Via M. Krzyżan

On finding that the Bismarck *had gone from Bergen, a force commanded by Vice Admiral Lancelot E. Holland consisting of the* Hood *and the battleship* Prince of Wales, *set out to intercept her. This photographs shows the* Hood *– Holland's flagship.*

The Bismarck *entering the Grimstadfjord on 21 May 1941, photographed from the* Prinz Eugen. *The battleship is still wearing camouflage, but upon receiving an order from the Fleet Staff, the existing camouflage was immediately changed to a uniform light grey, better matched to the surroundings in the Denmark Strait.*

Via M. Skwiot

region was also slowly deteriorating, heavy rain clouds coming in from the south-west, and fog forming above the mountains of Norway.

About 23:00 the German squadron altered formation, the destroyers now taking the lead, with the *Bismarck* and the *Prinz Eugen* following behind. After 23:00, they signalled Group North asking about British capital ships at Scapa Flow. The wind speed rose before midnight to Force 4 on the Beaufort scale, blowing from the south-west. Group North informed Lütjens that five British aircraft were flying along the cliff coast some 10km (6 miles) north of Bergen and had dropped bombs and flares over Kalvanes Bay. This attack had been the result of the noon reconnaissance by the Spitfire. The British obviously still believed that the German ships were in the fjords near Bergen. However, Admiral Lütjens' flotilla was already gone.

The Admiralty had to send reconnaissance aircraft immediately to locate the *Bismarck* regardless of the weather, and a Maryland of 771 Sqn Fleet Air Arm shortly took off from Hatston in the Orkney Islands. The aircraft reached the fjords in Norway and reported the absence of the battleship and the rest of the group. More patrols were sent out to search the Norwegian coast from Stavanger to Bergen. Further reconnaissance was ordered between the Shetlands and the Faeroe Islands; this was to be carried out by Sunderland flying boats fitted with ASV radar. Catalina flying boats were to patrol the Denmark Strait and the southern coast of Iceland.

En route for the Denmark Strait

Having left Norwegian waters behind around 03:00, Admiral Lütjens decided to send the destroyers, which had until then been providing his anti-submarine screen, back to Trondheim. At 04:20, Lütjens ordered the commander of the 6th Destroyer Flotilla, Hinrichs, to take his ships back to base. When the destroyers reached the latitude of Trondheim, they turned toward the coast, which they approached on the following day, while the heavy ships were sailing 410km (220 nautical miles) west of Trondheim on a course of 320 degrees. Following the earlier guidelines, Lütjens ordered both ships to maintain the same course and speed. The ships soon came within the range of British air reconnaissance, and steps had to be taken to make sighting them more difficult. At 09:30, the *Bismarck* radioed Group North for information on enemy naval activity in the area. While waiting for a reply, the group continued north as ordered, heading for Jan Mayen Island. The commander of Group North, Generaladmiral Carls, had a different opinion on the choice of the route into the Atlantic. He wrote in the Group's diary: 'I would also like to recommend to the Fleet Commander, if there is a choice of either the Danish route or the southern passage, that he choose the latter, as I believe it to be the most appropriate, as well as saving time and distance.' His intention was that on leaving Norway, Lütjens' group should sail through the gap between Iceland and the Faeroe Islands if the weather was favourable (i.e. bad). However, since the weather in the area was good, Lütjens decided to move further north to rendezvous with the tanker *Weissenburg* as planned at point 'Hans' (70°N, 1°W).[1] This might have been the result of the Admiral's previous experience during Operation *Berlin*. On 28 January 1941, after encountering the leading units of the Home Fleet between Iceland and the Shetlands, Lütjens had turned the *Gneisenau* and the *Scharnhorst* north. He had delayed the passage into the Atlantic by just a few days, and had passed through the Denmark Strait at the beginning of February. It was probably because of the fog, often present in that area, that he had from the very beginning favoured this route for Operation *Rheinübung*. Besides, he did not have to consider the risk of a chance encounter with British battleships in this passage, which might have been more likely off the Faeroe Islands as they were closer to Scapa Flow.

Photo by Busch, via AJ-Press

The Prinz Eugen *at anchor in the fjord, with a trawler in the foreground and a tanker further back. Because of the lack of anti-torpedo nets, they were protecting the warships.*

[1] *The* Weissenburg *was radioed by the SKL to immediately leave her operational square on refuelling Lutjens' ships. She was to be replaced by the tanker* Heide, *which was already proceeding toward Jan Mayan Island with full tanks.*

Four minutes later Admiral Lütjens was informed by Group North and the ship's B-Dienst that the British had not yet issued an order to search for his ships in the open sea. What had been noted, though, was increased radar activity in the northern square, which seemed to indicate that the enemy had focused on searching for the ships off northern Norway and in the Norwegian Sea. This state of affairs let him safely move further north and set a course for the Denmark Strait. Another report, at 10:53, said that enemy aircraft were patrolling northern Norway, opposite to the direction in which the squadron was moving. Moving at 24 knots, the ships were now 370km (200 nautical miles) from the Norwegian coast and completely out of range of British air patrols. At 12:37 came a message that a periscope had been sighted, and an air raid and submarine alert was sounded aboard the *Bismarck*. The squadron altered course to port and zigzagged for half an hour. No further alarms occurring, the ships resumed their previous course. The weather was slowly deteriorating; at 16:00, they encountered slight fog. Admiral Lütjens was hoping that it would be still covering the area during their attempt to break out into the Atlantic. The weather forecast for the next 24 hours, received by the *Bismarck*'s senior meteorological officer, Dr. Heinz Externbrink, was favourable to the Germans. At the same time, the weather to the north-east of Iceland was getting worse. The forecast said it would reach as far as the southern end of Greenland. This was promising for the Germans, who hoped that the patrolling British cruisers were not yet equipped with radar.

At 18:00, the group ran into rain clouds. The weather broke, with strong winds beginning to blow from the north-west. Visibility rapidly dropped to 300–400m (330–440 yards) and fog gradually settled in. Both ships maintained their relative positions and communicated via signal lamps. In order to mark the vessels' positions, small navigational lights and searchlights were switched on. When the fog grew very thick, a large stern searchlight was switched on aboard the battleship to help the *Prinz Eugen* keep her position. They soon reached an area where the nights were light, and now they were able to proceed at 24 knots. At 23:04, Admiral Lütjens received three very important messages from Group North. The first said that their discovery by the enemy had not been confirmed. The second referred to a reconnaissance of Scapa Flow made on 22 May. It said that there were still four battleships at the base and one aircraft carrier plus six light cruisers and numerous destroyers. The third message regarded enemy forces that had not yet commenced operations, and which, it should be assumed, would not do so the next day either. Even if the British set out from Scapa Flow immediately, they could not reach the German squadron in Norwegian waters. With such optimistic prospects, Lütjens decided not to refuel off Jan Mayen Island and set a westerly course, wanting to pass through the Denmark Strait as soon as possible. At 23:22, they turned toward the Strait. Unfortunately,

From the Prinz Eugen *archives*

In their leisure time, some of the Prinz Eugen's *crewmen fishing from the ship.*

The Prinz Eugen *departing the Norwegian fjords on 21 May 1941. To prevent easy identification, this picture has been retouched by a censor.*

Via CAW

the information about the situation at Scapa Flow sent to the *Bismarck* by Group North was incorrect. Owing to low cloud over the base, the German reconnaissance wrongly assessed the forces spotted there. The truth was that the British had already responded. The still only partially completed battleship *Prince of Wales* and the battlecruiser *Hood* had been dispatched from Scapa Flow under the command of Vice Admiral Holland. They set a course for Iceland, knowing that the Germans could only pass through the Denmark Strait or between the Faeroe Islands and Iceland.

Alert at Scapa Flow

Toward the end of May 1941, the British noticed increased German air reconnaissance activity in northern waters, between Jan Mayen Island, Iceland and Greenland. They supposed the Germans wanted to find the exact boundary between the floating and fixed ice in order to ensure safe passage for their ships. German ships had only three routes in that area to break out into the Atlantic. The safest route was via the Denmark Strait, so the commander of the Home Fleet, Admiral Sir John Tovey, ordered on 14 May that a detailed weather and ice report be made for the Jan Mayen region. The report mentioned only two safe options for a cruise from the south or south-east; the other passages were blocked by ice floes. At the same time he was also receiving other reports on German naval traffic – one about German tankers headed for Norway, and another raising a false alarm that an airborne landing on Iceland was being prepared. He believed that such information was to mislead the British and divert their attention from the real thing, the Denmark Strait. He assumed that the German activity was connected with another attempt to move capital ships into the Atlantic. His first move was to send the heavy cruiser *Suffolk* to the waters off Iceland on 18 May. She was to patrol both passages near Iceland that the Germans might choose. He also ordered that the heavy cruiser *Norfolk*, with Rear Admiral W.F. Wake-Walker aboard, depart Hvalfjord in Iceland and join the *Suffolk*.

He issued these orders on the afternoon of 21 May; accordingly, the *Norfolk* and the *Suffolk* watched the Denmark Strait from the north. A group of warships comprising the *Hood*, commanded by Captain R. Kerr and with the squadron commander Vice Admiral Lancelot E. Holland aboard, and the *Prince of Wales*, under Captain J. Leach, with an escort of six destroyers left Scapa Flow on the evening of 21 May and headed for the base at Hvalfjord in Iceland. Having refuelled there, they were to take up a good position for an interception of the German group as it was trying to pass through either the Denmark Strait or between Iceland and the Faeroes. This latter area was being patrolled by the cruisers *Manchester* and *Birmingham*, which

The Bismarck *shrouded in Arctic fog, seen from the* Prinz Eugen.

Via M. Skwiot

alternately called at Skaalefjord to refuel. The cruiser *Arethusa*, commanded by Captain Chapman, was also to come under Wake-Walker's command.

The following warships were stationed at Scapa Flow: the battleship *King George V*, commanded by Captain W. Patterson and the flagship of Admiral Tovey; the cruisers *Galatea*, *Aurora*, *Kenya* and *Neptune*; and three destroyers, which were joined by three more that evening. There was also the aircraft carrier *Victorious*, commanded by Captain H.C. Bovell. A few days before, on 15 May, she had been commissioned and had been prepared for sea at Liverpool. On her first mission, she was to take forty-eight Hurricane II fighters to Gibraltar. She had two squadrons onboard for fighter cover and anti-submarine defence: No. 800Z, comprising six Fulmar II fighters; and No. 825, comprising nine new Swordfish Is, three of which were equipped with radar. On 20 May, she had completed preparations for this mission, but it had been cancelled when the German warships had been photographed at Bergen. Captain Bovell had been ordered to unload the forty-eight Hurricanes and join the Home Fleet at Scapa Flow. When the *Victorious* arrived, Admiral Tovey informed the commander of 825 Sqn, Lieutenant-Commander E.K. Esmond, that being one of the best, his squadron had been chosen to carry out a torpedo attack.

The commanding officer of the Hatston naval air station, Captain Henry L. St. Fancourt, decided on the evening of 22 May to send aircraft on a reconnaissance sortie to the fog-bound coast of Norway. One of the pilots, Lieutenant Noel E. Goddard, was flying, as he reported, over the sea toward the fjord where the German warships had been photographed. He found nothing at their anchorage, but came under heavy anti-aircraft fire over Bergen. Despite this trouble, he managed to send a message that the ships had left the fjords. At 20:00, Admiral Tovey was told that the German flotilla had been sighted passing the Kattegat. Surprised, the admiral was thinking hard about the next move of the German ships. It seemed obvious – the report said about two large vessels escorted by three destroyers and five ships. However, the greatest mystery in all this was to him the fact that a convoy of eleven merchant ships was accompanying them. He saw four options open to the enemy, the most probable being that the merchantmen were being escorted just by chance, and that after they detached, the group would be continuing on its own. Still, in such a case there were two alternatives: either the German warships were conducting regular escort operations and would return to the Baltic on completion of their task, or – more probably – a new operation had begun and it was an attempt to break out into the Atlantic. This latter would be confirmed by the earlier intelligence reports and by the fact that, according to information obtained, there was a strong probability that the German ships had called at Bergen. In this case several possibilities had to be considered. Upon analysis of all existing options, Admiral Tovey was certain that the ships were trying to make a dash through the Denmark Strait. He well remembered the recent one by the *Scharnhorst* and the *Gneisenau* under the command of Admiral Lütjens that had taken place in February.

Admiral Tovey decided to wait with his flotilla at Scapa Flow until the Germans moved on from Bergen. At 20:00, he received a message from Hatston about their departure, and he no longer waited to see what would happen. On 22 May, at 22:45, his warships sailed. His force now comprised the flagship *King George V*, the aircraft carrier *Victorious*, the cruisers *Galatea*,

Aurora, *Kenya*, *Neptune* and *Hermione*, and seven destroyers. The destroyer *Lance*, under Lieutenant Commander R. Northcott, had to turn back due to boiler trouble. On leaving Scapa Flow, the group set a north-west course to the Faeroe Islands to patrol the area south of the 62-degree parallel and to block this way to the German ships. The reserve battlecruiser *Repulse* was at first to have joined the cruisers patrolling the passage between the Faeroe Islands and the Shetlands, but in the end the admiral decided to have her in his group. She set out from the Clyde and on 23 May joined the British warships on patrol south of the Hebrides.

It was very difficult to determine the exact position of the German ships because a long time had passed between their being sighted in the Skagerrak and the message about their departure from Bergen. The weather was in favour of the Germans, getting worse and worse, and their radio silence denied the British that means of locating them. What worried Admiral Tovey most, though, was that the Germans might sneak unnoticed between the patrols. Such a situation might have occurred during the relief of ships in the patrolling zones. They had to refuel from time to time, and as there were no tankers, they did it at bases – either Skaalefjord or Hvalfjord. The strategy Tovey chose placed his main force on parallel 60° N. It was a good point to intercept the Germans if they were trying to pass off Iceland; it was also a good point to return to if the German ships were coming from the west. Twenty-nine hours had passed

Via IWM

The commander of the Home Fleet, Admiral Sir John C. Tovey, photographed aboard the battleship King George V.

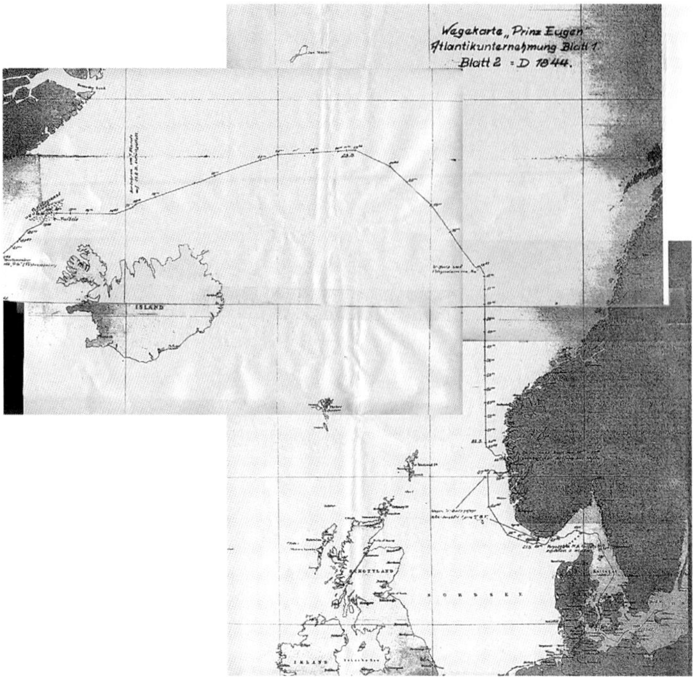

Original map from the heavy cruiser Prinz Eugen's *war diary. Note the German group route marked – until entering Denmark Strait.*

From J. Rico collection

since they had been photographed at Bergen, and all trace of them had been lost.

Contact

On the morning of 23 May 1941, the *Bismarck* and the *Prinz Eugen* reached the Denmark Strait. The weather was very favourable – fog, rain and ever-strengthening winds were perfect for an unnoticed passage by the ships. The forecast for the next twenty-four hours was also promising. The weather was changing rapidly, and visibility grew worse with every passing minute. At 11:15 came an order from the Fleet Command for all the batteries onboard to be at readiness, including the anti-aircraft guns, while approaching Iceland. At noon, the group was at 67° 28' N and 19° 28' W, about 140km (75 nautical miles) to the north of Iceland. The course was changed to 250 degrees in order to bypass a British minefield and drifting icebergs. At 14:22 came bad news from Group North: the weather had grounded all aircraft, preventing any reconnaissance of the ice boundary in the Denmark Strait. But likewise the same bad weather prevented the British from sending their aircraft in search of the German warships in the North Sea, the Denmark Strait, and the passages between Iceland, the Faeroe Islands and the Shetlands. The Germans were now sailing along the ice boundary on a north-eastern course toward the entrance into the strait. All of a sudden, at 15:00, the fog embracing them lifted and visibility increased to 400–500m (450–550 yards). The ships were now passing through areas of alternately good and bad visibility. The battleship's crew became more alert. At 17:30 came an order from the Fleet Command that the magnetic compasses be adjusted and allowances made for declination. In the meantime, the radar of both warships had been continually scanning the horizon. At 18:11, an alert was issued because the radar had plotted an unidentified 'warship' to starboard. They altered course towards the unknown ship, but eleven minutes later it turned out to be an iceberg. Such false alarms became more frequent as the voyage continued. About 19:00, the Germans reached the floating ice boundary and began to meander, trying to avoid icebergs, which could damage the ships' hulls and propellers. Visibility

Heavy cruiser Prinz Eugen*'s Kapitän zur See Brinkmann at the bridge; to the left is his staff officer.*

From A. Jarski collection

in the Strait was about 3 miles, with small patched of fog in places. Another alert was soon issued on the *Bismarck*.

At 19:22, the ship's hydrophones detected a ship at a distance of 1.3km (1,400 yards). Only radar detection was possible because the rangefinders could not find the object in the fog. No more than a dim shadow of a warship was plotted on the screen. The entire main battery prepared to open fire. The gunners waited for the target co-ordinates from the fire control centre. In the meantime, the radar once again plotted the unidentified warship approaching at high speed from the south (or south-west). Her identification was quite difficult, though, owing to the thick fog. When visual contact was eventually made, the warship was seen to have a solid superstructure and three funnels. She was shortly identified as a British heavy cruiser, and later also her name was found out: this was the heavy cruiser *Suffolk*, commanded by Captain R.M. Ellis.

Via AJ-Press

Anti-aircraft crew of the Prinz Eugen *sleeping at their posts while approaching the Denmark Strait.*

On watch on the Prinz Eugen's *bridge: sitting first from the left is the cruiser's First Gunnery Officer.*

Photo by Busch, via AJ-Press

Having set a south-westerly course, the *Suffolk* began another patrol. At 19:22, Seaman Alfred Newall sighted the German warships passing between icebergs and raised the alarm. They were sailing on the same course as their ship, 13km (7 nautical miles) to starboard. The captain had his ship increase speed in order to identify the enemy and notified the Home Fleet about it. He also ordered that the radar be switched on, because in view of the short distance between them, he expected the enemy to open fire. Coming out of the fog, the *Suffolk* suddenly found herself close to the *Bismarck*, which was sailing ahead of her. When Captain Ellis realized what he was dealing with, without hesitation he retired back into the fog. He then let the enemy steam further away from him in order to be able to follow her.

Precious minutes, vital for both sides, passed as their codebreakers intercepted and decoded the enemy's messages. They were racing against time – he who knew more about the other was in a better position when the fight began. The B-Dienst on the *Prinz Eugen* intercepted and almost immediately deciphered a signal transmitted by the *Suffolk*. The British were reporting one battleship and one cruiser 7 miles (11km) away at 20° N, on a course of 240 degrees. The *Suffolk*'s report was also decoded on the *Bismarck*. The exactly-determined position of the German ships clearly

Via IWM

Able Seaman Newall of the cruiser Suffolk, *the first to sight the* Bismarck *on 23 May 1941.*

The cruiser Suffolk *patrolling in the Denmark Strait in May 1941.*

Via IWM

indicated that the British warship was equipped with radar, which was a great surprise to the Admiral, who had not suspected that the *Suffolk* might be so equipped, believing that the British did not yet possess shipborne radar, only land-based equipment. The truth was that the *Suffolk* had been fitted with the newest location-finder and a Type 284 radar. At 20:15, Admiral Lütjens reported to Group North the sighting of an enemy heavy cruiser in square AD 29, following his battleship on the port side. As it later turned out from the intercepted messages, it was the *Suffolk* that was following the *Bismarck* at the limit of visual range. Immediately upon receiving the first message, Group North's Generaladmiral Carls ordered that Luftflotte 5 carry out a reconnaissance of Scapa Flow.

At 20:20, another alert was sounded aboard the *Bismarck* and full ahead rung up. The forward radar plotted the enemy at 6,400m (7,000 yards). Lindemann told his crew through the intercom that another enemy ship had appeared, this time on the port side, and that the battleship was going into action. The *Bismarck* was already at battle stations. Shortly, a three-funnelled heavy cruiser emerged out of the fog. Informed about the sighting of the German ships by the *Suffolk*, the cruiser *Norfolk* had headed at full steam toward the enemy. However, a slight navigational error caused her to suddenly appear out of the fog in front of the Bismarck. Going at 30 knots, the *Norfolk* (commanded by Captain A.A.L. Philips) came right under the battleship's guns. On realizing the danger, the ship at once tried to find shelter in the nearest fogbank. The *Bismarck* was quick enough to fire a few salvos in her direction, though, and the shells fell quite close. The *Norfolk* immediately headed back at full speed into the safety of the fog. The outcome of this engagement was as follows: three of *Bismarck*'s salvos fell short, one salvo landed astern of the target, and the others went over. Although a few shell fragments hit the cruiser's side, they did no harm. The *Norfolk*'s captain decided to remain hidden in the fog until his ship was at a safe distance behind the German ships, intending to join the *Suffolk* later and follow the enemy warships closely at the limit of their radar's range.

Admiral Lütjens had his ships alter formation so that the battleship's heavy guns could bear on the British cruisers. The latter stayed behind in fog, at a safe distance from the German ships, with the *Suffolk* to starboard and the *Norfolk* to port, and most importantly, maintaining radar contact with the enemy. The seemingly unimportant engagement soon showed its effect on the further course of the operation. The shock of the *Bismarck*'s own salvoes had damaged the forward radar beyond shipboard repair. Therefore, at 20:44, the German ships carried out a routine manoeuvre in which one ship took the place of another, the aftermost ship turning out of line and increasing speed to take the place of the leading ship, which fell astern of her. While performing this manoeuvre, the *Bismarck* had a problem with her rudder, which jammed in a full starboard position, and as the *Prinz Eugen* passed the battleship, the latter moved towards the cruiser. At one point both ships were heading for a collision but the quick reactions of the cruiser's captain, Kapitän zur See Brinkmann, prevented the ships from hitting each other, and the *Bismarck*'s rudder problem was soon corrected.

The German ships were now steaming at 30 knots in the dimness of the Arctic night through fog, snow and rain. The *Suffolk* and *Norfolk* maintained visual and radar contact with them, with the *Suffolk* to starboard, where visibility was very good, and the *Norfolk* to port, in thick banks of fog. The British cruisers kept Admiral Tovey informed about the position of the enemy group. Their reports were immediately decoded on both German ships and landed on Lütjens' desk five minutes later. Smokescreens produced every so often to lose the pursuers were of no help; radar contact continued to be maintained. The British radar signals were in turn picked up on the *Bismarck*. Admiral Lütjens had to suppose that he would shortly have a concentration of British forces standing in his way. Irritated by this situation, he decided at 22:00 to undertake offensive action. Concealed by a rain squall, the *Bismarck* turned 180 degrees to take the pursuing *Suffolk* by surprise. To the Germans' surprise, however, the heavy cruiser was not there as expected as they emerged from the squall. The *Suffolk* had noticed the manoeuvre on her radar screen and immediately turned and steamed away from the *Bismarck* at full speed. Admiral Lütjens noticed the *Suffolk*'s evasive action and abandoned further pursuit, ordering the ship back on her previous course. The *Bismarck* turned once again and took her position in the formation. The *Suffolk* had by then made another manoeuvre, but Lütjens did not attempt to give chase.

Via IWM

The Suffolk *on patrol in the Denmark Strait.*

The cruiser Norfolk *in 1940.*

Via IWM

On the evening of 23 May, Vice Admiral Holland was the nearest to the southbound German warships with his group of two capital ships with four destroyers as escort. The worsening weather and rough seas were making navigation difficult. The flagship *Hood* received the *Suffolk*'s message about the sighting of the enemy. Holland immediately consulted his staff and ordered a change of course so as to cut off the German ships. At about 20:00, Holland's warships increased speed to 27 knots. The destroyers were to follow the battleships as fast as possible, but they were falling behind more and more. At 22:00, both British warships began preparations for the impending battle. Based on the latest reports from the cruisers, Holland thought that the enemy was some 185km (100 nautical miles) away from him. The battle plan assumed that the battleships *Prince of Wales* and *Hood* would concentrate their fire on the *Bismarck*, and the heavy cruisers *Norfolk* and *Suffolk* would deal with the *Prinz Eugen*. For the time being, neither of the cruisers was notified of this because radio silence had been ordered. Twelve minutes after midnight, Holland altered course by 45 degrees and reduced speed to 25 knots. In the meantime, the German ships had run into a heavy storm just before midnight. Visibility plummeted to one mile, and the British cruisers' radar signal unexpectedly ceased to transmit. Informed of this, Holland decided to maintain his current course until 02:10, and if there still was no contact, to head south. Contact with the German ships was not restored within the time specified by the Vice Admiral, and both British warships turned to port, sailing parallel to the coast of Greenland.

PHASE TWO OF OPERATION *RHEINÜBUNG*

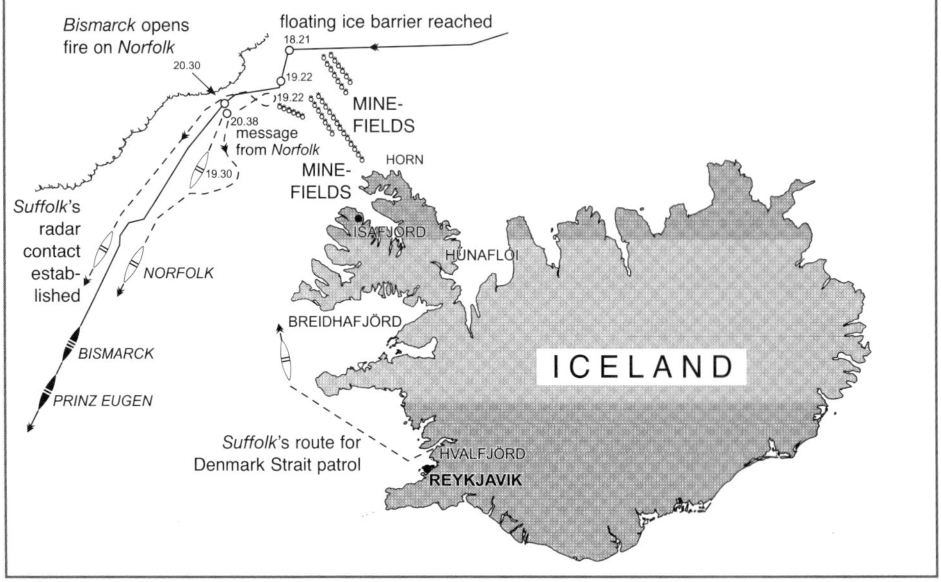

First Blood

Just before midnight on 23 May, the German force encountered fog but continued on at 30 knots. However, heavy snowfalls obliged them to slow down to 27 knots, as visibility was limited and proceeding at high speed in these conditions was dangerous due to the proximity of the floating ice boundary. The frequent anomalies appearing on the radar screens might have prevented a small iceberg being picked up in time, and the results of a collision could have been fatal. Furthermore, the British cruisers were still following behind, and the Germans expected to lose them in the favourable weather. However, they could not hope to change their course significantly, as the passage was rather narrow. The enemy could only have been lost in fog and snow at high speed or by a manoeuvre with a change of speed. The pursuing British ships had to keep their distance very carefully so as not to come within range of the German guns. The German ships' changes in speed obliged them to do the same, and there was a possibility that they might be shaken off whilst doing so. In the meantime, the *Prinz Eugen* changed her position in the formation – having been following the *Bismarck* on her port side, she now took up position to starboard. Before 02:00, course was altered to 220 degrees and speed increased back to 30 knots. At 02:28, the *Prinz Eugen*'s radar picked up a British cruiser following behind the Germans. Action stations was sounded, but the alert was cancelled at 03:58 due to the long range.

The *Hood* and the *Prince of Wales* were slowly approaching the enemy. Vice Admiral Holland was expecting to intercept the German warships soon. At 02:05, he turned so that he was now sailing on a course parallel to them, putting him in a better position to attack. Then, Holland ordered the commander of the *Prince of Wales* to turn on his Type 284 radar, but unfortunately mechanical failure put it out of action. At 03:40, both warships set a speed of 28 knots in order to catch up with the enemy as soon as possible. After some time, the *Hood* signalled a change of course. The manoeuvre performed was supposed to position the battlecruiser at a more convenient angle to the enemy for firing, allowing her to fire full salvoes. The weather around the Denmark Strait was improving, visibility having increased to about 18km (10 nautical miles). The British crews assumed battle stations. At 04:00, the distance between the two groups of warships had decreased to less than 37km (20 nautical miles). However, it still took more than an hour for the distance between them to close by only 7.5km (4 miles), as both groups were sailing on nearly parallel courses, Lütjens' warships steering 220 degrees and Holland's 200 degrees.

There was no suspicion whatever aboard the German battleship that British capital ships

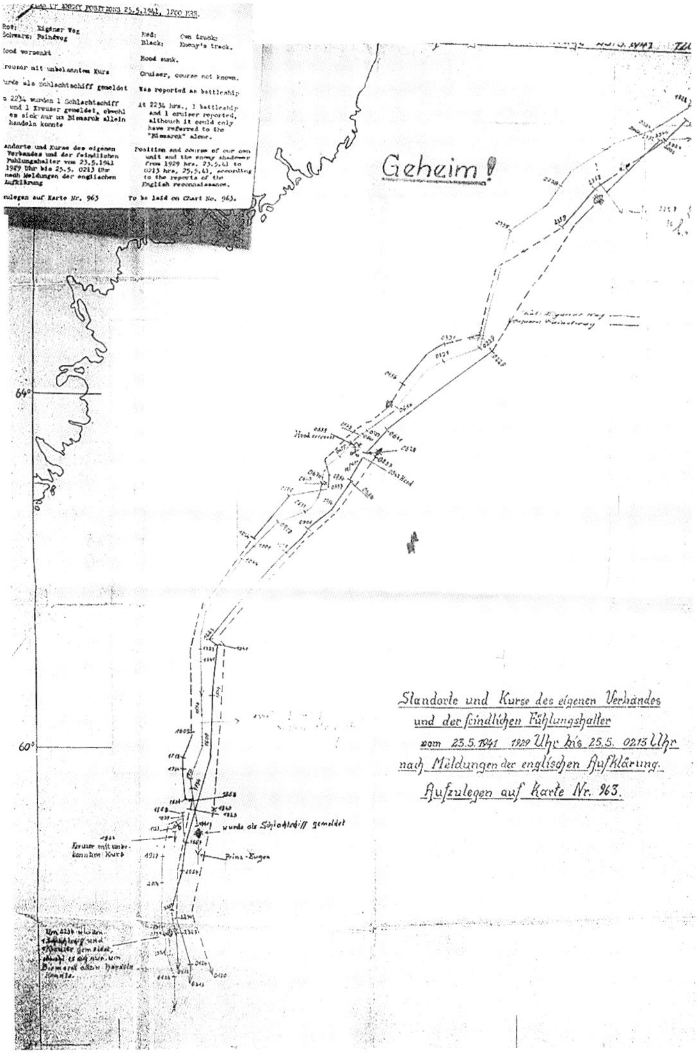

A map from the war diary of the heavy cruiser Prinz Eugen*: German group route on 24 May 1941.*

From J. Rico collection

were approaching and would shortly cross her path. On the morning of 24 May, the German squadron was sailing at 27 knots on a south-westerly course of 220 degrees, with the *Prinz Eugen* in the lead and the *Bismarck* following behind. There was increased alertness on the bridge and at all lookout positions, with a close watch being maintained on the south-eastern horizon. At 04:07, Kapitänleutnant K. Flindt, the sonar officer, notified the *Prinz Eugen*'s captain that the hydrophones had picked up the sound of an unidentified warship bearing 286 degrees. Nothing had yet been seen on the horizon and no British warships were expected to appear from that direction. Initially it was believed to have been the noise of one of the British cruisers shadowing the Germans. However, the noise was picked up again at 04:25 bearing 195 degrees, its source being vessels on the port side. Flindt analysed his data and reported to the bridge the detection of the sound of the turbines of two warships approaching fast on a course of 280 degrees. All the lookouts on the *Bismarck* kept scanning the

The King George V, *the flagship of the commander of the Home Fleet, Admiral Sir J. Tovey.*

Via CAW

Via IWM

The battlecruiser Hood *– the pride of the Royal Navy – during her voyage in the stormy Atlantic. She was sunk in the battle of the Denmark Strait.*

The first opponent and at the same time victim of the combat between the British and German warships in the Denmark Strait was the battlecruiser Hood.

Via IWM

Via IWM

The second opponent of the German force – the Prince of Wales, *which could have met the same fate as the* Hood, *had the battle lasted longer.*

south-eastern horizon for over an hour, the direction from which the enemy was to appear.

At 05:10, Vice Admiral Holland ordered action stations aboard the British warships. The enemy was sighted at 05:35. Two minutes later, the Admiral ordered the ships to turn 40 degrees to starboard in order to close the range. At that moment, neither of the British warships was in a position to open fire. The change of direction allowed them to come closer to the enemy, but was not good for an engagement because the Germans were ahead and to starboard so the aft turrets of the main batteries were unable to bear on the enemy.

At 05:21, the German group suddenly altered course to 170 degrees but after a few minutes the warships returned to 220 degrees. Sixteen minutes later, the observers of the *Prinz Eugen* sighted the first vessel and identified it as a heavy cruiser. At 05:39, Group North sent the *Bismarck* a decoded signal from KG3 (the *Suffolk*) transmitted to Scapa Flow at 04:56, which gave the German ships' exact position, course and speed. Seeing that the enemy possessed this information about his warships, Admiral Lütjens had no option but to fight. At 05:47, the German ships' instruments detected more vessels on the port side. Two minutes later, they saw columns of smoke from two fast approaching warships. The sun was slowly rising, and the enemy could be seen far away ahead of them. Action stations was sounded on the German warships. In the foretop, the *Bismarck*'s first gunnery officer, Korvettenkapitän Adalbert Schneider, initially identified the vessels as heavy cruisers. He passed this information on the target to the forward conning tower, to the second gunnery officer, Korvettenkapitän Helmut Albrecht, but he believed they were either battlecruisers or battleships. The third gunnery officer on the *Bismarck* was at the main fire control centre within the armoured citadel. It was he who collected all the data about targets, and after computation passed them on to the gun turrets. The fourth gunnery officer, Kapitänleutnant von Müllenheim-Rechberg, had the relatively lightest job, posted at the aft fire control position and tasked with keeping an eye on the actions of the British cruisers following the battleship.

Aboard the *Prinz Eugen*, the first gunnery officer, Kapitänleutnant Jaspers, was at his post carefully observing the emerging warships when he was joined by the second gunnery officer, Kapitänleutnant Schmalenbach. They saw four objects through their optical instruments, with three on the port side and one to starboard. Two of them, approaching side by side, were making very high speed. Jaspers and his comrade were at first convinced that these were not battleships but rather heavy cruisers of the *Exeter* or *Birmingham* class, and as such did not believe the British would attempt an attack.

Via IWM

The King George V *anchored at Scapa Flow.*

The British warships were slowly but steadily covering the distance which separated them from their opponents. The *Bismarck*'s main guns were loaded and waiting for an order to open fire from Admiral Lütjens. This, however, did not come. Second after long second passed, the suspense was growing higher, and the attacker was determinedly coming closer. The first salvoes were fired at 05:53. It was the British who opened fire first, while still at a very acute angle to the Germans. The *Hood* directed her entire fire at the leading German warship, which turned out to be the *Prinz Eugen* after she had taken up this position the evening before. The *Prince of Wales* engaged the rear German vessel, the *Bismarck*, although Holland had ordered both ships to concentrate on the leading enemy ship. Heavy waves were breaking over the battleship's forward turrets, preventing the turret rangefinders from locating the

Some of the last photographs of the Hood, *taken from the* Prince of Wales *just before the battle in the Denmark Strait.*

Via IWM

The captain of the Prinz Eugen, *Kapitän zur See Brinkmann, on the bridge watching the approach of the British warships.*

Photo by Lagemann, via AJ-Press

target, so fire had to be directed by the 4.5m (15ft) rangefinder mounted atop the bridge.

After the first salvo had been fired, the *Bismarck*'s crew expected an immediate order to return fire but the intercom was still silent. The First Officer's tentative comments that the enemy had opened fire and that their salvoes were well concentrated failed to have an effect. Irritated by this suspense, Korvettenkapitän Schneider requested the bridge for permission to open fire. Lütjens, though, was still hesitating. In the meantime, the enemy had suddenly turned to port, exposing her entire side to view. Korvettenkapitän Albrecht then saw that one of their opponents was the battlecruiser *Hood*. Korvettenkapitän Jaspers of the *Prinz Eugen* also now knew they were not just being engaged by heavy cruisers. Lütjens still did not give the order. The British warships were gradually closing on their port side. They were clearly visible, the foremost one having a long superstructure with two heavy gun turrets. The British fired another salvo two minutes later. Now very impatient, Lindemann turned to Admiral Lütjens and requested permission to open fire. The Admiral finally gave it, and Lindemann passed the order through the intercom. Likewise Brinkmann of the *Prinz Eugen* gave the order to open fire at 05:55. Both German warships concentrated on the leading British vessel, the *Hood*. Lindemann ordered that rapid fire should be opened the moment the target was straddled. On observing the first salvo, Schneider made a slight correction of range and inclination, ordering a 400m correction and shooting in 4-hm salvoes. The second salvo straddled the enemy ship. Well aimed, it resulted in an immediate order to fire broadsides. Schneider passed word to the computation room, constantly observing the *Bismarck*'s fall of shot. During the engagement, the captain of the *Prinz Eugen* ordered torpedoes to be launched. This order was given simultaneously with the order to open fire, but no torpedoes were launched. Brinkmann repeated the torpedo order at 06:01 but they were still not launched.

The *Hood* was not wasting time, either. Her very first salvo landed near the *Prinz Eugen*, raising great columns of water into the air. Since they hindered the observation of the exact place where the projectiles landed, another salvo immediately followed. When the Germans opened fire, Vice Admiral Holland changed the ship's course 20 degrees to port to bring her closer to the enemy and bring the after turrets to bear. At this point both sides recorded their first damage of the engagement. In the exchange of fire, the *Bismarck* was hit in the bows, while the *Hood* was hit by fire from the *Prinz Eugen* at 05:57. The heavy cruiser's second and third salvoes had straddled the British battlecruiser, and a shell from her fourth salvo hit the *Hood* on the boat deck, close to the mainmast, starting a fire and detonating 4in ammunition stored there. The fire spread rapidly through the aft superstructure and could be seen clearly against the ship's outline. At 06:00, Holland altered course by a further 20 degrees to port.

Aboard the *Bismarck*, Korvettenkapitän Schneider precisely controlled the fire from his ship, making the appropriate corrections. In reply he heard confirmations of hits passed

The Bismarck *beginning the battle with the* Hood. *This photograph was taken from the stern of the* Prinz Eugen, *and the barrels of her 'D' turret are on the right. During the battle, the German ships changed places so that the* Prinz Eugen *moved from in front of to behind the* Bismarck.

Via IWM

from the fore computation room. Suddenly, the men on the *Prince of Wales* saw the *Hood*'s bow slowly tilt a few degrees to port. Then she disappeared behind a wall of water. The fifth broadside from the *Bismarck* had hit the *Hood* at the mainmast on the starboard side. It was

Photo by Lagemann, via M. Skwiot

The Bismarck *firing her first salvo at the* Hood, *photographed from the* Prinz Eugen.

A sequence of salvos from the Bismarck's *main forward turrets at the* Hood.

Photo by Lagemann, via IWM

Via IWM

This photograph was taken right after the Hood *was blown up and shows the burning wreckage of the battle-cruiser (on the right of the picture) and the* Prince of Wales *sending up a smoke-screen.*

Salvoes fired from the Hood *fall astern of the* Prinz Eugen.

Photo by Lagemann, via AJ-Press

then that the unexpected happened. At 06:01, the *Hood* first shook, and then, after a few seconds, there was a powerful explosion. An immense yellow flame rose into the air, and yellow-white fragments blazed at the foot of the mast. The explosion took place between the aft mast and the second funnel. The small white bursts were probably fragments of molten metal seen against clouds of black-yellow smoke. Wreathed in smoke, the *Hood* disappeared from sight. In the dark veil that surrounded her, flashes of multiple explosions could be seen. Debris was thrown into the air with great force and was falling into the water around the stricken ship, including her 1,000-ton main turrets that had been blown out of their barbettes by the massive explosion, and smaller-calibre shells, scattered by the blast, were exploding in the air around her. A 380mm shell from the *Bismarck* had penetrated the *Hood*'s armour and exploded in one of the aft magazines, setting off approximately 100 tons of cordite. From the *Bismarck*, it appeared that the stern half of the *Hood* had simply ceased to exist, blown to pieces. The remaining half of the ship was rapidly sinking. Suddenly, the bow rose up, almost vertically, and then silently slipped below the waves. There was no trace left of the proud, 48,000-ton HMS *Hood*.

The *Prince of Wales* could not pick up survivors as she now became the target of the German ships. With Holland gone, the most senior admiral present was Wake-Walker aboard the *Norfolk*, who was now in command. He could not send the *Suffolk* to rescue any survivors from the *Hood* as she had the best radar equipment and had to maintain contact with the Germans. He therefore ordered the four destroyers of Holland's escort, which was not far behind, to conduct rescue operations. The destroyers formed line abreast and began their search. After two hours, lookouts aboard the *Electra* spotted the first remains of the sunken *Hood* – pieces of wood and oil slicks on the water. They then picked up three survivors from the battlecruiser, Able Seaman E. Tilburn, Ordinary Seaman A.E. Briggs and Midshipman W.J. Dundas. The destroyers spent another

The Bismarck *passing the* Prinz Eugen, *with the cruiser on her starboard side. This photograph was taken immediately after the sinking of the* Hood, *when the battleship shifted her fire onto the* Prince of Wales.

Via IWM

Photo by Lagemann, via AJ-Press

A salvo fired from the Prince of Wales *falls ahead of the* Bismarck*'s bow.*

A salvo fired by the Hood *falls between the* Bismarck *and the* Prinz Eugen.

Photo by Lagemann, via AJ-Press

Photo by Lagemann, via AJ-Press

The Bismarck *firing at the* Prince of Wales.

A drawing depicting the dramatic battle between the German and British warships in the Denmark Strait.

Via CAW

From the Blohm & Voss archives, via Jörg Schmiedeskamp

The Bismarck *photographed from the* Prinz Eugen *while firing another salvo at the* Hood.

Captain Leach, commander of the Prince of Wales.

Via IWM

One of the survivors of the Hood *– Able Seaman Tilburn.*

Via IWM

hour searching for survivors but found no more.[2]

When the *Hood* sank, the *Bismarck* trained her guns onto the remaining target, the *Prince of Wales*. Brinkmann on the *Prinz Eugen* also ordered his guns to switch to the second vessel. The gun directors turned. As the *Hood* exploded, the *Prince of Wales* had turned 20 degrees to port in order to avoid the rain of debris. During this action, the third and fourth salvoes from the *Prince of Wales* straddled the *Bismarck*, and it was probably then that she received two serious hits. Meanwhile, the forward turret on the *Prince of Wales* jammed after the first salvo. The battleship continued to fire every now and then from her remaining guns until she made a turn. At 05:59, the *Prinz Eugen* opened fire, delivering a broadside at the *Prince of Wales*, whereupon she continued with her fore and aft batteries. At 06:02, the British battleship fired her ninth salvo at the *Bismarck*, while the range between them had dropped to 18,300m (20,020 yards). It was then that the *Bismarck* opened fire with her secondary armament, quickly scoring hits on the *Prince of Wales*. The *Prinz Eugen*'s secondary batteries also joined in, and fire control was shifted to the aft director. From there, the target's bearings were passed to 'Cäsar' and 'Dora' turrets; this continued until both ships ceased fire at 06:09.

[2] *It is difficult to determine the exact complement of the* Hood. *The first messages claimed that along with the ship perished Vice Admiral Holland, Captain Kerr, 92 officers, 1,152 seamen, 161 marines, 4 Australian sailors, and 7 men of other nationalities, including 4 Poles in the rank of podchorazy (officer cadet).*

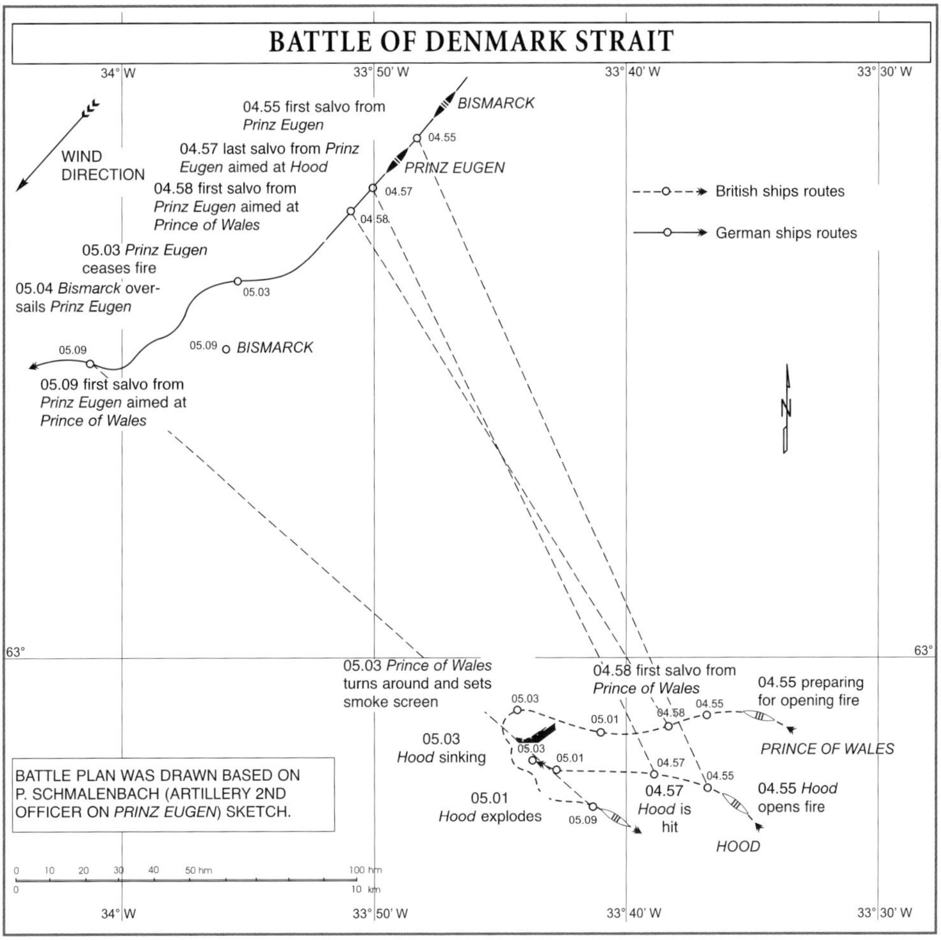

The British battleship had been on the same course as the *Hood* and was probably at a similar range, so Korvettenkapitän Schneider could engage her with minimal corrections. The two ships were on convergent courses and the range between then had soon dropped to 14,000m (15,300 yards), and the German's fire quickly yielded results. The *Prince of Wales* was first hit below the waterline, then at 06:02, while she was passing by the sinking wreckage of the *Hood*, a 380mm shell from the *Bismarck* hit the starboard side of her compass platform. First it hit the armour plate, which it totally smashed above the bridge. Then it went through the platform's structure and came out at the port corner. An auxiliary door leading to the platform was destroyed; the same happened to the platform's roof and armour plate. The ship was very lucky that the projectile did not explode, but in passing through the platform it destroyed a 44-inch searchlight position. The shell destroyed or damaged all the instruments and cabling in its path, cutting off all communication with the compass platform. Most of those on the platform were killed: only Captain Leach escaped serious harm, and the navigation officer was slightly injured. At the same time, a 150mm shell hit above the navigation room, went through, and exploded outside. The splinters pierced a drinking water gravity tank placed on top of the platform and the boiling water flooded the rooms below. In the navigation room, the

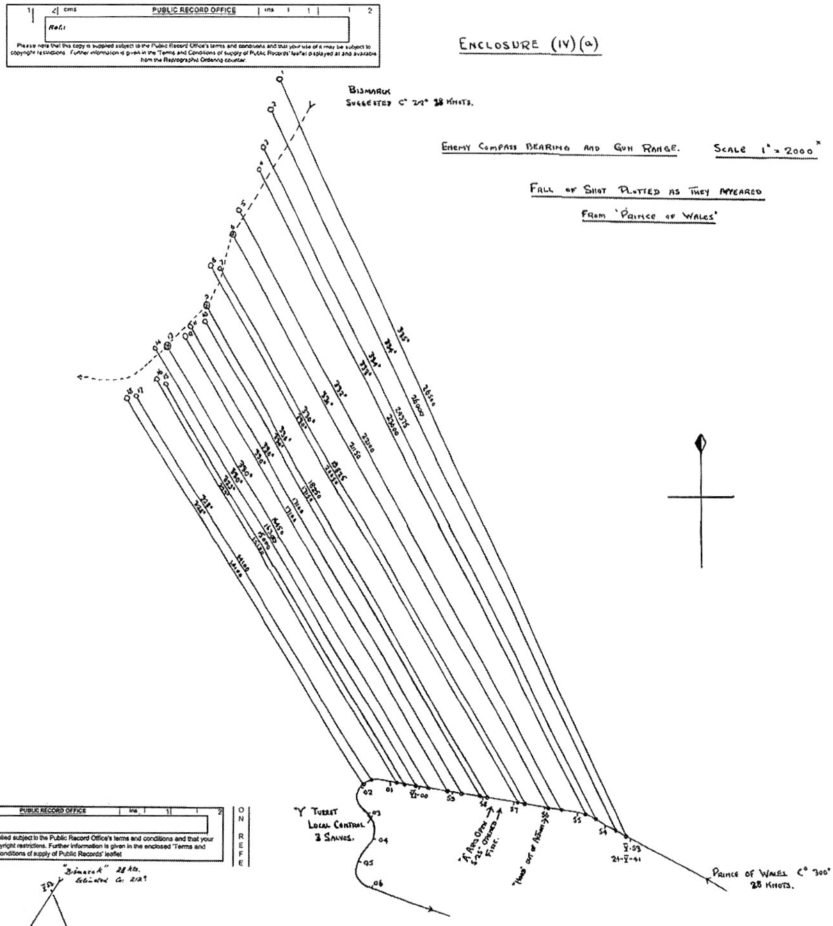

Exhibit B

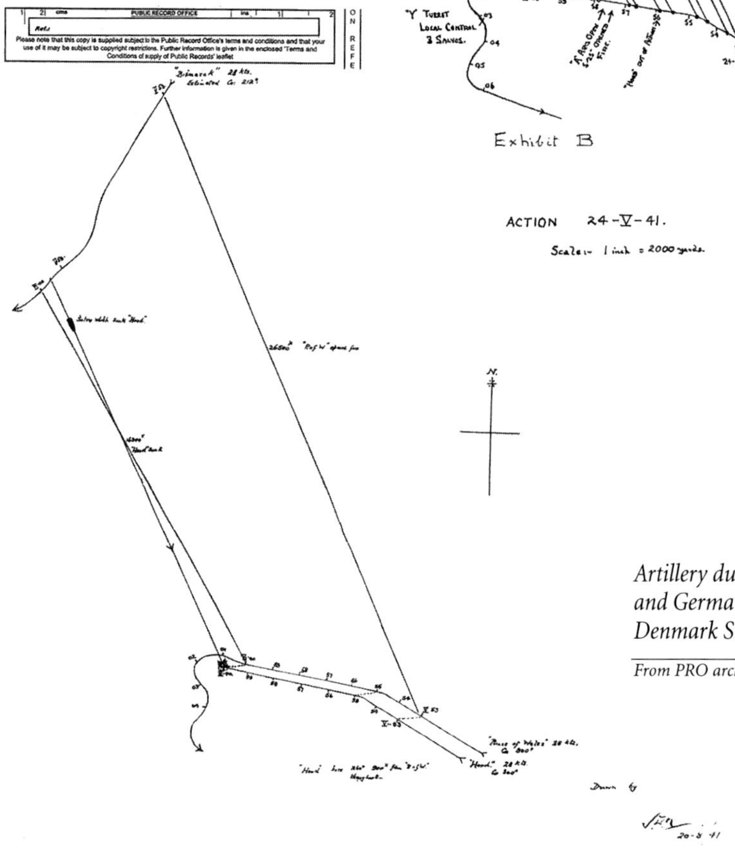

Artillery duel between the British and German group in the Denmark Strait, 24 May 1941.

From PRO archive

-2-

Evidence of Lieutenant William Norman Kennedy, R.N.V.R. (contd.)

Did any turret fire after the fire and before the explosion?

Yes, the forward turret.

(An honest, cautious witness.)

EVIDENCE OF ROBERT E. TILBURN, PJX.153249., A.B.
late of H.M.S.HOOD.

The witness was cautioned in accordance with K.R. Chapter 11.

Where were you at the time of the action?

Sheltering underneath the forward bridge on the port side; just before the port forward U.P. mounting; Position "P" on Exhibit "M".

On which deck?

The boat deck.

Tell us what happened from the time the HOOD opened fire.

We opened fire with the 2 forward turrets and fired about 2 or 3 salvos, when there was a hit by the midship U.P. (at "Q" on Exhibit "M".)

Would you say it was one or more shell that hit.

Just one, Sir.

Would you say it was a big one or a small one?

A small one, because I don't think the deck was very thick and I think a big one would have gone through.

Could you say whether this shell penetrated the deck or not?

I don't know.

Continuing his evidence the witness said -

A fire started - it was a very fierce blaze - pinkish colour, with not much smoke.
(Witness picked out the colour as No.6 on Exhibit 2.)

What was your impression of what this fire was caused by?

My idea was the U.P. ammunition had caught fire because some ammunition exploded. It may have been the ammunition lockers..

Do you know if the U.P.guns were loaded?

Yes, Sir, they were.

Was it your impression that they went off as a result of this hit?

They did not all go off at once - but my impression is that they did at various intervals. There were two U.P.ammunition lockers just abaft the mounting and 2 - 4" ammunition lockers just abaft L.I.4" H.A.mounting.

/24

-3-

Evidence of Robert E. Tilburn, PJX.153249. A.B. (Contd.)

Could you say exactly where the fire seemed to start?

No, it was somewhere between L.I. and the U.P.mounting.

Which way did it seem to spread?

It did not seem to spread at all. It kept on blazing while we were in action but it did not seem to spread to the picket boat or anywhere else, though I cannot say definitely whether the picket boat took fire or not. Anyway, it did not come before L.I. 4" mounting.

Could you see men dealing with the fire?

No. There was an order given to put the fire out, but it was countermanded almost immediately because of the ammunition exploding.

Can you describe the nature of these explosions?

They were fairly small explosions, rather like a big Chinese cracker. I heard the explosions but could not see any results of them. The order to put the fire out was given and countermanded by Petty Officer Bishop who was a Gunners Mate in charge of the 4" guns.

Have you any idea how long this fire went on burning?

No,Sir.

Did the HOOD fire any of her turrets while this fire was burning?

Yes.

Do you know which turrets?

"A" and "B". After the fire had been going on for a good while it fired about 6 salvos altogether, when we started turning round to port and we were hit somewhere, and the whole ship shook and a lot of debris and bodies started falling all over the decks. She started going down by the stern and slowly going over to port. As she tilted over at an alarming angle I got up from where I was and jumped on to the forecastle which was nearly under water at the time. I took off my gas mask and coat, and the water, which was coming over the forecastle, washed me over the side. As I was in the water swimming I looked back at the ship and I saw her coming over on top of me. Some part of the mast struck me on the legs and I was partly pulled down by it, but I managed to cut my seaboot off and free myself, and when I came to the top just the bows were stuck out of the water, practically vertical, and then she slid under.

How much of the bows could you see?

Before the foremast breakwater.

I suppose you were not alone when the explosion occurred?

I was with three other men. One was killed, one was hit in the side or the stomach, I believe, and I presume the third was blown away because I never saw him again.

Did you feel any particular blast yourself?

No, Sir.

How do you think these men were hit?

I don't know.

Did you see any other people alive in the water besides the 2 who were saved with you?

Nobody at all, alive or dead.

/36

Reports from the interrogations of the witnesses to the sinking of the Hood.

Via A. Jarski

-4-

Evidence of Robert E.Tilburn, PJX.153249. A.B. (Contd)

Could you see any flame or smoke of this explosion?

There was a lot of grey smoke, just hanging around the ship, but otherwise I did not see anything of the explosion.

Was there much noise accompanying the explosion?

No, it was just as if the guns had fired.

Did you hear any noise of men shouting after the explosion?

No, Sir, there was dead silence after the explosion.

Have you any personal knowledge of where this last hit occurred or if there was more than one hit?

I do not know, but some of the bodies I saw falling were those of Officers.

Did the bodies start coming down before you heard the explosion, or after?

Directly afterwards as if they were part of the explosion itself.

Can you describe the movement of the ship when the explosion occurred?

She shuddered and then seemed to stop altogether.

Were you thrown off your feet?

Actually I was lying down all the time.

Are you absolutely certain of the position of the first hit so far as you have described it?

Yes, Sir.

Did you know if all HOOD'S turrets fired during the action?

Only "A" and "B" turrets.

Did you form any impressions of the direction in which the debris and bodies came from?

I could not tell.

Could you see any of the after part of the ship after the explosion?

No.

The mainmast must have been noticed. Did you notice that?.

No, Sir, I did not notice anything further aft.

With regard to the first fire, could you tell if it spread aft or not?

I have no idea how far aft.

Did you get any impression that the ship had broken in two?

No Sir.

Do you know if the mantlet doors for the torpedo tubes in HOOD were closed or open at the time?

I had nothing to do with Torpedoes.

-5-

Evidence of Robert E. Tilburn, PJX.153249. A.B. (Contd.)

Do you know where the petrol stowage in HOOD was. Can you show us on the diagram?

(Witness indicated positions on both sides abreast the mainmast, close abaft the after 4" mounting.)

I think there were 2 or 3 ten gallon drums and a big drum on a slipway.

Do you know if the big tanks each side were released before the action started?

I do not know.

Have you any reason to suppose there was a fire below the boat deck?

No, Sir, except when I was going into the water there was just one flash of flame came round between the control tower and "B" turret - it came just above the forecastle deck.

Did you form any idea as to whether the shock on the ship was upwards, fore and aft or athwart ship?

I could not tell.

Were any men standing near you?

There were none standing.

Did you smell anythin after the explosion?

No.

Could you give any rough estimate of the time from the explosion until you went into the water?

About a minute.

Did you know whether the foremast was intact?

I could not tell.

Did you notice any oil on the water after the HOOD had sunk?

Yes, there was oil on the water.

Was any of the oil burning?

There was one fire some distance away but none of the oil near me was burning.

Could you feel any vibration of the HOOD'S engines where you were lying.

Yes.

Do you think she slackened speed at any time between the original fire and the explosion?

No, Sir.

Did you hear any escaping steam after the explosion?

No, Sir.

Did you see any debris floating on the water after the HOOD had sunk?

Yes, there was a lot.

Reports from the interrogations of the witnesses to the sinking of the Hood.

Via A. Jarski

-6-

Evidence of Robert E.Tilburn, P/J.153249 A.B. (Contd.)

Could you recognise any of it?

There were a lot of long steel tubes, sealed at both ends.

Could you say very approximately their length and diameter?

Roughly 15 ft. long and 1 ft. diameter.

Could you say the colour of these tubes?

Rusty.

Can you describe how the ends of these tubes were sealed?

All the ends I saw were sealed, like the bottom of a bottle - slightly concave - apparently of the same metal as the rest of the tube. I saw about 10 of these.

Could you describe any of the other debris that went up first, apart from the bodies'?

No, Sir.

Can you remember any more details of the first hit?

We felt the slight shock when the shell hit us and then the fire broke out.

Can you remember any of the remarks of your guns crew at the time?

One of them said "that has hit us somewhere."

Can you tell us any more about the final hit?

There was just a tremendous vibration and the debris falling down.

Were you able to see any splashes at that same time?

No.

Have you any idea if the U.P.ammunition already in the guns went off or not?

That is what I was meaning when I said the U.P.ammunition was going off.

Can you explain to us why you are so certain that "X" and "Y" turrets never fired.?

From the sound, and the fact that there were no flashes from aft; also by the vibration of two guns firing instead of four.

Did it cross your mind when you saw the first fire that it was possibly petrol?

No, because I thought it was too far forward for petrol.

What was your impression of the cause of the fire?

My impression was that it was the U.P.ammunition in the gun that was on fire.

/78

-7-

Evidence of Robert E.Tilburn. P/J.153249 A.B. (Contd.)

What do you think the explosions were coming from in the fire?

From the U.P.ammunition exploding in the gun.

When the shell arrived which started the fire, did you hear any noise or see any splinters flying up.?

No Sir.

The evidence of Ord. Signalman A.E.Briggs, P/J.157404 was next taken, after which A.B.Tilburn was recalled.

Robert E.Tilburn P/J.153249. A.B. (Contd.)

After the explosion did you notice any smoke boiling out of the water?

No.

Can you give us a little more information as to what positions the ship took up as she sank?

When I was on the forecastle deck she had a heavy list to port - about 10 or 15° - and she was down by the stern. When I was in the water I saw from the after funnels forward and her bows were well out of the water, heeling over at an angle of about 60°. I could not say whether the mainmast was there or not. I then started swimming away and the mast hit me and when I looked again all I could see was the starboard side of the bow nearly vertical.

Is there anything else you would like to tell us?

When I was on the forecastle I noticed a badly twisted bolt of pom pom practice ammunition. It was just by me.

Do you know where the practice pom pom ammunition was stowed?

There was one stowage just abaft the mainmast and there was one either side of the forward end of either battery in the superstructure.

Do you know anything about the supply for the 4".?

It came up through the hatch abreast the after funnel.

Do you know if this hatch was open or shut?

It was shut. I had asked the Officer for orders and he had told me to leave it shut.

Do you know where the spare U.P.ammunition was stowed?

In lockers along the forecastle.

NOTE: A very clear headed and intelligent witness, but it is doubtful if he is correct about "A" and "B" turrets only having fired.

Secret **INTERCEPTED CYPHER MESSAGE**

To: Admiralty
C-in-C H F
C.S.1.

27/5/41.

Cypher

Area 1.

27 MAY 1941

From: PRINCE OF WALES.

Method of Receipt (W/T, T/P, H/M, etc.)

IMMEDIATE.

Your 2317B/25?.

Burnt camouflage account has been compiled from preliminary examinations record. Further scrutiny? may disclose some minor inaccuracies.

At 0535/24 HOOD and PRINCE OF WALES in close order course 240° 28 knots sighted enemy hulls down on similar courses bearing 335°, BISMARCK astern lighter?' ship. Within gun range turns brought the enemy (?) 30°.

HOOD ordered G(?) I C just before opening fire at 0553. Range approximately 25,000 yards.

Part 1. T.O.O. 0948/27

PRINCE OF WALES opened fire at 0553 and ½. BISMARCK replied with extreme accuracy on HOOD, second or third salvo straddled and fire broke out in HOOD in vicinity port? after 4 inch gun mounting. Lighter ship engaged by PRINCE OF WALES. PRINCE OF WALES's opening salvo at BISMARCK observed over, sixth seen to straddle. At this time PRINCE OF WALES had 3 14inch guns in action. Y turret would not? bear.

Part 2. T.O.O. 0957/27

Fire in HOOD spreading rapidly to main mast. A * turn for 2 blue opened a valve? at PRINCE OF WALES 9th salvo and HOOD has a further 2 blue flying when she was straddled again and at 0600 a huge explosion occurred between after funnel and main mast. She sank in 3 to 4 minutes. C.O. PRINCE OF WALES saw whole incident. HOOD had fired 5 or 6 salvos but falling shot was not seen possibly because this coincided with the firing of PRINCE OF WALES's guns.

Part 3. T.O.O. 1001/27

PRINCE OF WALES's starboard 5·25 inch battery was now in action. Course had to be altered to starboard to avoid remains of HOOD; meanwhile BISMARCK shifted main and secondary fire quickly and accurately to PRINCE OF WALES. A heavy hit was felt almost immediately and at 0602 compass platform was hit, and majority personnel killed. Navigating Officer was wounded; Commanding Officer unhurt.

Part 4. T.O.O. 1010/27

Additional or Special Distribution:— T.O.O.

* 2 blue i.e.alter course 20° to port together. Final T.O.O. 1029/27

T.O.R.

To be completed on Cypher Log copy only, "Nil" being inserted if applicable :—

Passed by P/G or H/M to

sonar equipment was totally destroyed. The splinters also damaged the anti-aircraft gun directors. Another 380mm projectile hit the seaplane- and boat-hoisting crane. On bouncing off, it burst against the aft funnel. Fragments of the funnel walls pierced the deck and damaged a seaplane on the catapult. The Walrus seaplane was immediately pushed overboard. The crane mechanism was destroyed and unusable. The splinters also hit the funnel, and the holes it had caused in ventilation shafts allowed the smoke to be sucked inside the ship. It also left all the boats onboard unusable. Another German shell struck on the upper deck; this one, however, failed to explode and was later removed. One 380mm projectile landed 25m (80ft) short of the ship's side and pierced it about 8m (26ft)

From A. Jarski collection

Correspondence (radiograms) sent from Prince of Wales *on 24 May 1941, regarding details of sinking of* Hood.

Series B.

CAPTAIN JOHN CATTERALL LEACH? M.V.O , ROYAL NAVY, H.M.S. "PRINCE OF WALES," called and cautioned.

1. Q. Are you Captain J.C.Leach, M.V.O., Royal Navy, of H.M.S. "Prince of Wales."
   A. Yes.

2. Q. Will you tell u s what you saw from the time the action started until the "Hood" sunk.
   A. Before the action started I was in station on "Hood's" starboard quarter at a distance of abou four cables. We had had a concentration signal and waited to open fire in our proper time sector after "Hood" had opene fire. The "Hood" opened fire first and in between the time that she fired and the time it was due for me to fire the German ships opened fire. I saw the first salvo from the German ships arrive near the "Hood" and about the second or third salvo I looked toward the "Hood" and saw a fire burning on the superstructure deck on the port side right aft. I did not actually see the fire start but I saw it a few seconds after it had started. From that time onwards I looked at "Hood" occasionally but I noticed that the fire spread quickly from the port after superstructure deck till it was extended from th after superstructure deck to about the mainmast. (Witness was given a model of the "Hood" which he placed at the correct inclination, which was 40° to the right).

3. Q. What was the colour of this fire and was it accompanied by much smoke.
   A. The colour was reddish yellow and there was a certain amount of smoke, but no more than I should expect to see from a fire of that size.

4. Q. Would you indicate the colour on either of these two papers.
   A. The bottom was redder than the top and was somewhere between "B" and "D" on Exhibit One.
   We opened fire half a minute approximately after "Hood" and as far as I recollect it was about the third or fourth salvo from the enemy which caused the explosion in "Hood." I happened to be looking at "Hood" at the moment when a salvo arrived and it appeared the to cross the ship somewhere about the mainmast. In that salvo there were, I think, two shots short and one over, but it may have been the other war round. But I formed the impression at the time that something had arrived on board "Hood" in a position just before the mainmast and slightly to starboard. It was not a very definite impression that I had, but it was sufficiently definite to make me look at "Hood" for a further period. I in fact wondered what the result was going to be, and between one and two seconds after I formed that impression an explosion took place in the "Hood" which appeared to me to come from very much the same position in the ship. There was a very fierce upward rush of flame the shape of a funnel, rather a thin funnel, and almost instantaneously the ship was enveloped in smoke from one end to the other. Subsequently beyond glancing in the direction of the "Hood" I was fully occupied in attending to other thingsand I had no very distinct impression of anything after that except that I formed the impression that the gunwale of the "Hood" was just showing outside the cloud of smoke and quite a short distance above the water, I should say about two to three feet. I am not certain what part of the ship it was.

5. Q. In other words the bit of the ship's side that you last saw appeared to be intact.
   A. Yes, it was an unbroken line, but only a very narrow strip of the ship above the water, and I am not at all certain what portion of the ship it was.

(continued ....

below the armour belt, flooding a fuel tank. This also failed to explode and remained there until the battleship docked at Rosyth.

The *Prince of Wales* took seven hits: three 380mm and four 203mm shells. The situation on the British ship was serious, the damage from direct hits threatening the loss of another ship. Throughout the engagement, the ship's main battery proved defective, and Captain Leach was feared he might be left without any serviceable guns. The ammunition rooms under the fore quadruple turret were flooded by water coming in from the upper parts of the turret. The only water outlets were blocked, and the water in it rolled from side to side with the rolling of the ship, soaking and damaging equipment. Under these circumstances, at 06:03, Leach decided to break off the action and

Page 2.

CAPTAIN JOHN CATTERALL LEACH, M.V.O. ROYAL NAVY, H.M.S. "PRINCE OF WALES," continued.

6. Q. Can you describe the colour of the flame of the explosion.
   A. I formed the impression that it was generally rather lighterin colour than the first one. Somewhere between "D" and "F" on Exhibit One.

7. Q. Can you tell us the shape of the first fire.
   A. It was an irregular flickering fire and I should say was not more than 12 or 14 feet high in general, there may have been ~~tons~~ tongues above that but generally speaking it did not impress itself upon me as being a very tall fire Gas or a particularly solid one.

8. Q. Did you see much debris thrown up by the explosion.
   A. Yes, a considerable quantity of all sorts.

9. Q. Did you see some big objects in the debris.
   A. Yes.

10. Q. What was the state of the first fire when the explosion occurred.
   A. I did not notice it, but looking back on it I should say that it was less noticeable than it had been a little while previously.

11. Q. Are your recollections of this incident pretty clear now.
   A. My recollections are quite clear on what I have told you up to the present.

12. Q. You have told us you saw the "Hood" open fire.
   A. Yes.

13. Q. Can you tell us more about her shooting.
   A. As far as I remember she opened fire from her forward turrets, but before she blew up she had fired from either "X" or "Y" and I think both.

14. Q. Have you available any exact times of the "Hood" catching fire and blowing up.
   A. No, not exact times.

15. Q. Can you find out for us the interval between "Hood" opening fire and her blowing up.
   A. Yes, I will get that.

16. Q. Did "X" and "Y" fire after the fire had started.
   A. I think so.

17. Q. For the previous board you made sketch of the "Hood". Do you consider this copy to be correct particularly as regards colour.
   A. The general impression is correct but I think the flame and smoke should have extended higher relative to the upper deck and the sides of the cone of flame were more nearly parallel.

18. Q. Can you indicate any more closely than you have already done where the base of the explosion started.
   A. It was definitely just before the mainmast in my opinion and about the middle line. I would like to emphasise the difference in appearance between the fire on the port side and the explosion. The former gave the impression of a fire burning on the upper deck with flickering flames as might be expected with the wind made by the ship's speed

(Continued...........

Reports from the interrogations of the witnesses to the sinking of the Hood.

Via A. Jarski

Page 3.

CAPTAIN JOHN CATTERALL LEACH, M.V.O., ROYAL NAVY, H.M.S."Prince of Wales". Continued.

18.cont. It did not give me any impression having come from between decks. The explosion gave the impression of a vast blow-lamp. I almost expected to hear the corresponding noise but I did not. I do not remember hearing any noise.

19. Q. Was the explosion a flash or had it duration.
   A. I should say it had duration and ~~though~~ that it had not ceased by the time the ship became obscured in smoke from one end to the other. I did not notice any considerable quantity of debris until after the smoke had formed.

20. Q. Could you say definitely whether the armoured doors of "Hoods" torpedo tubes were open or shut.
   A. No.

21. Q. Have you any impression on that point.
   A. No.

22. Q. Did you at any time see any holes in the "Hood's" ship's side.
   A. No.

23. Q. So far as you can remember was the "Hood" still going at the same speed when she blew up.
   A. Yes, I am sure of this.

24. Q. Did you feel any shock to your own ship.
   A. None.

25. Q. Did you see anything in the debris which could possibly be portions of "X" or "Y" turrets.
   A. I remember seeing one fairly large plate very high in the air. Whether it was armoured plate or thin plate I do not know.

26. Q. Did you notice if "X" and "Y" turrets were intact at the time of the explosion.
   A. No, but I did not notice that there were any signs of damage. My impression was that "X" and "Y" were quite widely separated from the explosion

27. Q. You have told us that the effect of the explosion was similar to a vast blow lamp. Was there just one gush of flame or a number of gushes.
   A. One.

28. Q. Are you an expert in the appearance of explosions.
   A. No, but I should say the fire on the port side was not typical of a cordite fire. As regards the explosion, I consider this was obviously caused by some explosive going off but I could not say what sort of explosive.

WITNESS WITHDREW.

LIEUTENANT COMMANDER GEORGE WILLIAM ROWELL. ROYAL NAVY. "H.M.S. PRINCE OF WALES." called and cautioned.

29. Q. Are you Lieutenant Commander George William Rowell. Royal Navy. of "H.M.S."PRINCE OF WALES".
   A. Yes.

(Continued..........

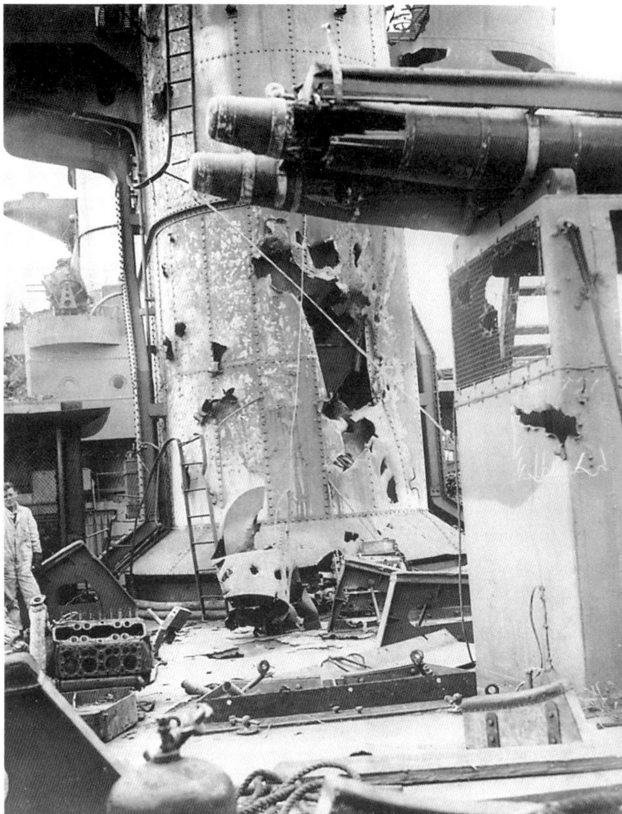

The damage sustained by the Prince of Wales *during the battle with the* Bismarck *and the* Prinz Eugen.

Via IWM

follow the enemy at a somewhat longer distance. Two minutes later, the *Prince of Wales* reduced her speed and made a smokescreen. During the fourteen minutes of the engagement, the British ship had fired eighteen salvoes at the enemy, scoring two direct hits; a few of the salvoes had fallen near the German battleship.[3] The cruiser's fire control noticed that after her eighth salvo the *Prince of Wales*, hidden behind a smokescreen, had changed her course to a south-easterly one. When she was 22km (24,000 yards) away, Admiral Lütjens ordered his ships to cease fire. At 06:10, an air alert was sounded aboard the two German ships when a Sunderland flying boat was sighted. The *Prinz Eugen*'s heavy antiaircraft battery commenced firing at the aircraft. It turned out later that the machine they attacked was Sunderland 'Z' of 201 Sqn RAF that had been watching the entire battle from above.

Back aboard the *Prince of Wales*, at 06:13, when she was making a turn behind her smokescreen, one of the 14in projectiles being loaded in 'Y' turret rolled off and blocked the turret's traverse. This put the turret out of action until 08:25, when the shell was removed. Only two guns were in service throughout that time, and it was only after five hours that nine of the ten guns had been unjammed. Captain Leach reported to the *Norfolk* that the *Hood* had been sunk. He also said that he would soon join the *Norfolk* 31km (17 nautical miles) astern of the *Bismarck*. He notified Admiral Wake-Walker of the damage the battleship had sustained, that 'A' and 'Y' turrets were out of action, and that her current maximum speed was 27 knots. Finally, he added that there was about 600 tons of water in the ship at the moment, this amount being likely to increase owing to leaks and damage below the waterline.

The British heavy cruisers shadowed the German battleship at a distance of 22–28km (12–15 nautical miles) proceeding on the same course as the German group and on either side of it. Holland's battle plan had assumed that the *Hood* and the *Prince of Wales* would be fighting the *Bismarck*, while the cruisers would take care of the *Prinz Eugen*. This was never put into practice, as the strict radio silence prevented Admiral Wake-Walker from being told about it. At 06:19, while pursuing the Germans, the cruiser *Suffolk* fired several 8in salvoes at the *Bismarck*, which fell short. After a few minutes the British cruiser held her fire owing to the ever-increasing range, as any further firing would have been a waste of time and ammunition.

Between 06:03 and 06:14, the hydrophones on the *Prinz Eugen* detected the sound of three torpedoes coming towards the cruiser. All three of

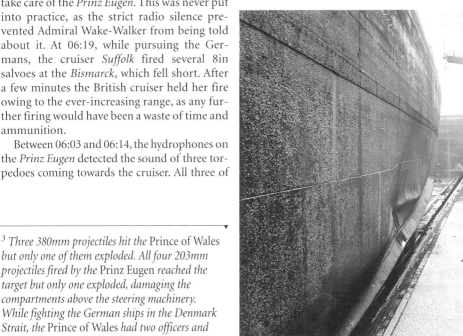

[3] *Three 380mm projectiles hit the* Prince of Wales *but only one of them exploded. All four 203mm projectiles fired by the* Prinz Eugen *reached the target but only one exploded, damaging the compartments above the steering machinery. While fighting the German ships in the Denmark Strait, the* Prince of Wales *had two officers and eleven enlisted men killed plus nine wounded.*

The damage sustained by the Prince of Wales *during the battle with the* Bismarck *and the* Prinz Eugen.

Via IWM

them were subsequently avoided. It was difficult to determine their source, as the ship was obliged to take evasive action owing to an enemy aircraft sighted on the horizon. Still, their bearings and range seemed to suggest at the time that they were launched from the *Hood* in long-range mode. Men aboard the *Prinz Eugen* spotted air bubbles marking the wake of the second and third torpedoes in the water.

The damaged *Prince of Wales* was gradually moving out of range of the German main batteries, which eventually allowed her to cease fire at 06:20. In the meantime, there had been a slight 'difference of opinion', so to speak, on the *Bismarck*'s bridge between Admiral Lütjens and Kapitän Lindemann. Witnesses to their conversation later mentioned a slight argument between the two concerning the future course of Operation *Rheinübung*. Lindemann wanted to continue the fight against the new opponent, which he would destroy with a 'single hard blow'. He was trying by all possible means to persuade the Admiral to begin another battle with what he considered an 'impaired' opponent but Lütjens rejected this. Engaging an enemy moving away in an easterly direction could, in his opinion, land them in a dangerous situation because it was from that direction that more enemy warships might arrive. The Admiral was aware that other British capital ships were steaming in their direction at the moment. He had no recent air reconnaissance data and was not in possession of the exact bearings of the British fleet which was after him. He therefore gave up the opportunity to sink the British battleship in favour of the original goal of attacking vital enemy convoys with very important supply shipments. Having been given command of the entire group, Lütjens did not have to justify his decision to the captain of the *Bismarck*.

When the battle ended, Brinkmann passed word to the *Bismarck*: 'Kapitän zur See to Admiral. No damage. Torpedo noises detected on port side from 245 degrees. Ship rapidly turned left.' At 07:05, Admiral Lütjens on the *Bismarck* reported to Group North: 'I have sunk a battleship in square AD 73.' The weather around Greenland was very bad, and the message reached Wilhelmshaven only about 13:00. At that time, Greenland was being affected by disturbances of the Earth's magnetic field. Owing to poor wave propagation, the German warships had problems with sending and receiving radio messages. The issue of torpedo noises detected by the *Prinz Eugen* reappeared at 07:23, when they were picked up on the port side coming from 245 degrees. The cruiser again rapidly turned to port to evade the torpedoes, returning to her previous course after four minutes.[4]

When the situation on the *Bismarck* was fully under control, all the officers on duty assembled at 08:30 in the mess in order to congratulate the First Officer on the sinking of the *Hood*. The battle in the Denmark Strait was a tactical success for Admiral Lütjens, but an hour after the battle Lütjens and Lindemann discussed the further course of the operation. Lütjens decided that the *Bismarck* had to call at Brest or Saint-Nazaire for necessary repairs without which they could not proceed with the operation. The undamaged *Prinz Eugen* was to continue the operation against convoys on her own.

[4] *Those might have been anomalies continuing from the day before, because the British war diaries do not mention any torpedoes having been launched.*

After the Battle

Damage to the *Bismarck*

The decision for the *Bismarck* to return to port was made on the grounds that her top speed was now only 28 knots and could fall to 26 knots in the future, since two boilers in boiler room No. 2 had been totally flooded and 5 per cent of reserve power was lost owing to a flooding of electric generator No. 4. Damage to forward sections and to outer tanks in boiler and machinery rooms caused the loss of the fuel they contained. If all that fuel was unavailable, the battleship's operational range would be reduced by some 2,040km (1,100 nautical miles). If the ship was to continue her mission, it was imperative that the damage to that section be repaired. Besides, the warships shadowing the *Bismarck* had superior radar equipment which allowed them to maintain direct contact, thus preventing the battleship from refuelling from a tanker while in radar contact.

During the battle, the *Bismarck* received three direct hits from 14in shells fired by the *Prince of Wales*. The first hit had the greatest influence on the further course of the operation. The shell hit the starboard side at the superstructure sections XX/XXI, exactly where the fuel tanks were. Then it travelled inside to make a hole in the bottom where sections XXI and XXII met. The torpedo bulkheads between sections XX and XXI as well as XXI and XXII were damaged. The resulting 1.9m (6ft) hole let about 2,000 tons of sea water into the forward sections of the hull. The shell also opened up a few compartments in the double bottom. The second hit was at section XIV below the armour belt, the shell exploding against the longitudinal torpedo bulkhead. As a result, the port electrical generator No. 4 was flooded. Because the bulkheads between this room and the adjacent port side rooms (boiler room No. 2 and its auxiliary compartment) were smashed, the sea water leaking in through the gaps thus created put the electric power plant out of action. Later on it was found that several fuel tanks and stowage compartments in the double bottom had also been damaged. The third shell passed through the ship, entering through a motor boat on the port side and out into the water on the starboard side. It did not cause any immediately evident damage, this only becoming noticeable later on. Its splinters had destroyed the hydraulic system powering the seaplane catapult. The shell exploded upon hitting the water, without causing any major damage. There were no casualties onboard the *Bismarck* during this engagement with the enemy.[5]

The crew immediately set to work repairing the damage. Meanwhile, the forward capstan room at

The forecastle of the Prinz Eugen *as it looked after the battle in the Denmark Strait. In the foreground are empty shell casings ejected by the cruiser's main guns.*

From the Prinz Eugen *archives*

TABLE 1
Fuel situation of the *Bismarck* from 07:00 hours 18 May to 08:00 hours 24 May 1941.

18 May – the *Bismarck* took on 8,100 tons of heating oil, of which 7,800 tons were to be burned. 200 tons were not loaded as planned due to a broken fuel hose. Operations with the *Prinz Eugen* from noon until late evening consumed 150 tons of fuel.

19 May – she left port at 02:00, entering the Baltic Sea. Sailing at 18 knots, she used up 400 tons of fuel.

20 May – the German force reached the Skagerrak and the Great Belt. Average speed between 00:00 and 21:00 around 17–18 knots. Departing the Skagerrak and southern Norway, speed was increased to 22 knots on average. Total fuel used was 432 tons.

21 May – sailing from the southern coast of Norway to Bergen (arrived at 10:30). Speed from 00:00 to 09:00 was 24 knots. It was reduced when calling at the fjord of Bergen. Anchoring between 10:30 and 19:30. Left the fjords 19:30–23:00 at low speed, increasing to 18 knots between 23:00 and 24:00. Total fuel consumption 425 tons.

22 May – the ship sailed toward the Denmark Strait at 24 knots. Total fuel consumption 640 tons.

23 May – continuing toward the Denmark Strait, reaching it at 18:21 with an average speed of 24 knots. At 19:22, the battleship was sighted by the *Suffolk*, and her speed then varied, ranging from 24 to 30 knots. Total fuel consumption 710 tons.

24 May – the cruisers *Suffolk* and *Norfolk* were in contact. At 05:53, the battleship engaged the *Hood* and the *Prince of Wales*. Speed during contact was almost 30 knots. Fuel consumption until 07:00 was 435 tons. Fuel contaminated and lost due to damage suffered – 1,000 tons.

Sailing at 30 knots, she used 1,000–1,100 tons of fuel daily with ten boilers steaming. From then on, the *Bismarck* had the fuel to make 2,000 nautical miles at 30 knots.

Fuel:
Available as of 18 May 1941: 7,800 tons
Used (+10%): 3,500 tons
Contaminated: 1,000 tons
Available as of 07:00 hours 24 May 1941: 3,300 tons

sections XX and XXI had become totally flooded. The rear bulkhead of section XX had to endure both the pressure of the water leaking in through the hole in the hull and that produced by the speed of the ship. In order to prevent the bulkhead collapsing, a group of carpenters supervised by the second damage control officer, Oberleutnant Karl Ludwig Richter, shored it up with stanchions. Groups of sailors under his command tried to enter the bow compartments through emergency doors, hoping that the pumps in the pump room could be switched on and the fuel there pumped out into the tanks adjacent to the boiler rooms. This proved impossible, as the pumps at section XX were already under water. The only remaining option was to try to use the neighbouring pumps at section XVII. However, these were much less efficient, and the intake valves turned out to have been damaged during the battle, rendering those pumps effectively useless. Thus the 1,000 tons of oil in the forward tanks were completely unavailable. Attempts were made to pump the fuel via the upper decks; however, this also failed and the idea was eventually abandoned.

Admiral Lütjens did not agree with suggestions made by the *Bismarck*'s captain to tilt the ship slowly to each side at reduced speed and then plug the holes in the hull with welded patches. Instead, he told Lindemann to first trim the ship, reduce speed, and then patch the hole in the hull. When the speed dropped to 22 knots, a patch was put over the hole, reducing the influx of water. The crew tried to pump the water out of the flooded rooms using portable pumps. The No. 4 generator at section XIV was completely flooded, which resulted in a reduction of power by half. The power supply for the various systems came from the other sources and did not affect the battleship's serviceability. The bulkheads in the port No. 2 boiler room and auxiliary compartments were sealed to prevent leaks. The initial success in stopping the flooding was short-lived, as vibration and soaking of the hammocks used to plug the holes opened up more leaks. When the water reached a height of 1.5m (5ft), the boilers had to be switched off. Another attempt to pump out the water was made during the night, but eventually the boiler rooms had to be declared unusable. The effects of the battle damage were gradually becoming evident. The *Bismarck* was 3 degrees down by the bow and had a 9 degrees list to port. The blades of the starboard propeller projected a little out of the water. Flooding the starboard ballast tanks at sections II and III reduced the list to port. These and all the other problems reduced the ship's speed to 28 knots. Also, leaking oil was leaving a trail in the ship's wake that could lead the pursuing enemy to her. This oil was from tanks in compartments at section XIV, and probably also at sections XX and XXI.

Lütjens' decisions

Admiral Lütjens decided to put in at Saint-Nazaire. Only there, in the giant Normandie Dock, could the *Bismarck*'s damage be repaired. The situation was becoming critical. With 2,000 tons of sea water having entered the hull, the battleship's speed was reduced by 3 knots following the shutting-down of two boilers. The fuel in the forward tanks was unavailable, and some of the tanks were leaking oil into the sea, leaving a visible trail. The Admiral was well aware that until British forces assembled, his ship would be constantly shadowed by the *Suffolk* and the *Norfolk* supported by the *Prince of Wales*. Lütjens had considered various options for the continuation of Operation *Rheinübung*. He thought about returning to Norway along the southern coast of Iceland and putting in at Bergen, which was only 2,040km (1,100 nautical miles) away, or Trondheim, 2,410km (1,300 miles) away. He also considered returning to Trondheim via the Denmark Strait; this would have meant 2,590km (1,400 miles) to cover. Considering the weather in the

[5] *Kapitänleutnant Hans Henning von Schultz, Intelligence Officer on the* Prinz Eugen, *says differently. His story is in accordance with the ship's War Diary. He says that the battleship gave optical signals to the cruiser at 09:50, the message being: 'Commander to commander. For your information, I have received two severe hits. One, at sections XIII and XIV, put the electric power plant No. 4 out of commission. Stoppable water is leaking into the port boiler room. The second hit – at sections XX and XXI at the bow, the projectile coming in on the port side and out on the starboard side through the lower deck. A third hit, in a boat – negligible. Besides that, I am fine. Five slightly injured'.*

Photo by Lagemann, via AJ-Press and IWM

The Bismarck *photographed on 24 May, after the battle in the Denmark Strait. During this engagement, the* Bismarck *received three direct hits with 14in shells fired by the* Prince of Wales. *The first of these was of the greatest significance for the further course of the operation – it hit the fuel tanks in the starboard bow, and penetrated the ship at an angle, coming out through the bottom and leaving a hole almost 2m (6.5ft) in diameter. Some 2,000 tons of sea water flooded the bow compartments. This picture, taken from the* Prinz Eugen, *clearly shows that the ship had become bow-heavy.*

Photo by Lagemann, via AJ-Press and IWM

strait and mostly poor visibility, this seemed feasible, but this option was abandoned in the face of the excellent British radar.

Moreover, the British fleet must have been alerted by then, and the Admiral had no idea of the position of the British battleships, except that they must be somewhere between his ships and Scapa Flow. Information received from Fleet Command had to be treated with caution, as it had been shown to sometimes be inaccurate by the unexpected appearance of the *Hood*, which had supposed to have been still moored in Scapa Flow. There still remained the option to sail east, to Saint-Nazaire, 1,110km (600 miles) further than Trondheim. The coming of night and the deteriorating weather conditions, with rough seas, made it seem possible that the shadowing British warships could be shaken off. It might then be possible to refuel from submarines or from tankers waiting in their operational zones. One more argument in favour of this option was the dry dock at Saint-Nazaire, suitable for the *Bismarck*.

About 10:00, Lütjens received more alarming news. During a routine exchange of visual signals with the *Prinz Eugen*, it turned out that the *Bismarck* had failed to receive the radio signals from Group North and SKL for the last two days. More strangely, they had been correctly received by *Prinz Eugen*. The information they contained concerned the current courses and locations of enemy warships as well as British convoys at sea. They additionally mentioned German submarine attacks on the convoys. The lack of confirmation of receipt by the *Bismarck* of the transmissions from headquarters and the forwarding of the messages addressed to the *Bismarck* by the *Prinz Eugen* obliged Admiral Lütjens to revise his plans. A 'deaf' flagship could not continue with the planned operation of raiding enemy convoys. She had to reach Brest or Saint-Nazaire as soon as possible. Brest was alerted in case it should prove impossible to reach Saint-Nazaire for some reason. It was only there, with shipyard facilities on hand, that most of the damage could be repaired and, most importantly, the communications equipment could be repaired.[6]

After 10:10, Lütjens ordered the *Prinz Eugen* to take up position astern of the *Bismarck* and check whether the oil leak had reduced. Lindemann requested Brinkmann to immediately report to him the effects of the leakage. The fuel quickly spread over the water, forming a visible trail large enough to be sighted by Sunderland or Catalina

From the Prinz Eugen *archives*

The Bismarck *astern of the* Prinz Eugen *after the battle.*

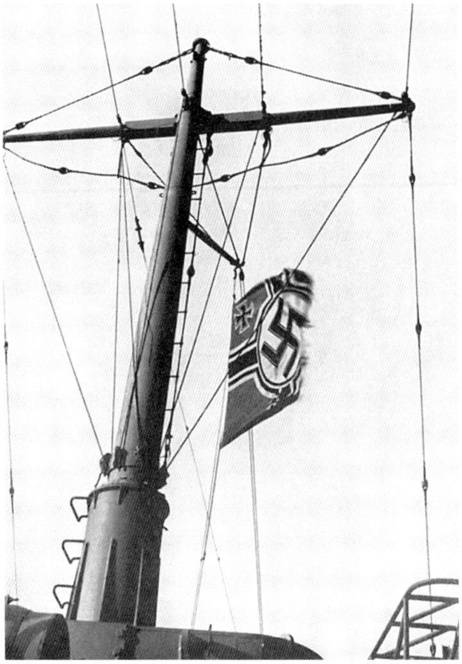

A torn flag on the Prinz Eugen *– a result of the battle.*

Photo by Schöppe, via AJ-Press

flying boats patrolling the area. The contaminated wake of the battleship was indeed soon spotted by a patrolling Sunderland and by the *Suffolk*. After an hour, the *Prinz Eugen* finished her inspection of the oil spill and returned to her previous position. The British side carried out similar procedures to check the damage sustained and the trail left by the *Prince of Wales*. The *Norfolk* and *Suffolk* followed her on both sides, observing the fuel leaking from her damaged tanks. The spill could easily be spotted by the German long-range reconnaissance aircraft, thus putting the *Prince of Wales* in a situation very much like that of the *Bismarck* – the hunter could easily become the hunted if her oil slick attracted U-boats patrolling in those waters.

At about 10:00, a Sunderland sighted the trail of oil from the *Bismarck* and reported it to the *Norfolk*, giving the current position and exact course of the ship. The decoded messages from the British warships constantly sent to the *Bismarck* by Group North confirmed that contact was being maintained by three enemy vessels. About 11:00, the weather began to slowly deteriorate. With passing squalls and patches of mist appearing ahead of the German ships, there was hope. The sun still broke through the dark clouds from time to time. The visibility between the *Bismarck* and her British pursuers at one moment increased to 37km (20 miles), then dropped. It was very difficult to keep visual contact, but they kept shadowing her at a distance of 35–37km (19–20 miles). They systematically reported to the Home Fleet the exact bearing, course and speed of the German ships. Just as regularly, with only a slight delay, Group North transmitted the decoded *Suffolk* radio intercepts to the German ships.

[6] *It is conceivable that the reason why the* Bismarck *failed to receive the signals was a defect in the radio receivers. The radio set might have been damaged during the battle with the* Norfolk *and later the* Hood. *Another possibility, human error, has to be rejected. The incoming and outgoing signals were double-handled by radio rooms A and B. Then they were processed by the communication centre. This ensured that errors were prevented and no messages were missed in the process.*

Bismarck Alone

Operation *Hood*

At 12:00 on 24 May 1941, the *Bismarck* reached position 60°50' N, 37°50' W, and from then on Operation *Rheinübung* was controlled by the Paris-based Group West. Only then, based on radio reports received by Group West from the *Bismarck*, did it become known what had happened in the Denmark Strait. The reports transmitted in the early morning had not been received until then because of bad propagation and magnetic disturbances around Greenland. Admiral Lütjens reported that between 05:52 and 06:37 the *Prinz Eugen* had received the *Bismarck*'s four reports to Group North. The first was 'Began fighting two heavy vessels', but this failed to reach the addressee, with further attempts failing also. It was confirmed at 07:05, when the *Prinz Eugen* received another *Bismarck* message, 'Sank a battleship in square AD 73'. At 12:38, Group West sent the ship part of a message received at 11:44 concerning the positions of U-boats and supply ships in the North Atlantic that had been subordinated to Lütjens. With an easterly wind and calm seas, at 13:00 both vessels changed course to 180 degrees and accelerated to 24 knots to facilitate the makeshift sealing of the *Bismarck*'s forward compartments. The weather in the Atlantic being forecasted to worsen soon, this moment of calm had to be used to do the necessary work.

After the battle, the three British ships continued to shadow the enemy. She was sailing on a south-westerly course with minor alterations until 12:40. Visibility fluctuated between as little as 3.7–5.5km (2–3 miles) to as much as 32km (17 miles). Radar contact was maintained at the limit of the *Bismarck*'s main battery range. Each change of speed or course was immediately reported by observers to Vice Admiral Wake-Walker, who in turn passed it on to Admiral Tovey aboard the *King George V*. The German ships soon entered a patch of mist and rain. Throughout the entire operation, the *Prinz Eugen* kept a safe distance from the British naval group. If the latter had come within the range of the enemy's guns, immediate action would have been taken by Admiral Lütjens on the *Bismarck*. It was almost 13:15 when the *Bismarck* received a radio message from SKL that an American Coast Guard vessel, the *Madoc*, had made her presence known in square AJ 3920. It was one of the many messages sent to the battleship to aid the admiral in making the best decision concerning the further course of the group and the operation. Before 13:50, Admiral Lütjens sent another message to SKL and to Group West, saying that he had entered square AK 11 at 14:00 and was in contact with the battleship *King George V* and two heavy cruisers. He also stated that he was not going to take any action before sundown.

The foredeck of the Prinz Eugen. *Aft of the conning tower, on the bridge, the lookouts are scanning the horizon. This picture was taken after the German ships had separated, when the* Prinz Eugen *was continuing the operation.*

Photo by Busch, via AJ-Press

About 14:20, Group North informed Admiral Lütjens about the pursuing British ships, which were sending messages about the exact bearings of the *Bismarck* and the *Prinz Eugen*, and that the commander of the British warships was onboard the heavy cruiser 1 UY (i.e. *Norfolk*). Because of the requirement to keep radio silence, Lütjens ordered that orders be transmitted to the *Prinz Eugen* visually. He gave detailed instructions as to how both ships were to separate. Although this was the principal purpose of the manoeuvre, it was also hoped to break contact with their shadowers. The *Bismarck* was to set a southerly course, and then turn west into an approaching rain squall. The *Prinz Eugen* was to maintain her course and speed for at least three hours after separating from the *Bismarck*. Having shaken off the British ships, she was to refuel from either the tanker *Belchen* or the *Lothringen*, and proceed alone. The separation procedure was codenamed Operation *Hood*. Apart from this, Lütjens radioed further orders (regarding the continuation of the operation) to the Commander-in-Chief of the U-boat force, Grossadmiral Dönitz. Submarines were to form a picket line to the west of the southern tip of Greenland in square AJ 68 and wait in ambush for his British 'shadows'. He gave detailed instructions and bearings to all the submarines put under his command. Lütjens intended the U-boats lie in wait for the enemy on the morning of 25 May. He hoped this would free him from his pursuers once and for all.

The course that the *Bismarck* had set would theoretically take her rapidly away from the area of British patrols and American air reconnaissance, but at 14:42 an unidentified aircraft was sighted astern. At first it was thought to be a Dornier flying boat, but when it did not give an identification signal, it was assumed to be hostile. It was indeed an American Catalina flying boat. The alarm was sounded, and the *Bismarck*'s anti-aircraft guns opened fire. Owing to engine trouble or more likely damage sustained, the Catalina made off to the north, disappearing from view at 16:30. All this time, the *Bismarck* continued to receive information from friendly reconnaissance reports and enemy intercepts helping Lütjens to predict the enemy's next move. He also got aerial reconnaissance reports on the course and speed of British convoys.

At 15:08, Admiral Lütjens gave the SKL and Group West more details of the battle off Iceland. His signal said that the battlecruiser *Hood* had been destroyed at 06:00 that morning following an exchange of fire which lasted no more than five minutes; that the battleship *King George V* had been hit several times by the German warships; and that the *Bismarck* had to sail at reduced speed because of flooding in the forward section of the ship.

The *Bismarck* was slowly coming into a heavy squall. Visibility dropped, and the admiral decided that it was the right time for the ships to separate as planned. At 15:40, he signalled the *Prinz Eugen* to 'perform the *Hood*'. The *Bismarck* increased speed to 28 knots, turned to starboard, and headed westward, while the *Prinz Eugen* held her course and speed. However, the attempt to separate failed owing to the bad weather not lasting long enough. Even though the *Bismarck* made a full circle, British vessels were again to be seen to starboard. At 15:59, she returned to her previous course, increased speed, and soon rejoined the *Prinz Eugen*.

At 16.44, the *Bismarck* received a message from Group North informing her about a change of the positions of U-boats in the nearest operational squares the battleship would be crossing. The signal gave the positions of eleven submarines as recorded at 08:00 on 24 May 1941. An hour later, intelligence officer Korvettenkapitän Reichard

Photo by Busch, via AJ-Press

Having evaded the British warships, the Prinz Eugen *was to refuel from the tankers* Belchen *or* Lothringen *and continue the mission on her own.*

The Commander of Group West, Generaladmiral Saalwächter.

Via CAW

contacted intelligence officer Kapitänleutnant von Schultz, asking whether he had also received the message with the positions of German U-boats. Because of the radio silence, he sent the question via visual signalling. Von Schultz replied that the information had not been received completely owing to the weather conditions and reduced visibility between the ships. At 17:36, the battleship received a message from the commander of the SKL, congratulating the admiral on the sinking of the *Hood* and informing him that Lütjens' messages to him of 06:32 and 08:01 hours had not been received until 13:40. Ten minutes later, the *Bismarck* intercepted another piece of good news from the Intelligence Headquarters to the Fleet Command praising the work of both the *Bismarck*'s and the *Prinz Eugen*'s decoding teams. Their achievements had been recognized at the highest levels, which was further confirmed by other messages to the Fleet Command intercepted by both ships.

In the evening, the German ships entered an area of thick fog, which reawakened hopes of a successful separation. The order to commence Operation *Hood* was once more signalled to the *Prinz Eugen*. At 18:14, the manoeuvre began as before. The *Bismarck* rapidly turned back, while the *Prinz Eugen* first headed west, and then north, to hide from the enemy in a squall. The *Bismarck* turned 180 degrees to starboard. Closing on the heavy cruiser *Suffolk*, she opened fire from all her main guns at a range of 18,300m (20,000 yards). The cruiser increased speed at once and made smoke. She was also quick enough to fire nine salvoes at the *Bismarck* before the latter withdrew. Sailing to port of the cruisers, the *Prince of Wales* also joined the fight about 18:46. Meanwhile, a few salvoes fired by the *Bismarck* landed some 900m (980 yards) to port of the *Suffolk*. According to British observers, the fire from the *Prince of Wales* failed to straddle the German ship. The *Bismarck* fired nine salvoes at the *Prince of Wales* during this engagement, without scoring any hits. As a result of this engagement, all three British ships found themselves on the port side of the *Bismarck* at 18:40. This time, the German ships had separated successfully.

Heading for Saint-Nazaire

At 19:50, Group West radioed Admiral Lütjens, replying to his signal of that morning about taking the *Bismarck* to Saint-Nazaire. They agreed that once he had broken contact with the enemy, he should make for the French port. They also informed him of the preparations being made at Brest to receive the battleship should that become necessary. It was assumed that steaming at 28 knots the *Bismarck* would manage to escape the British warships pursuing her. However, at that time Group West was completely unaware of the Bismarck's fuel problems or the damage she had sustained. The *Bismarck* soon received another report: an American aircraft carrier was probably present in the area. All the anti-aircraft battery crews took their stations. In the evening, at 19:58, Lütjens sent SKL a radio message informing them about the short engagement with the battleship, which the Germans still identified as the *King George V*, and that the *Prinz Eugen* had managed to separate from the *Bismarck* during the action. The battleship also confirmed having visual contact with the shadowing enemy. At 20:56, she sent a message to inform Group North about radar contact with the enemy, her shortage of fuel, and a change of course. The inability to use the fuel in the forward tanks forced him to choose the shortest route to Saint-Nazaire. This new course resulted in a change in the orders to the U-boats that had been in the area for the past twenty-four hours. Lütjens cancelled the order for them to form a picket line off Greenland, but kept them at his disposal.

With the *Hood* sunk and the *Prince of Wales* damaged, the British were not in a good position. Admiral Tovey hoped that the German ships would not head back for the Denmark Strait but continue southward. This would have enabled him to bring more capital ships into the area and set up an ambush. However, in order for this to succeed, the battleship's speed had to be reduced and the distance between the German squadron and the slower British warships reduced at all costs, to prevent the *Bismarck* and the *Prinz Eugen* from escaping Tovey's ships under the cover of night. At 15:09 the admiral ordered his aircraft carrier *Victorious* escorted by four cruisers to set the most appropriate course that would allow her to take a position 185km (100 nautical miles) from the German ships. From there, she was to mount a torpedo attack on the *Bismarck*. The admiral planned for the final battle to take place the next morning, just after sunrise, assuming that the *Bismarck*'s speed was successfully reduced by that time, and that the battleship *King George V* and the battlecruiser *Repulse* made contact with the enemy by 08:30, an hour-and-a-half after the sun came up. He could not depend on the *Prince of Wales*, since she, like the *Bismarck*, was having fuel trouble and, on top of that, two turrets unusable and a completely wrecked bridge. She had to sail at an economical speed of 22–24 knots, and every time the *Bismarck* speeded up, she was left further and further behind. Still, until the main force arrived, the *Prince of Wales* was needed as a potential opponent to the *Bismarck*. The Germans were unaware that Tovey had forbidden her to become involved in a battle. She was only allowed to engage if directly fired at by the *Bismarck*. The fuel situation on the other pursuing ships was also unfavourable. For example, the *Repulse*, which had a short exchange of gunfire with the Germans, was left with only as much fuel as was needed to reach Newfoundland. The escorting destroyers were worse off, and they had been long since been sent to Reykjavik to refuel. The battleship *Rodney*, commanded by Captain Frederick Dalrymple-Hamilton, with three escorting destroyers was to the south of her, and was to join her at about 10:00 sailing on a south-easterly course. An hour later, Tovey's group was to be joined by the westbound battleship *Ramilles* under Captain Arthur Read. Thus, at the decisive moment, the British admiral was to have at his disposal one aircraft carrier and four capital ships that were capable of opposing the *Bismarck*.

Along with the *Victorious*, the entire group under Rear Admiral Alban T.B. Curteis aboard the cruiser *Galatea* increased their speed to 28 knots and set such a course as to find themselves 185km (100 miles) from the enemy at 21:00. However, earlier events had thwarted these plans. The *Bismarck*'s short engagement with the *Prince of Wales* had put her now on a westerly course, and as a result, it was impossible to reach a position suitable for a torpedo attack before 23:00. The rear admiral ordered that a torpedo attack be prepared for 22:30, when the enemy would be less than 222km (120 nautical miles) away. Another problem was that the *Victorious* had been only recently commissioned, and some of her air crews, especially those of the Fulmars of 820 Sqn, had had less than a week of practice. The Swordfish pilots of 825 Sqn were in a better position. An attack undertaken by inexperienced pilots in such weather conditions and after so few hours on the aircraft carrier would have obviously been doomed to failure. The only hope lay in the experience of the Swordfish pilots, who had already taken part in a few sorties. At 22:10, nine Swordfish took off from the *Victorious*. At 23:00, they were followed by three Fulmars, and three more at 01:00, right after sunset, tasked with watching the target until sunrise because the next torpedo attack had been scheduled for the morning. The 825 Sqn formation was led by Lieutenant Commander Esmonde. The Swordfish were equipped with radar to assist navigation in such difficult weather conditions.

The weather was very bad during take-off. The carrier's flight deck was rolling and pitching in the strong, north-westerly wind, but the aircraft got off successfully and set a course of 225

The first group of torpedo-armed Swordfish took off from the aircraft carrier Victorious *in order to prevent the* Bismarck's *escape into the safety of Brest.*

Via IWM

degrees. The slow Swordfishes were shortly joined by the Fulmars, and the combined force headed towards the *Bismarck*'s reported current location. At 22:30, the formation made radar contact with the battleship sailing ahead of them on a south-westerly course. Lieutenant Commander Esmonde made a circle and located the other warships in the area: *Suffolk*, *Norfolk*, *Prince of Wales* and USS *Madoc*. The *Bismarck* was 11km (6 miles) from the aircraft and any advantage of surprise, which the pilots had hoped for, had now been lost. Esmonde divided his formation into three groups and commenced his attack.

It was almost 23:30 when the day's second air raid warning was issued aboard the *Bismarck*. Despite the late hour, there was still daylight. Several aircraft were approaching from the bow quarter in a tight formation preparing to attack the ship. The heavy anti-aircraft crews were ready. As the nine torpedo-carrying Swordfish came upon the battleship, all the anti-aircraft guns immediately opened fire. One of the forward 380mm guns and the 150mm guns also joined in, the *Bismarck*'s captain hoping that their shell splashes would hinder the attacking aircraft. The Swordfish, though, smoothly bypassed the obstacles and were gradually closing in on the ship.

The tactics employed consisted of launching torpedoes from several directions at the same time so that even if one was successfully evaded, the others could not be. Since Esmonde's machine was hit, the commander was obliged to change this tactic. He proceeded with the attack and decided to drop the torpedo when in a good position. Only the incredible, almost suicidal, determination of the pilots was responsible for the continuation of the attack. The aircraft were flying at 2m (6.5ft) above the water and dropped their torpedoes at only 400–500m (450–550 yards) from the target. The battleship increased speed to 27 knots and began to zigzag in order to evade the torpedoes, in which she succeeded brilliantly. The other group, led by Flight Lieutenant P. Gick, came in from the starboard side, which proved rather unsuitable for an attack. He then circled over the target to choose a better angle. His wingmen carried on their attack, dropping their torpedoes off the starboard bow, the *Bismarck* avoiding these too. A moment later, the two aircraft of the third group flew in from the port side. These were piloted by Flight Lieutenant H.C. Pollard, and Flying Officer R.G. Lawson. Despite the heavy anti-aircraft fire from the battleship, they had a good angle of approach. Still, like the previous aircraft, they were unable to reach the *Bismarck* at the moment. It was then

Via IWM

Swordfish onboard the Victorious *waiting for a take-off order against the* Bismarck. *The photograph was taken on 24 May 1941.*

that Percy Gick unexpectedly appeared. The Swordfish he was flying came at low level from the bow quarter and dropped its torpedo amidships. His appearance caught the Germans unawares, leaving them no time to take evasive action. The torpedo hit but exploded on the battleship's armour belt, which absorbed the entire force of the blast, thus leaving the ship unharmed.

Steaming at a high speed and skilfully steered by Matrosenhauptgefreiter Hans Hansen, the *Bismarck* took only one torpedo hit during the aerial attack. It hit her starboard side at the level between sections VIII and X, the explosion raising a huge fountain of water. Oberbootsman Kirchberg, standing next to the starboard 105mm anti-aircraft gun, was thrown against the hangar wall by the force of the blast and killed. Damage control later found no major damage, and the ship returned to her previous course. However, increasing speed to 27 knots had raised the water pressure on the hull, and this, coupled with the evasive manoeuvres during the attack, had forced off the patches applied to the damaged bow and flooding resumed. After the action, the ship was heavier by the bow. The vibrations caused by the firing of her guns and the torpedo hit on the starboard side

TABLE 2
825 Sqn pilots who took part in the attack on the *Bismarck* on 24 May 1941.

Subsection	*Aircraft*	*Pilot*	*Observer*	*Radio gunner*	*Result of action*
1st	(5)A+	Lt Cdr (A) E.K. Esmonde, RN	Lt C.C. Ennever, RN	PO(A) S.E. Parker, RN Fx.76360	Port bow
1st	(5)C	S-Lt (A) J.C. Thompson, RN	A/S-Lt R.L. Parkinson, RN	PO(A) A.L. Johnson, RN D/Jx.146558	Port bow
1st	(5)B	Lt N.G. MacLean, RNVR	T/S-Lt (A) L. Bailey, RNVR	NA D.A. Bunce, RN, SFx.631	Port side
2nd	(5)F+	Lt P.D. Gick, RN	S-Lt (A) V.K. Norfolk, RN	PO(A) L.D. Sayer, RN Fx.76577	Port bow
2nd	(5)G	T/Lt (A) W.F.C. Garthwaite, RNVR	T/S-Lt (A) W.A. Gillingham, RNVR	LA H.T.A. Wheeler, RN Fx.189404	Starboard bow
2nd	(5)H/V4337	S-Lt (A) P.B. Jackson, RN	A/S-Lt D.A. Berrill, RN	LA F.G. Sparkes	Starboard quarter
3rd	(5)K	Lt (A) H.C.M. Pollard, RN	T/S-Lt (A) D.M. Beattie, RNVR	LA P.W. Clitheroe, DSM, RN P/Jx.135706	Port quarter
3rd	(5)L	T/S-Lt (A) R.G. Lawson, RNVR	A/S-Lt F.L. Robinson, RN	LA I.L. Owen	Port quarter
3rd	(5)M	S-Lt (A) A.J. Houston, RNVR	T/S-Lt (A) J.R. Geater, RNVR	PO(A) W.J. Clinton, RN	Didn't find the *Bismarck*

A slow Fairey Swordfish torpedo bomber was the first to set off to attack the Bismarck. *Its antiquated appearance earned it the nickname of 'Stringbag'.*

Via IWM

Via IWM

The Victorious *turning into the wind and preparing aircraft for take-off.*

The Victorious *launching aircraft – this photograph was taken during a later period, when the ship was operating in Norwegian waters.*

Via IWM

resulted in a gap appearing in the bulkheads between the port No. 2 boiler room and the electric power plant. Flooding in the bow increased, and another boiler room was taking in water. At 23:38, Lütjens informed Group West about the air attack from a British aircraft carrier in square AK 19. The bad weather at the time delayed the transmission of radio messages to headquarters, and having no confirmation of receipt, the admiral ordered that they be re-sent until they were confirmed. After midnight, the battleship sent another message about the torpedo attack, and a little later, at 00:28, about the single torpedo hit taken on the starboard side which had turned out to have done no real damage. As the Swordfish from the *Victorious* carried out their attack on the battleship, the British ships that were following her temporarily lost visual contact. After the attack, the *Bismarck* reduced speed so that emergency patches could be fitted to the bow. This allowed the British to come closer to her and, more importantly, reduce the distances between their own ships.

Lacking radar, the Fulmars were less successful in locating the battleship, only one making contact and then not for long. The Swordfish had difficulty finding the *Victorious* on their return flight, and two crews had to ditch but were picked up safely by auxiliary vessels a few days later. The sun set at 00:52, leaving the aircraft to attempt to land back aboard ship in pitch darkness. On top of that, the ship hit a squall which completely hid her from view. Admiral Curteis had ordered his ships to change course towards the returning aircraft to help them to land, and the carrier's commander, Captain Bovell, took the risky decision to use searchlights to illuminate the approach for the pilots, which might well have attracted

Force H, under the command of Vice Admiral Sir James Somerville, was based in Gibraltar. Their mission of escorting a troop-carrying convoy in the Atlantic was cancelled, and on 24 May 1941 the force joined the hunt for the Bismarck. *Shown in the picture is the aircraft carrier* Ark Royal.

Via CAW and IWM

Photo by Busch, via AJ-Press

A bit of leisure time for sailors aboard the Prinz Eugen.

U-boats, but he had no choice. It was vital that the aircraft and their crews be recovered, as another attack was scheduled for sunrise. These measures allowed all the Swordfish to safely land on the carrier between 02:00 and 02:30, with the last Fulmar that had been watching the *Bismarck* landing at 03:06. From that moment, Admiral Tovey could only depend on reports from the British warships shadowing the *Bismarck*.

The Home Fleet's Hunt

Escape

The evening of 24 May 1941 found most of the Home Fleet at sea, under the direct command of Admiral Tovey on board the *King George V*. Having received the bad news of the sinking of the *Hood*, the Admiralty directed all the ships in the vicinity of the *Bismarck* against her. Tovey considered all possible options available to Admiral Lütjens. There were three conceivable routes the German battleship could take. She could rendezvous with a tanker off the westernmost point of Greenland. She could also – if she had sustained damage during the battle of the Denmark Strait, of which Tovey had no confirmation in the reports he had received – head for western France or back to Germany. Tovey felt it was most likely that the *Bismarck* was refuelling off Greenland. The British warships at sea at the time were not advantageously positioned and it took some time to assemble them all near the *Bismarck*. The loss of the *Hood*, which had been considered the symbol of the Royal Navy's power, called for the sinking of her defeater by all means. To make matters worse, the fast-steaming *Bismarck* was gradually pulling away from her pursuers. Tovey and his group were on a north-westerly course in order to cut the *Bismarck*'s way if she tried to turn back that way. The enemy was in the meantime slowly moving away on a south-westerly course.

After midnight, the *Bismarck* maintained her course, with the British 'shadows' astern and to port at a safe distance but maintaining radar contact. At 02:48, the *Bismarck* received a radio message from Group West. They agreed with Admiral Lütjens' first point, this being the change of course to Saint-Nazaire. As to the second point, they gave the admiral the positions of U-boats at his disposal in squares BE 6420, BE 6620 and BF 4420. After 03:00, Admiral Lütjens decided to make one more attempt to shake off his pursuers. The battleship increased her speed and turned to starboard at 03:06, first heading west, then changing to north-west at about 03:40. Ten minutes later she made a turn north and, having described almost a full circle, set an easterly course to Saint-Nazaire. The British had in the meantime been zigzagging in fear of German submarine attack. At 03:06, they had just commenced a turn to port when the German battleship rapidly turned to starboard and increased her speed. Before they realized this, radar contact between the *Suffolk* and the *Bismarck* was lost at about 03:30. Ten minutes later, after another alteration of course, the battleship had finally moved out of the British cruiser's radar range. The *Suffolk* had been zigzagging for a while and was used to

LOSING CONTACT WITH THE *BISMARCK*

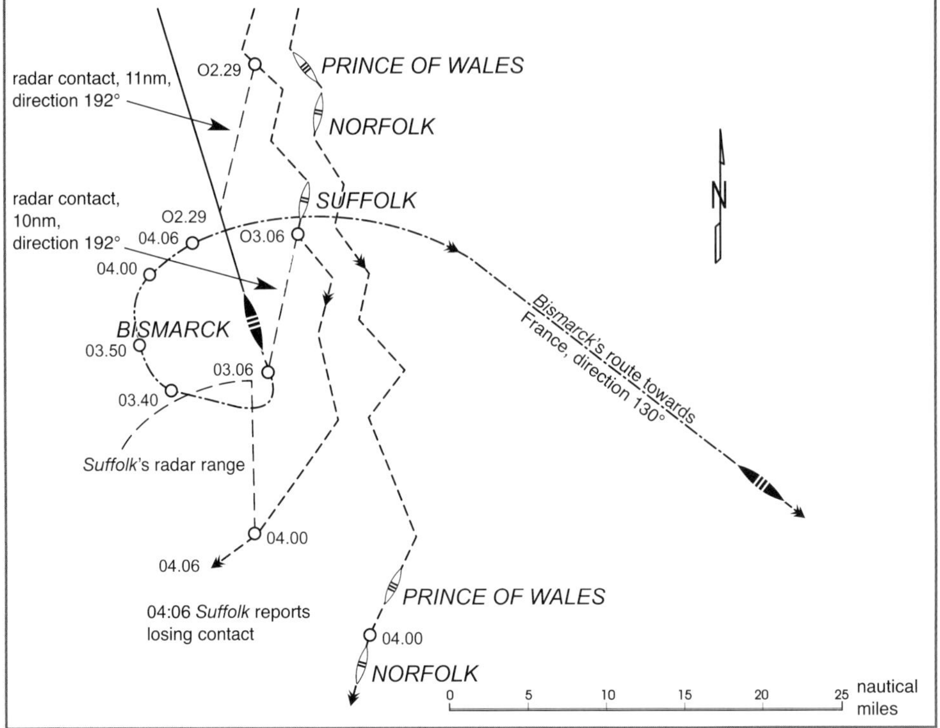

regularly losing contact with the enemy during this manoeuvre. With the *Bismarck* maintaining a steady course, the British had always regained contact after a while. However, in this case, the unexpected increase in speed and change of course helped the Germans to lose contact with the pursuers. The latter expected to regain it at about 03:30, but at 04:01, the *Suffolk* had to report that she had definitely lost contact with the German battleship.

After contact had been lost, Rear Admiral Wake-Walker on board the *Norfolk* increased speed and began a search for the German battleship on the starboard quarter. This lasted until 11:00 and did not yield any results. The rear admiral told Admiral Tovey that the battleship had probably turned 90 degrees west, made a circle outside the range of his group, and headed east. At 06:20, Admiral Tovey ordered that the *Prince of Wales* join his group of warships and participate in the search for the *Bismarck* to the west. The *Suffolk* was to search to the north. Rear Admiral Curteis was instructed to launch aerial patrols from the *Victorious* and, along with the cruisers, comb the north-west quarter, in which the last contact with the *Bismarck* had been recorded. But the entire search, aided by the radar-equipped Swordfishes from 825 Sqn, was to no avail.

At the same time, the Admiralty made decisions the consequences of which might soon have proved fatal. The greatest possible number of warships in the Atlantic at that moment had to be mobilized to join the search for the German battleship, or more ought to be quickly brought in from other areas. There were several convoys in the North Atlantic escorted by battleships, heavy cruisers and destroyers. It was decided that these warships would detach from their convoys to take part in the search. The heavy cruiser *London*, commanded by Captain R.M. Servaes, which was escorting a convoy from Gibraltar to Great Britain, was ordered to leave it and relocate to the area near 25° 30′N and 42°W. Based on intercepted signals, the Admiralty expected to find the German tanker from which the *Bismarck* might try to refuel at these bearings. The area to the south-west of Tovey's flagship was being searched by the battleship *Ramilles*. The battleship *Rodney*, operating off Iceland, was also dispatched to look for the Germans, but due to bad weather she was trailing behind the *King George V*. Vice Admiral James Somerville's Force H was stationed at Gibraltar. Their mission to escort a convoy of troopships in the Atlantic was cancelled and the force was deployed for the hunt for the *Bismarck* on 24 May. It consisted of the battlecruiser *Renown*, the aircraft carrier *Ark Royal*, the cruiser *Sheffield*, and six destroyers. At that time, they were about 2,400km (1,300 nautical miles) away and were ordered to intercept the *Bismarck* from the south-west. After the unexpected loss of radar contact, Admiral Tovey was forced to begin his hunt anew.

Although this attempt to shake off his pursuers had been successful, Admiral Lütjens was not aware of it, since the *Bismarck* was still picking up British radar signals. Therefore, suspecting that the British knew his bearing and still had radar contact, he did not maintain radio silence, thus allowing them to intercept his signals. After 07:00, Lütjens radioed Group West, saying that the enemy had radar contact in square AK 55. Ironically, this very message contributed to the final loss of contact by the British. It was, of course, intercepted and led to an error in calculating the current position of the *Bismarck*. As a result, the British warships were sailing farther away from her at the moment. Another piece of good news sent by Group West at 08:46 and received by the *Bismarck* at 10:42 was a decoded message from the *Suffolk* (K3G) revealing that at 02:13 the cruiser was still in contact with her. Then three-

Via CAW and IWM

Force H, under the command of Vice Admiral Sir James Somerville, was based in Gibraltar. Their mission of escorting a troop-carrying convoy in the Atlantic was cancelled, and on 24 May 1941 the force joined the hunt for the Bismarck. *Shown in the picture is the aircraft carrier* Ark Royal.

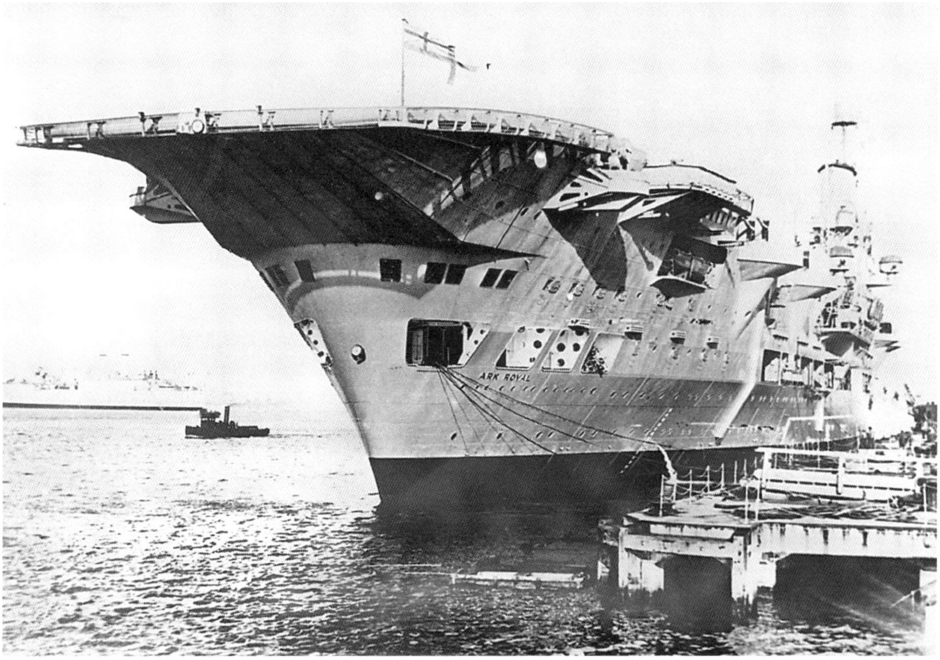

A Swordfish hunting for the Bismarck.

Via IWM

character tactical messages were intercepted giving no information about her position. This convinced Group West that contact with the British had been lost. The German battleship had a radio-location finder for locating radar signals emitted by enemy equipment. On receiving such signals, it notified its operators about the contact by means of visual and audio signals. It was also capable of finding the wavelength, frequency, power and estimated source of the impulses. It was therefore practically impossible to make a mistake in the processing of intercepted radar signals. The only possible causes of data errors were weather anomalies, reflection of waves, and natural perturbations of the Earth's magnetic field. It is possible that the *Bismarck* actually entered such a zone and, somewhat strangely, was receiving impulses from the *Suffolk*. Right after 09:00, Lütjens sent four signals to Group West, giving further details of the battle off Iceland and the ship's damage. He also informed them that the *Bismarck* was still picking up British radar signals. At 10:00, radio silence was ordered on the battleship.

About 11:30, Admiral Tovey received an urgent message from the Admiralty informing him that the *Bismarck* had been located, and he was given relevant data collected from land-based RDFs in Britain, Iceland and Gibraltar. Based on these, the *King George V*'s Navigation Officer, Captain F. Lloyd, calculated the position of the German battleship, the result being marked on the ordinary Mercator projection map instead of the gnomonic chart.[7] In consequence, considering the difference between the two grids, the calculated position appeared more northerly than was the case. Admiral Tovey radioed the new position of the German battleship and ordered all the pursuing vessels to set a north-easterly course. Instead of getting closer, his ships were now moving away from her.

At 12:00, Admiral Lütjens decided to address his men. He had them gather near the loudspeakers because he wanted to inform them about the current situation and the concentration of ever-stronger British forces around their battleship. He recognized the crew's effort put into the sinking of the *Hood* and expected them to continue to act as bravely, daringly and with the same utter determination in the coming battle. He called on them to choose no course other than victory or death. The senior officers were well aware that the British were concentrating around them not only warships from British bases but also all that were operating north of the Equator. Lütjens' address to his men badly affected their morale – they were particularly anxious about the growing concentration of British forces around the *Bismarck*, as this was making their chances of reaching the safety of French ports smaller with every passing hour. To make things worse, the higher-ranking staff officers of the fleet, among others, put on lifejackets, which they would not take off until the end. With the battleship having been obliged to change her course owing to the damage sustained, and now sailing toward French ports, Lütjens' speech deprived the men of trust in the *Bismarck*'s combat capabilities which she had proven when fighting with the *Hood*. Recognizing the effects that Lütjens' speech had on the crew, the ship's commander decided to raise the spirits of the

Via IWM

Another warship constituting part of Force H was the battleship Renown.

[7]*The gnomonic map projection displays great circles as straight lines, thus the shortest route between two locations in reality corresponds to that on the map. This is achieved by projecting, with respect to the center of the Earth (hence perpendicular to the surface), the Earth's surface onto a tangent plane. The least distortion occurs at the tangent point. Less than half of the sphere can be projected onto a finite map. Since meridians and the Equator are great circles, they are always shown as straight lines.*

RAF Coastal Command carried out long-range reconnaissance of the North Atlantic throughout Sunday, 25 May 1941, by Catalinas of No. 210 Sqn based in Iceland.

Via MAP

'young crew'. An hour after the Admiral's address, Lindemann addressed the men through the intercom, assuring them that the enemy would certainly be evaded and the French harbour reached very soon. He firmly believed in the 'crew's spirit' and that they were in a position to defeat the next opponent they would encounter. These two very different speeches caused what might be called 'murmurings' among the officers and crew. Still, his words had the intended result: they chased away the fears and boosted the sailors' morale. Most of them returned to their duties in a cheerful and optimistic mood. Some of the young crewmen had a positive attitude, believing that their battleship was a lucky one and could not come to any harm.

The Admiralty in London was constantly analysing signals from the *Bismarck*, trying to find her exact position as quickly as possible. In the afternoon, Tovey was presented with the results of the verification of the ship's bearings. They seemed to clearly show that she was sailing on a southerly course toward the Bay of Biscay. The admiral admitted that there must have been an error in the previous analysis. After an exchange of results with the Admiralty, some argument and hesitation, he changed course at 18:00, heading for the French coast. At the same time, he ordered that air patrols be dispatched in search of the *Bismarck* in the direction of her assumed route to Saint-Nazaire. RAF Coastal Command carried out a long-range reconnaissance of the North Atlantic throughout Sunday, 25 May, by Catalinas of 210 Sqn based in Iceland. The mission was to extend into the next day.

In the afternoon, the *Bismarck*'s crew set to work disguising their ship. It was decided that another 'funnel' should be set up in order to make her outline resemble that of the British battleship *Prince of Wales*. The next enemy to be contacted would see the *Bismarck* as a two-funnelled British capital ship. With the expectation that the Allies would continue to fly reconnaissance sorties to locate her at sea, such a disguise, considerably modifying the outline of the battleship, could help mislead the enemy and allow the Germans to sail on undisturbed. The 'conversion' of the German battleship to a 'British' one was not at all so easy as it at first seemed. The erection of the extra funnel brought some activity to the life that the crew were leading onboard. If an enemy was to fall for the *Bismarck*'s disguise, it needed to be convincing; it also had to be done quickly. But there was another problem with the disguise: the British battleships were being escorted by destroyers, whereas the *Bismarck* was alone. A few additional ships could not be improvised like another funnel. Therefore, the disguise was unlikely to achieve its purpose. Besides this, Admiral Lütjens was being troubled by one more problem – the fast-depleting fuel supply. The ship was moving at an economical speed of 20 knots, which theoretically should allow her to reach the French ports. If speed had to be increased to 28 knots, the ship would not make Saint-Nazaire, running out of fuel about 300km (160 miles) from port, although at this distance she would have been under Luftwaffe air cover. The ship was slowed down to 12 knots and repair work commenced in the forward sections. Damage control teams would go down into the flooded compartments and open the valves on the fuel tanks. It was very hard work – the divers worked in completely flooded rooms that were also contaminated by the fuel from the damaged tanks in the bow compartments. However, their toil resulted in a few hundred tons of the fuel becoming available. In order to reduce the load on the bow and reduce pitching, the naval engineering office suggested that the bow anchors and chains be jettisoned, but the ship's captain rejected this as the anchors would be indispensable for getting into Saint-Nazaire.

In the meantime, the dummy second funnel was being erected. It was to be mounted on the flight deck, forward of the main hangar. Made of metal, wood and tarpaulin, after assembly it was quickly painted grey. It did look almost like a real one. Some combinations of British identification signals were also prepared in case of contact with the enemy. However, the Chief Engineer, Korvettenkapitän (Ing.) Walter Lehman, had another problem, even more serious than the battleship's fuel shortage and the unavailable reserves in the bow tanks. The danger was sea water, which was leaking into boilers. As a result of the flooding of port No. 2 boiler room, the water used by the No. 4 electric plant became contaminated with sea water, which quickly posed a threat to the No. 3 turbine. Salt water entering the system and carried with vapour to turbines will

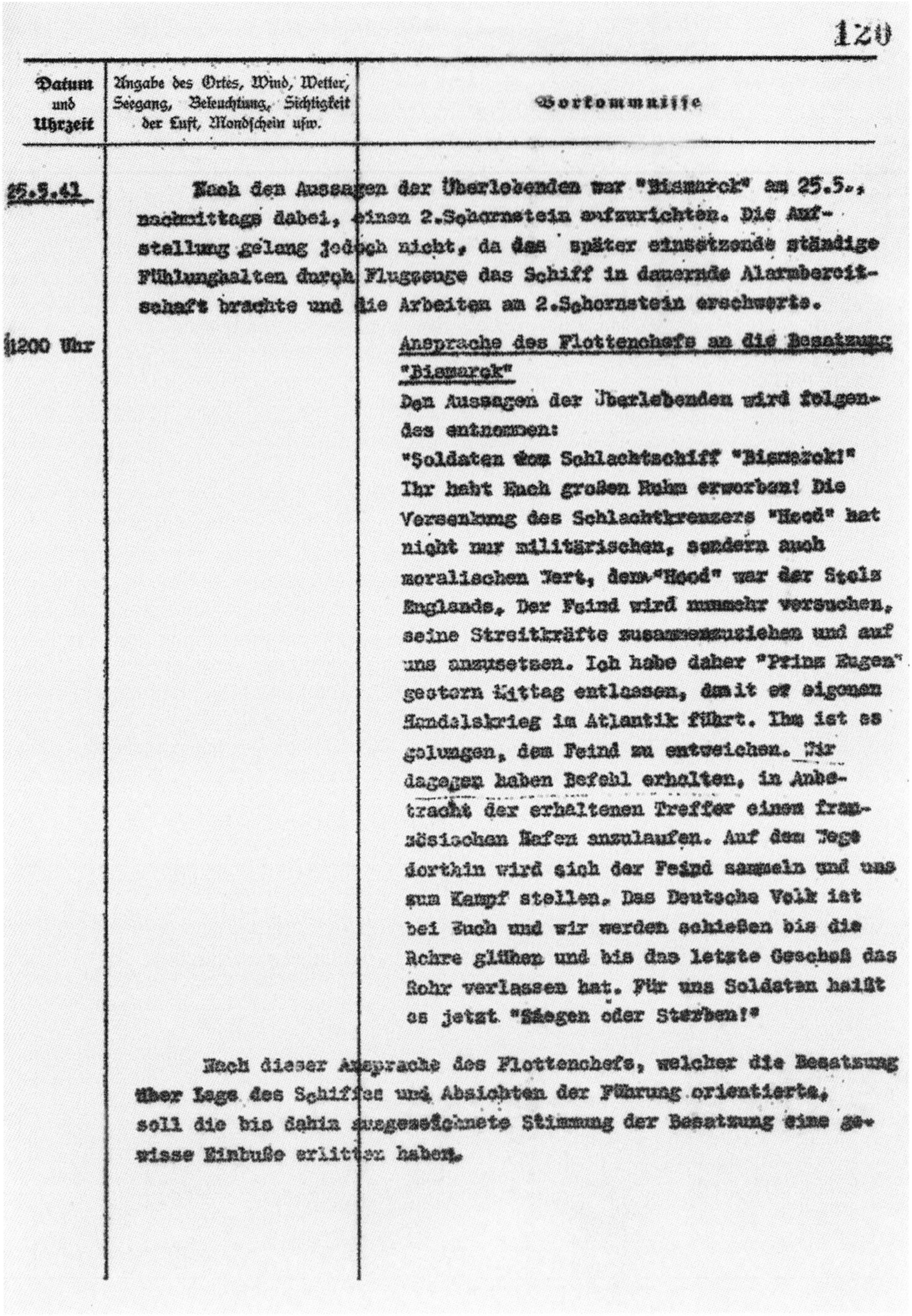

120

Datum und Uhrzeit	Angabe des Ortes, Wind, Wetter, Seegang, Beleuchtung, Sichtigkeit der Luft, Mondschein usw.	Vorkommnisse
25.5.41		Nach den Aussagen der Überlebenden war "Bismarck" am 25.5., nachmittags dabei, einen 2.Schornstein aufzurichten. Die Aufstellung gelang jedoch nicht, da das später einsetzende ständige Fühlunghalten durch Flugzeuge das Schiff in dauernde Alarmbereitschaft brachte und die Arbeiten am 2.Schornstein erschwerte.
1200 Uhr		Ansprache des Flottenchefs an die Besatzung "Bismarck" Den Aussagen der Überlebenden wird folgendes entnommen: "Soldaten vom Schlachtschiff "Bismarck!" Ihr habt Euch großen Ruhm erworben! Die Versenkung des Schlachtkreuzers "Hood" hat nicht nur militärischen, sondern auch moralischen Wert, denn "Hood" war der Stolz Englands. Der Feind wird nunmehr versuchen, seine Streitkräfte zusammenzuziehen und auf uns anzusetzen. Ich habe daher "Prinz Eugen" gestern Mittag entlassen, damit er eigenen Handelskrieg im Atlantik führt. Ihm ist es gelungen, dem Feind zu entweichen. Wir dagegen haben Befehl erhalten, in Anbetracht der erhaltenen Treffer einen französischen Hafen anzulaufen. Auf dem Wege dorthin wird sich der Feind sammeln und uns zum Kampf stellen. Das Deutsche Volk ist bei Euch und wir werden schießen bis die Rohre glühen und bis das letzte Geschoß das Rohr verlassen hat. Für uns Soldaten heißt es jetzt "Siegen oder Sterben!"
		Nach dieser Ansprache des Flottenchefs, welcher die Besatzung über Lage des Schiffes und Absichten der Führung orientierte, soll die bis dahin ausgezeichnete Stimmung der Besatzung eine gewisse Einbuße erlitten haben.

A page from the reconstructed war diary of the Bismarck, *quoting Admiral Lütjens' address to the crew of the battleship.*

Via the Bundesarchiv

quickly damage the turbine blades. Since all the high-pressure boilers required more fresh water in order to meet the requirements of all the systems, the entire production of this water was directed from the evaporator to the four condensers of the main turbines and auxiliary boiler.

Information about the concentration of the British fleet around the *Bismarck* was passed to Admiral Lütjens by the codebreakers of his ship and of Group West. Also, based on the intercepted signals, Lütjens found that his second opponent in the Denmark Strait had not been the *King George V* but her sister-ship *Prince of Wales*. He knew that he was being hunted by the battleships *King George V*, *Ramillies* and *Rodney*, the battlecruiser *Repulse*, and a number of cruisers and destroyers. With the equipment on board, it was difficult to accurately determine the positions of the British warships. He could only speculate on their probable courses based on their last known positions. Admiral Tovey's force was actually about 185km (100 nautical miles) astern of the *Bismarck*. The aircraft carrier *Victorious* and four cruisers were behind them and searching the waters to the east. The heavy cruisers *Norfolk* and *Suffolk* looked more to the west. There was a lack of more detailed information – neither Group West nor the intelligence were very informative in this respect.

Having lost contact with the enemy, Admiral Lütjens sent two signals to Group West. In the first one, he informed them that radar contact with the enemy had been broken. In the other, he confirmed this situation and ordered radio silence so that the enemy could not locate him. During the day, Lütjens received two messages from Germany. Both were addressed to him personally and both concerned his birthday. Lütjens' first birthday greeting came from

Via IWM

Oil leaking from the Bismarck *can be seen on the surface of the sea.*

Admiral Raeder. The second message, received on the battleship at 16:47, was from the Führer himself. In the evening, Group West informed Admiral Lütjens that the Luftwaffe was ready to provide aerial cover for the battleship upon her crossing 25°W, and that there were three destroyers standing by. The *Bismarck* was supposed to send a notification to Group West immediately upon crossing the 10 degree line.

On the evening of 25 May 1941, Kapitänleutnant K. Mihatsch was on duty on the bridge. He believed that the battleship was very likely to reach the French coast and Saint-Nazaire. With a constant speed of 28 knots, this chance was estimated to be 50 per cent. Most of the British ships were astern of the *Bismarck*, whereas Force H was ahead of her. The other ships, sailing singly, were closing in on her from every possible direction. The only defence the ship had was to maintain her speed or if possible increase it. If the battleship were to be unfortunate enough to lose speed or manoeuvrability, the slower British battleships would soon catch up and, most probably, commence a heavy and concentrated attack. The aircraft carrier *Victorious* also posed a serious threat, another attack from her squadrons being expected to take place before sunset. However, there still was no certainty as to whether that would happen or not, since the current position of the *Victorious* was as then unknown. Worse still, British submarines were scattered along the entire west coast of France, and this threat had to be taken into consideration as well. The news soon spread on the battleship that radar contact with the enemy had been broken, one of the most comforting reports that the officers and the crew had received in the last few hours. The fact was a great relief for the crew, as contact had lasted for thirty-one long, uninterrupted hours.

Via IWM

Dennis Briggs, the pilot of the Catalina *that spotted the* Bismarck *on 26 May 1941.*

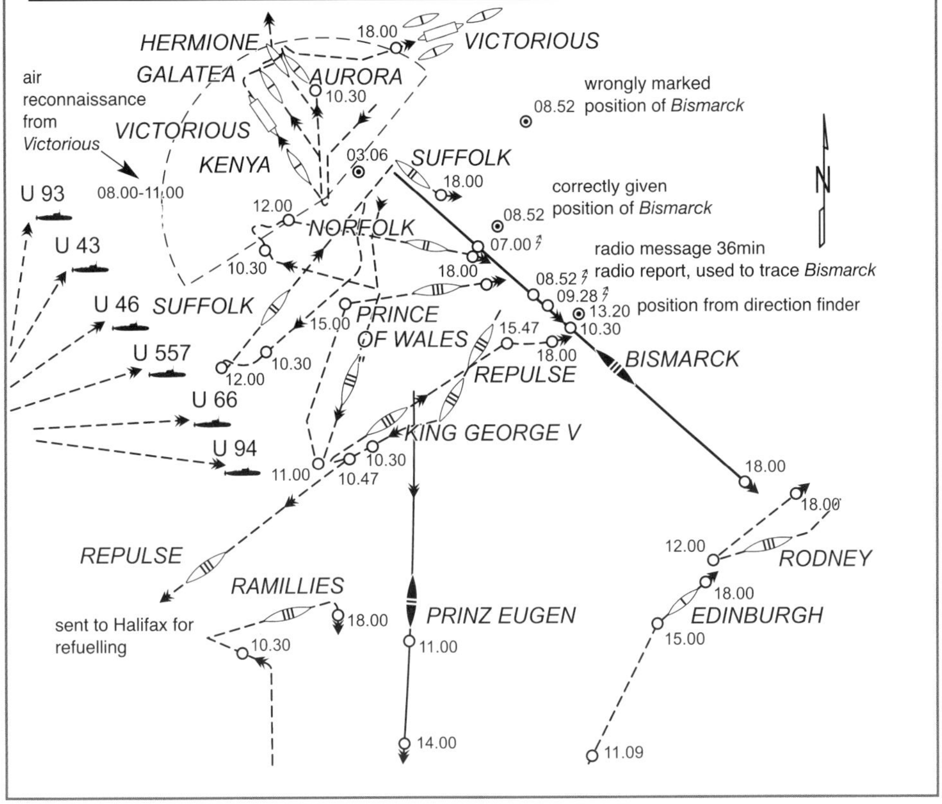

FINDING THE *BISMARCK*

Contact

On 26 May, RAF Coastal Command continued the large-scale search for the *Bismarck*. Catalinas, Sunderlands and Hudsons kept patrolling the Denmark Strait to the south of Iceland and the passage between the Faeroes and Iceland. These sorties were flown despite very bad weather. Apart from that, two patrols were dispatched in the direction of France, toward where the *Bismarck* was probably steaming. At 03:00, two Catalinas took off from the Lough Erne base in Northern Ireland to search for the *Bismarck*. One of these, coded 'Z' of 209 Sqn, was piloted by Dennis Briggs, with his co-pilot, American Pilot Officer Leonard B. Smith, sitting next to him. This aircraft was to perform a search to the south. The other Catalina, 'M' of 204 Sqn, was to patrol the area to the north. Further air patrols were mounted consisting of Beauforts, and these, too, were dispatched to reconnoitre the probable path of the German ship. Additionally, Kaldadarnes base kept five Beauforts of 22 Sqn at readiness, eight of 42 and two of 22 Sqns waited at Wick, ten of 217 Sqn at St Eval, and eight of 42 Sqn at Leuchars. All the Bomber Command aircraft were also kept on stand-by. In order to definitely cut off the *Bismarck*, six British submarines patrolled between Brest and Saint-Nazaire.

Sailing on a south-westerly course, the *Bismarck* was slowly coming nearer to the French coast. At 02:11, a message received from Group West gave instructions about a blue flag to be hoisted for the U-boats operating in squares BE and BF to make their identification of the battleship quick and

The heavy cruiser London *(commanded by Captain R.M. Servaes), which was escorting a convoy from Gibraltar to Britain when it was ordered to detach and join the search for the* Bismarck.

Via CAW

easy. All the U-boats were told that this flag would not be taken down by the *Bismarck*. An hour later came another radio message from Group West containing details on the docking of the warship, and the anti-aircraft and anti-submarine defences of Saint-Nazaire, which were superior to those of Brest. The battleship regularly received weather reports from weather patrols and reconnaissance aircraft. Individual air units were assigned different frequencies so as to reserve special channels for communication with the *Bismarck*. In the morning, the intercom informed the crew that they were maintaining course to Saint-Nazaire. The commander estimated that the ship should enter the U-boat area of operations and be within air reconnaissance range by noon; later on, the Luftwaffe would protect the ship. This news had a very positive effect on the crew. Almost everyone's thoughts were now turned to the French harbour. None of them suspected that their dash could end differently.

Force H moved on a north-westerly course during the night. The sea was rough and the wind increased, with very poor visibility. Admiral Somerville was obliged to reduce the speed of the whole group, first to 24 knots, then down to 17 knots after midnight, on 26 May. At 08:35, the aircraft carrier *Ark Royal* launched a reconnaissance flight after the *Bismarck*. The mission of the ten Swordfish mission was to search the western waters ahead of the aircraft carrier. Six of the machines were carrying extra fuel in drop tanks. Fulmars were also intended to fly a reconnaissance sortie but the weather prevented it. The wind was blowing at Force 7, and the rough sea was causing the ship to pitch by as much as 15m (50ft). Take-off for the Fulmars was impossible, and it was very dangerous for the Swordfish to fly out, not to mention return. On finding the *Bismarck*, the aircraft were to take position astern of her and keep Admiral Tovey informed about her course and position.

High above the clouds, the Catalinas were making their monotonous flights along their assigned routes. The weather in the North

Atlantic was not very good, clouds hanging low above the water, with patches of clear sky to be found in some places. At 10:15, the co-pilot of the Catalina 'Z', the American Smith, thought he had spotted the *Bismarck* below them. He was not sure, though. Dennis Briggs made an appropriate manoeuvre and took a more convenient position for closer observation. Sitting in the aircraft 700m (2,300ft) up, Smith once again saw the German battleship through a gap in the cloud, 500m (550 yards) away from them. They immediately reported the location of the *Bismarck* to base. The report contained the exact position of the aircraft and its current flight path – they were about 1,280km (690 nautical miles) to the west of Brest.

At 10:30, an air alert was sounded aboard the *Bismarck* and her anti-aircraft batteries soon opened fire on the Catalina, but after a moment the aircraft disappeared into low cloud and fire was ceased. Lindemann considered the possibility of launching a seaplane to drive the enemy off, but he rejected this as the rough sea would have made it impossible to recover the plane safely afterwards. The few minutes' fire had scored a few hits on the flying boat. Fifteen minutes later, the British Catalina lost contact with the battleship. Its report had been intercepted and immediately decoded by both admirals – Tovey aboard *King George V* and Saalwachter at Group West. At 11:56, the decoded Catalina report was radioed from Group West to Admiral Lütjens on the *Bismarck*. All the British warships under Admiral Tovey's command were nearby, but none could take a direct part in the engagement. The battleship *Rodney* and her destroyer escorts had missed the *Bismarck* by some 90km (50 miles) and were still moving away from her. The cruiser *Edinburgh* was 83km (45 nautical miles) from the

Via CAW

The cruiser Sheffield *barely escaped being sunk by friendly carrier aircraft in a near-fatal mistake on 26 May 1941. It was only the quick reactions of the cruiser's captain that saved her from the six torpedoes coming at her.*

Consolidated Catalina flying boat – one of the many that took part in the attack on the Bismarck.

From MAP archive

Via IWM

The battleship Rodney *took part in the hunt for the* Bismarck.

After the Bismarck *was located, the* Sheffield *was tasked with shadowing her at close range to keep Admiral Tovey informed of the battleship's movements.*

Via IWM

German vessel. The 4th Destroyer Flotilla crossed the *Bismarck*'s path about 55km (30 miles) behind her. The battleship *King George V* was 217km (135 miles) to the north of her. Only the *Rodney* was in her vicinity. The battlecruiser *Renown* was 250km (112 miles) to the south-east of the German ship.

After the receipt of the Catalina report, a Swordfish from Ark Royal piloted by Flying Officer J.V. Hartley located the *Bismarck* at 11:14. Seven minutes later, it was joined by another Swordfish with Flying Officer Callander at the controls. These two were ordered to keep an eye on the battleship. They kept shadowing her, reporting her course and speed. In the meantime, the *Ark Royal* dispatched two more aircraft equipped with radar and drop tanks. The Catalina had reported damage to the fuselage and the possibility of losing contact with the battleship. This the British could not afford to let happen. As it soon turned out, the reported position of the Catalina contained an error of 37km (20 nautical miles). The one given by the aircraft of the *Ark Royal* was correct and this was passed on to all the British ships hunting the *Bismarck*. The reconnaissance aircraft loitering above the battleship were soon joined by the Catalina piloted by Briggs. Admiral Tovey was somewhat surprised by the reports from the aircraft. The pilots were only reporting restored contact with the *Bismarck* – there was no sign of the *Prinz Eugen*.

At 11:54, Admiral Lütjens sent a signal to Group West, reporting the presence of aircraft with fixed landing gear near the *Bismarck*. The admiral inferred from this that there must be an enemy aircraft carrier nearby escorted by another heavy vessel. The *Ark Royal*'s aircraft were fired at when they approached the *Bismarck*, just like the Catalina before, but they would not be scared away. A minute later, the Admiral sent

In the meantime, the lone Prinz Eugen *continued the operation.*

Photo by Busch, via AJ-Press

Group West a message that the battleship had entered square BE 27.

A fatal mistake

The only warships close to the German vessel were the ships of Force H under Somerville. Admiral Tovey was unable to commence a decisive battle without first forcing the *Bismarck* to reduce her speed. Besides, low fuel obliged him to recall the *Prince of Wales* and the *Victorious* along with their escorting destroyers. The *Suffolk* was also withdrawn from the operation, all those vessels having to sail to bases for refuelling. The admiral ordered that the battlecruiser *Renown* of Force H not take part directly in a battle with the *Bismarck*, fearing that she might go the same way as the *Hood*. In the end, he was only left with the aircraft carrier *Ark Royal* and the thirty Swordfish aboard her. Compared to the *Victorious*, the *Ark Royal* was much better off. She had the best pilots with experience of many combat sorties. Since early morning, the *Ark Royal* had been deploying constant air patrols to the north. After the *Bismarck* had been located, the Vice-Admiral decided to carry out an immediate torpedo attack on the ship. However, bad weather in the Atlantic and the fact that his Swordfish were already airborne shadowing the *Bismarck* made such an attack impossible at the moment. He ordered the cruiser *Sheffield* of his escort to set a new course and position herself astern the *Bismarck*. She was to maintain uninterrupted contact with the battleship because the degrading weather was making it probable that the reconnaissance aircraft would have to be recalled. When the Swordfish from the morning reconnaissance sortie returned to the aircraft carrier, preparations began for a torpedo attack.

As fourteen Swordfish were being prepared for the sortie, the *Sheffield* commenced the task she had been assigned. This lasted till 14:50, when the aircraft led by Lieutenant-Commander J.A. Stewart-Moore took off from the British aircraft carrier. During the briefing on the *Ark Royal*, it was emphasized to the pilots that their task was to reduce the battleship's speed. They should concentrate on attacking her stern, targeting the propellers and steering gear. After the briefing, the ship's commander, Captain Loben E. Maund, informed the crews that there were no other vessels in the waters between them and the *Bismarck* 74km (40 miles) to the south. However, this was not the case – to port of the battleship, the cruiser *Sheffield* was sailing in her wake, and it was she that appeared ahead of the British torpedo aircraft. The consequences of the incorrect information given to the pilots was serious. After obtaining radar contact at 15:20 with the target 37km (20 miles) away, the aircraft prepared to attack. The Swordfish dived from out of the clouds toward what they took for the *Bismarck*, but they were puzzled by the absence of anti-aircraft fire. They launched eleven torpedoes against the *Sheffield* before she received a warning from the aircraft carrier. It was only owing to the quick reactions of the cruiser's commander, Captain Larcom, that his ship managed to accelerate to full speed and evade six of the torpedoes heading in her direction. Five others exploded in the water due to faulty magnetic pistols. Two exploded the moment they hit the water, the rest shortly after. This was not the end of the problems for the *Ark Royal*'s commander: three of the aircraft crashed on their return from the sortie and the wreckage had to be thrown over the side in order to clear the deck for the other aircraft. Luckily, there were no casualties.

Meanwhile, the fuel situation of all the British ships had become critical. The British were therefore doing their utmost to slow down their

German opponent. They needed more time to refuel their ships and bring more vessels into the area. Tovey knew that if the *Bismarck* was not slowed down by the night of 26 May, she would escape. Another, this time successful, torpedo attack on the German battleship was now the only possibility of catching her. The *King George V* was already coming to the limit of her operational range – she had only 32 per cent of her fuel remaining, which was only enough to return to base. Besides, he was without the anti-submarine escort provided by destroyers. The *Rodney* with three destroyers were the nearest, but these could have joined him only by the next morning. There were many German U-boats operating in these waters, and several more had been dispatched from bases in France to support the *Bismarck*. The *King George V* had to dash to base in order to avoid their torpedoes. At 17:05, she reduced her speed to 22 knots to conserve fuel and let the *Rodney*, which was following in her wake, catch her up.

❦

Night Approaches

Achilles heel

At 18:20 on 26 May, Admiral Tovey sent Somerville more bad news: if the *Bismarck*'s speed was not reduced by midnight, the *King George V* would break off the pursuit and return to base. The battleship had been shadowing the *Bismarck* from the Denmark Strait for the four days and nights, covering more than 3,700km (2,000 nautical miles). The decision to break off was difficult to accept but there was no alternative. Only the *Rodney* remained to face the German battleship in a direct combat; she continued to follow the *Bismarck* with her destroyer escort. Having received this message, Somerville decided to carry out another torpedo attack. The *Ark Royal* crews prepared for the next sortie. This time the torpedoes' magnetic pistols were replaced by more reliable contact pistols. The first take-off was scheduled for 18:30 but it was only at 19:15 that the *Ark Royal* was turned into the wind and the sortie launched. A formation of fifteen Swordfish led by Lieutenant Commander T.P. Coode got airborne, took up formation ten minutes later, and headed toward the *Sheffield*. This time the encounter was uneventful because the pilots knew that a friendly cruiser was in their path. On finding her, the pilots were to obtain the bearing to the *Bismarck*, which was sailing ahead of her, and then mount an attack.

Before the British aircraft located the *Bismarck*, she had received a message from Group West timed at 18:55. It said that the ship was still outside the range of the German air forces and she could not depend on them for protection. The only defence could be provided by the submarines heading in her direction. At 19:50 one of these, *U-556* under the command of Korvettenkapitän Wohlfarth, was near the British warships that were pursuing the *Bismarck*. Sailing on the surface, the boat spotted the battlecruiser *Renown* and the *Ark Royal* steaming at high speed. Unfortunately, the U-boat had no torpedoes left and was unable to attack. A report was immediately sent to headquarters that an enemy battleship and an aircraft carrier had been sighted in square BE 5332 on a course of 115 degrees sailing at high speed. Another submarine was *U-48* in square BF 71. At 20:23, the *Bismarck* ordered her to head at full speed towards the *Sheffield* and, as a message of 19:54 laconically stated, 'commence operations against her'. A successful torpedo attack could get rid of one more British radar-equipped warship that was constantly vectoring aircraft and warships on the *Bismarck*.

Just before 20:00, the *Ark Royal*'s Swordfish arrived over the *Sheffield*. The first vectoring of the aircraft onto the *Bismarck* was unsuccessful. Thirty minutes later another attempt began – this time they succeeded. The formation approached

TABLE 3
Pilots of Squadrons that took part in attacks on *Bismarck*, on 26 May 1941.

Section	*Sqn*	*Aircraft*	*Pilot*	*Observer*	*Radio gunner*	*Attack*
1st	818	5A/ P4219?	Lt Cdr T.P. Coode, RN	Lt E.S. Carver, RN	PO W.H. Dillnutt	Port
1st	818	5B+	T/S-Lt (A) E.D. Child, RNVR	S-Lt (A) G.R.C. Penrose, RN	LA R.H.W. Blake	Port
1st	818	5C/L9726	T/S-Lt J.W.C. Moffatt, RNVR	T/S-Lt (A) J.D. Miller, RNVR	LA A.J. Hayman, Jx.151230	Port, stern hit
2nd	810	2B+	Lt D.F. Godfrey-Faussett, RN	S-Lt (A) L.A. Royall, RN	PO(A) V.R. Graham, F.55072	Starboard
2nd	810	2A+/ P4131?	S-Lt (A) K.S. Pattisson, RN	S-Lt (A) P.B. Meadway, RN	NA D.L. Mulley	Starboard
2nd	810	2P	S-Lt (A) A.W.D. Beale, RN	A/S-Lt (A) C. Friend, RN	LA K. Pimlott, RN SFx.392	Port bow, amidships
3rd	818	5K	Lt (A) S. Keane, DSC, RN	S-Lt (A) R.I.W. Goddard, RN	PO(A) D.C. Milliner Fx.77749	–
3rd	810	2M	S-Lt (A) C.M. Jewell, RN	–	LA G.H. Parkinson	–
4th	820	4A	Lt H.G. Hunter, MiD, RN	Lt Cdr. J.A. Stewart-Moore, RN	PO(A) R.H. McColl, DSM, Fx.76319	Port
4th	820	4B	S-Lt (A) M.J. Lithgow, RN	T/S-Lt (A) N.C.M. Cooper, RNVR	LA J.R. Russell	Port
4th	820	4C/V4298+	S-Lt (A) F.A. Swanton, RN	T/S-Lt (A) G.A. Woods, RNVR	LA J.R. Seafer	Port
5th	820	4K/ L7643?	Lt (A) A.S.S. Owensmith, RN	A/T/S-Lt (A) G.G. Topham, RNVR	PO J. Watson, Fx.76318	Starboard
5th	820	4L/ P4204?	S-Lt (A) J.R.N. Gardner, RN	T/S-Lt (A) J.B. Longmuir, RNVR	–	–
6th	820	4F	S-Lt (A) M.F.S.P. Willcocks, RN	S-Lt H.G. Mays, RN	LA R. Finney, Jx.156354	–
6th	820	4G	S-Lt (A) A.N. Dixon, RN	T/S-Lt (A) J.F. Turner, RNVR	LA A.T.A. Shields	Starboard

the German battleship from astern. It was almost 20:30 when an air raid alert was issued aboard the ship on sighting the British aircraft at high altitude. They soon re-arranged their formation and began a co-ordinated attack at 20:47. They approached the ship in groups of two and three aircraft. The *Bismarck* threw up a wall of fire, with the main and secondary batteries joining in as

Via IWM

Vice Admiral Sir James Sommerville with the captain of the Ark Royal, *Captain L.H.E. Maund, aboard the British aircraft carrier.*

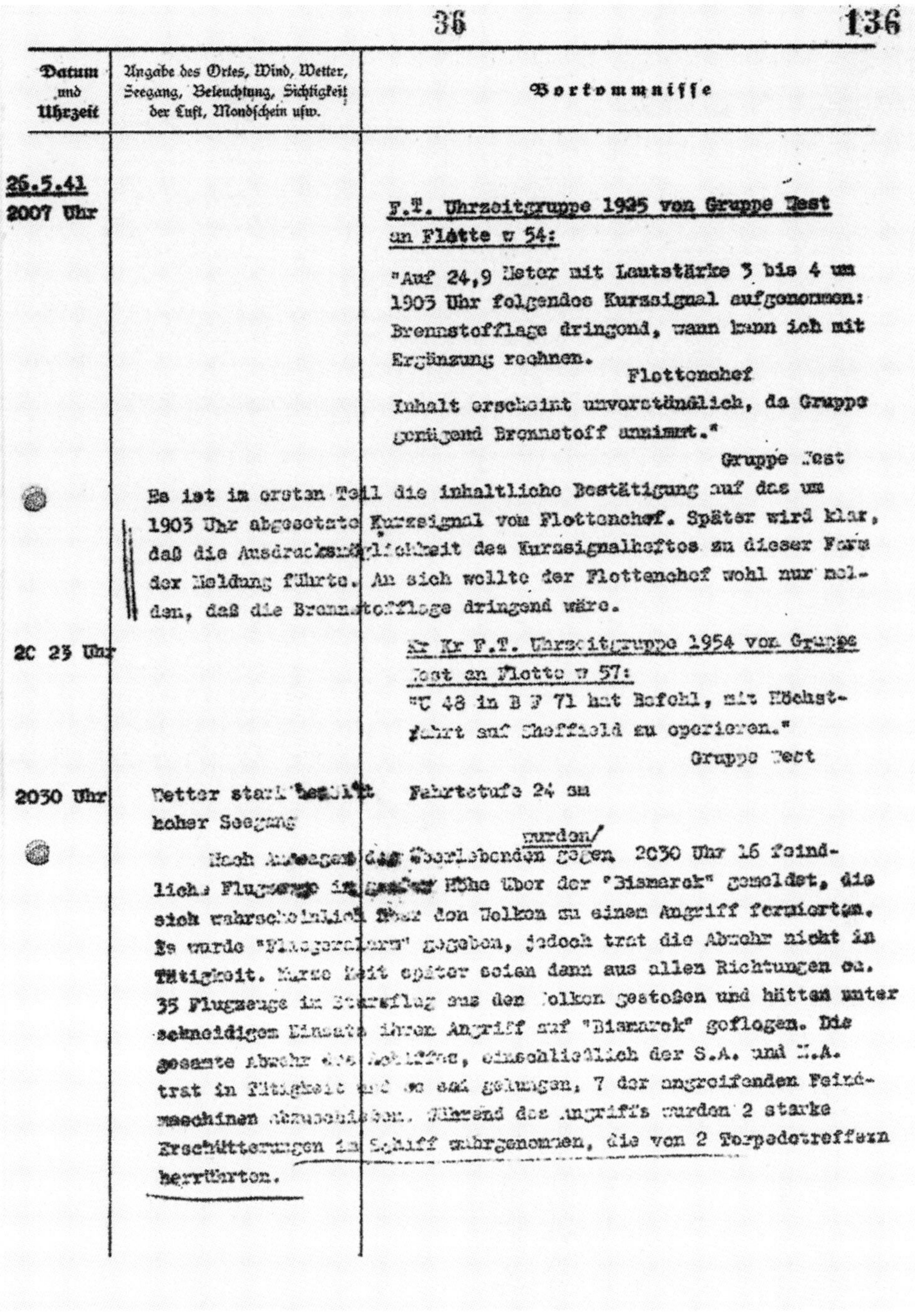

36 136

Datum und Uhrzeit	Angabe des Ortes, Wind, Wetter, Seegang, Beleuchtung, Sichtigkeit der Luft, Mondschein usw.	Vorkommnisse
26.5.41 2007 Uhr		F.T. Uhrzeitgruppe 1935 von Gruppe West an Flotte v 54: "Auf 24,9 Meter mit Lautstärke 3 bis 4 um 1903 Uhr folgendes Kurzsignal aufgenommen: Brennstofflage dringend, wann kann ich mit Ergänzung rechnen. Flottenchef Inhalt erscheint unverständlich, da Gruppe genügend Brennstoff annimmt." Gruppe West

Es ist im ersten Teil die inhaltliche Bestätigung auf das um 1903 Uhr abgesetzte Kurzsignal vom Flottenchef. Später wird klar, daß die Ausdrucksmöglichkeit des Kurzsignalheftes zu dieser Form der Meldung führte. An sich wollte der Flottenchef wohl nur melden, daß die Brennstofflage dringend wäre.

Datum und Uhrzeit	Angabe des Ortes, Wind, Wetter, Seegang, Beleuchtung, Sichtigkeit der Luft, Mondschein usw.	Vorkommnisse
2025 Uhr		~~Kr Kr~~ F.T. Uhrzeitgruppe 1954 von Gruppe West an Flotte v 57: "U 48 in B F 71 hat Befehl, mit Höchstfahrt auf Sheffield zu operieren." Gruppe West
2030 Uhr	Wetter stark bedeckt hoher Seegang	Fahrtstufe 24 sm

Nach Aussagen der Überlebenden wurden/ gegen 2030 Uhr 16 feindliche Flugzeuge in [illegible] Höhe über der "Bismarck" gemeldet, die sich wahrscheinlich über den Wolken zu einem Angriff formierten. Es wurde "Fliegeralarm" gegeben, jedoch trat die Abwehr nicht in Tätigkeit. Kurze Zeit später seien dann aus allen Richtungen ca. 35 Flugzeuge im Sturzflug aus den Wolken gestoßen und hätten unter schneidigem Einsatz ihren Angriff auf "Bismarck" geflogen. Die gesamte Abwehr des Schiffes, einschließlich der S.A. und M.A. trat in Tätigkeit und es sei gelungen, 7 der angreifenden Feindmaschinen abzuschießen. Während des Angriffs wurden 2 starke Erschütterungen im Schiff wahrgenommen, die von 2 Torpedotreffern herrührten.

A page from the reconstructed Bismarck *war diary with information about the* Bismarck *having been hit by two torpedoes dropped by the Swordfish of the* Ark Royal.

Via the Bundesarchiv

The destroyer Cossack *– the flagship of the 4th Destroyer Flotilla under Captain Vian.*

Via IWM

before. The German strategy aimed at damaging the greatest possible number of enemy aircraft, as every aircraft carrier had a limited number of them. If they were put out of action, the ship would be unable to deploy them against the *Bismarck* again, and she would be of no further danger to them. Even though the *Ark Royal* still had Fulmars on board, they could not take off in such weather.

The Swordfish were attacking at low level, coming through the wall of flak and dropping their torpedoes as close to the target as possible. The first passes proved ineffective, as the battleship managed to avoid all the torpedoes, keeping up heavy fire at the attacking aircraft. As the attack was coming to an end, Pilot Officer J.W. Moffatt's machine dropped a torpedo which hit the *Bismarck* in the stern at 21:05. The torpedo exploded against the unarmoured side of the ship's hull, tore open the plating and caused water to flood the steering gear compartment and jammed the rudders. The damaged plating made it impossible to free the rudders, which were eventually stuck at 12 degrees to port. The battleship's list increased and she began to turn. At 21:15, another torpedo struck her amidships. This was launched by Pilot Officer A.W. Beale's aircraft. When the Swordfish ended the attack at 21:25, Lieutenant Commander Tim Coode sent the first report to the *King George V*, saying that he had not noticed any hits scored on the *Bismarck*. It was the last chance that Tovey had to stop the German battleship. In the meantime, the *Sheffield* had taken advantage of the confusion and come closer to the *Bismarck*, which fired a few salvoes in her direction but all fell short. The British cruiser turned around at once and increased her speed, making smoke. The *Bismarck* then ceased fire. Most importantly, visual contact between the ships had been lost.

The impact of the exploding torpedoes shut off the safety valve in the starboard turbine room of the *Bismarck* – the main turbines shut down immediately. The ship gradually slowed down from 24 to 13 knots. The force of the explosion raised the stern up, and the ship rolled on the waves a few times, shaken by slow vibrations. When the valve was reopened, the steam re-entered the turbines. The floor in the central machine room had been warped and now projected about 0.5m (19in). Water was entering the machine compartment through a damaged port shaft alley. The damage control centre was notified about the stern having taken a torpedo hit. Repair crews from all over the ship immediately set to repairing the damage. Damage Control Team No. 1 under the command of Obermaschinist W. Schmidt took care of the stern. Upon examination, they found that the battleship had a hole in the hull which was so huge that the seawater entering through it had immediately flooded all the three steering compartments. The crew working in these rooms had been forced to evacuate at once. The water had risen very high. The damage control team were unable to check what damage the steering gear itself had suffered because the armoured hatch above the steering room had been shut, but this had failed to prevent the adjacent compartments from being flooded, as the water was entering everywhere through cable passages and cracks in the transverse bulkheads. An attempt to pump the water out of Section III failed because there was no electric power in this part of the ship.

Supervised by two engineers – Kapitänleutnant G. Junack and Oberleutnant H. Giese – and assisted by carpenters, the repair teams set to work. The transverse bulkhead from the hatchway to the steering gear was shored up with stanchions. The teams managed to get to the hatchway above the steering gear room. They tried to dive in order to reach the upper 'tweendeck and release the steering machinery. The attempts failed, though, and the hatch was eventually shut. Trying to switch to manual steering did not yield the expected results, either. The sailors picked for this task found the compartment totally flooded on reaching it. Only after several hours of combined effort did they manage to free one of the rudders. The other one, however, remained stuck in the turned position. During that time, the uncontrollable battleship had already made a semi-circle. Her course had changed from south-

Via IWM

Captain Philip Vian on the Cossack's *bridge during torpedo exercises in 1940.*

easterly to north-westerly, and she was inevitably getting closer to the enemy.

Captain Lindemann tried alternative ways of steering the ship by varying the rotation of the propellers to get the *Bismarck* back on her course. It was rather difficult for the men in the machinery compartment to follow his orders – the ship was at battle stations throughout and all the doors were tightly sealed. The temperature in the compartment had risen to 50°C and work in such conditions was much harder, which will become especially obvious when one considers the fact that the machinery operators worked in leather overalls. The only success that Lindemann achieved through his attempts was to turn the battleship into the wind and set her back on her north-westerly course. Fortunately for the ship, the attack had not affected the propellers and this kept her manoeuvrable to at least some extent. During a meeting called to address this problem, it was proposed to the captain that divers should cut off the jammed rudders or change their positions from over the side of the ship. To cut off the entire rudder would in practice be equivalent to their being held in the neutral position. The ship could then be steered by altering the rotation of the propellers. The Chief Engineer, Walter Lehmann, and his assistants were positive that it was a feasible option. There was only one small problem – finding volunteers who would perform the task. The sea was very rough, and there was nothing for the diver to catch hold of around the rudder, where the current was very strong. Even the most experienced diver lowered on a safety rope would find it extremely difficult to cope with the task, not to mention the great risk of such an enterprise. Thus one of the slight chances that were left for the battleship was eventually rejected, one of the reasons being the lack of the necessary light diving equipment. The ship had only been supplied with submarine escape breathing apparatus. The possibility of blowing the rudders off with explosives from inside was also rejected – an uncontrolled explosion might have damaged the nearby propellers and the stern section of the hull.

Via IWM

Only the battleship Rodney *remained, her main armament being a match for that of the German battleship in a direct engagement.*

The main armament of the Rodney.

Via IWM

A new idea soon emerged of how to restore the ship's manoeuvrability. Some of the crewmen were trying to weld a kind of auxiliary rudder to the starboard side amidships, near the main hangar. The hangar's door was sacrificed in order to place it deep enough. This auxiliary rudder was to be set at an angle of 15 degrees, which would have been more or less equal to the 12 degree inclination of the rudder at the stern. Thus fixed, the new rudder would have offset the main rudder's inclination to port, allowing subsequent steering of the ship through the use of the propellers. Again, the adverse weather conditions led to the rejection of this idea also.

After the pessimistic report from Lieutenant Commander Coode, the *Sheffield* reported the interesting fact that the *Bismarck* had altered course to the south-west. The British admiral found it hard to believe that the German battleship was steaming right in his direction. He initially thought that Captain Larcom must have been mistaken. However, the report was shortly confirmed by reconnaissance aircraft that were following the *Bismarck*. The only reasonable explanation was that the ship had after all received a torpedo hit and was now badly damaged. He immediately directed the battleships *King George V* and *Rodney* southward, in the *Bismarck*'s direction. About 22:30, the aircraft returned to the *Ark Royal*. At the short debriefing, the pilots told Captain Maund that the battleship had been hit amidships. The last reconnaissance aircraft watching the enemy ship had in the meantime returned to the aircraft carrier in the gathering darkness, and from that moment Tovey could not expect any more information about the opponent. Contact with her could now only be made by Captain Philip Vian's destroyers. The damaged *Bismarck* was slowly moving in the direction of the British warships, and Tovey ordered his ships to alter course so as to avoid a collision with the Germans in the dark. At 22:30, the *Rodney* set an even more northerly course, and later changed it to westerly.

On the evening of 26 May 1941, Admiral Tovey had bad news for Somerville: unless the Bismarck *slowed down by midnight, the* King George V *would break off the pursuit and return to base because she had been chasing the battleship from the Denmark Strait, having covered a total of more than 2,000 nautical miles over the past four days and nights.*

Via IWM

A little later, Tovey received a report from the commander of Force H, Vice-Admiral Somerville, that the German battleship had probably been hit by another torpedo in the stern on the starboard side. He also reported that the *Bismarck* must have sustained damage to the shafts or propellers, since she had not altered course for a considerable time. Shortly before 01:00, Admiral Tovey received the last report from the aerial reconnaissance. This said that after the torpedo attack, the *Bismarck* made two complete circles and then headed north. In discussion with his officers, Tovey considered all the conceivable alternatives of repairing the *Bismarck*'s damage which might have been implemented after she had been hit in the steering gear compartment. Although such a hit was usually not very likely, it could have happened to the *Bismarck*. Tovey soon instructed Somerville to keep his force at a distance of 37km (20 nautical miles) astern of the enemy. He feared that a shorter range would expose the *Renown* to the danger of the accurate fire of the excellent German gun crews, who had already exhibited their skills in the battle with the *Hood*. At about 02:30, Admiral Tovey ordered that the 4th Destroyer Flotilla, now shadowing the German battleship, use flares for more accurate determination of the *Bismarck*'s position. However, an unusually dark night and a squall made that impossible and Tovey could not be certain of the enemy's position. He decided to wait about two hours to commence the action in daylight.

Vian's destroyers attack

The closer was the French coast, the greater became the threat from German U-boats. This worried Tovey because his flagship *King George V* had been sailing without the escorting destroyers, which had turned back as they were running out of fuel. The *Rodney* and her three destroyers were the only hope now. She had not yet joined up with the flagship and it was hard to say how long she could operate on the fuel she had. On the evening of 25 May, Admiral Tovey requested the Admiralty for another destroyer group to escort the *King George V* and the *Rodney*. It was not so easy to fulfil this request because most of the destroyers had by then almost emptied their fuel tanks and were on the way back to base. The only destroyers nearby were those of the 4th Flotilla, escorting Convoy WS-8B. On the previous day, they were about 550km (300 nautical miles) from the *King George V*. On the night of 26 May, the squadron commander Captain Philip Vian received orders for the destroyers *Sikh* and *Zulu* along with his flagship *Cossack* to provide escort for the *King George V*, whereas the destroyers *Maori* and *Piorun* were to join the *Rodney*. The destroyers immediately detached from their convoy. Later they received the signal from the Catalina which had found the *Bismarck*. After calculating the bearings, it turned out that the *Piorun* and *Maori* were the closest to the German battleship. They were striving to head in the enemy's direction at full speed but the strong wind and rough sea hindered their efforts. At about 21:40, the destroyers noticed the *Sheffield* under fire from the Germans. On receiving the exact bearings, they steamed on to intercept, locating the German ship at 22:30.

Action stations was sounded aboard the *Bismarck*. The main and secondary batteries were ready to receive the enemy. At 22:42, the *Bismarck* fired three salvoes at the *Piorun* at a range of 12,500m (13,760 yards), the shells falling very close to the Polish destroyer. During the half-hour long engagement, the destroyer was trying to close the range between them to be able to launch torpedoes. This was very difficult, though, considering the state of the sea. The darkness, pouring rain and overcast hampered the observation

Via IWM

The Norfolk *while patrolling the Denmark Strait in May 1941. Like the flagship, she was also taking part in the chase of the* Bismarck.

Submarines were sent to retrieve the Bismarck's *war diary and film of the battle in the Denmark Strait. As can be seen in the second picture, it was difficult to operate in the stormy waters of the Atlantic, not to mention taking documents from the battleship.*

Via CAW

of targets by both the Germans and the British. The German fire was being directed by the second gunnery officer, Korvettenkapitän Albrecht, and was as effective as the existing conditions allowed. The majority of the salvoes were aimed quite well, which obliged the *Piorun* to withdraw at once to a safer distance. In the meantime, other destroyers had joined the battle, carrying out individual torpedo attacks. There was little hope of success, as the destroyers would have had to attack throughout the night at close range, subject to the enemy's fire. A direct hit from the *Bismarck*'s main battery would have blown a small destroyer to pieces. A total of sixteen torpedoes were launched at the Germans under constant fire from the *Bismarck*'s main battery, with shell splinters raining down on the destroyers' superstructure, but no hits were scored. They finally broke off their attacks about 01:00. The task now was to maintain unbroken contact with the *Bismarck* during the hours of darkness that followed and, more importantly, to keep firing flares.[8]

Attempting to evade the torpedoes being launched against her, the *Bismarck*, 'staggering' by propeller-rotation control, was trying to maintain a more or less straight course despite her jammed rudder. Overloading of the machinery and the rapid changing of the propeller rotation from 'ahead full' to 'back full' resulted in a stoppage of the starboard turbine. Initial attempts to raise steam and get it to work were unsuccessful. Only when all steam was directed at the highest-possible pressure into the turbine's nozzle did it restart. Still, from this moment, the battleship's speed slowly but

[8] *Later, the crew of the destroyer* Maori *claimed to have scored at least a single torpedo hit on the* Bismarck. *However, it should rather be believed that it was just wishful thinking on the part of the* Maori *sailors because there is no mention of any hits in the* Bismarck's *War Diary.*

steadily dropped. From a theoretical maximum of 31 knots, the *Bismarck* was now steaming at 10–12 knots.

The destroyers ceased firing flares at 03:00 in the morning. Continuing to do so would have been dangerous, since the *Bismarck* quickly directed her secondary battery guns at the destroyer which was firing flares and easily straddled the ship. Further flare-launching could have ended in severe damage or even the sinking of the destroyers. They were seen from the battleship about 06:00, at a moment when almost all of them surrounded her. Their subsequent torpedo attacks did not score any hits. The fire delivered from the *Bismarck* was not effective, either.

The final hours aboard the Bismarck

After the attack by British aircraft, Admiral Lütjens reported to Group West at 21:05, informing them about the torpedo hit received in the stern in Square BE 6192. Ten minutes later, he sent out another radio message about being hit by another torpedo, this time amidships. After a while, he also added that the ship could not be steered. Talking to Captain Lindemann and Chief Engineer Lehmann, he was made aware of the exact situation of the ship: it was far from being satisfactory, the jammed rudder and loss of speed allowing the pursuing warships to come closer. From this moment, the *Bismarck*'s chances for a successful getaway were growing smaller from one minute to the next. The only remaining hope was the approaching U-boats, which might in theory stop the enemy. However, this could not be relied on too much, as the Atlantic was very stormy and torpedo attacks on the British ships in those condition were more than likely to fail. As such discussions continued on the bridge, feverish work was taking place below, the crew trying to repair the damaged rudders and raise steam in the boilers. Lindemann was also trying to work out an alternative means of manoeuvring the crippled battleship.

Up on the admiral's bridge, Lütjens regularly read intercepted messages being sent between various commanders as well as those addressed to him personally. From these, he learnt the number, positions and courses of the British warships that were pursuing him, including one aircraft carrier. An intercepted report to headquarters from *U-566* told him that the aircraft carrier in question was the *Ark Royal*, with the battleship *King George V* sailing nearby with the commander of the Home Fleet aboard. At 22:05, Group West radioed the Admiral that eight U-boats currently in Square BE 6192 had been ordered to support him. At the same time a message was intercepted from the British ships addressed to the commander of the 4th Flotilla and Force H announcing that operational orders would soon be issued to them. Being able

Admiral Tovey's 'eyes' – the cruiser Sheffield.

Via IWM

to decode them, Admiral Lütjens would learn about the enemies' plans and could take steps to counteract them. However, this remained only theory because putting it in practice would require an undamaged ship capable of high speed. One and a half hours later, Lütjens radioed Group West again, reporting that the *Bismarck* was surrounded by the *Renown* and light British forces. Shortly after 23:00, Group West radioed that the Luftwaffe would be flying reconnaissance on 27 May covering the area between 46° and 48°30' as well as the area north of Brest. The report also emphasized that the earliest possible take-off time for the aircraft was 04:30, whereas bombers would only be able to set off at 06:30. This news was received on the battleship at 23:45. At the same time Group West only now received the previous message of 21:40 about the critical circumstances that the *Bismarck* was faced with and about the failure of steering gear making manoeuvring impossible. Finishing his message, Lütjens stated that the *Bismarck* would fight to the last shell.

At 00:14, the commander of the Kriegsmarine, Grossadmiral Raeder, radioed Admiral Lütjens on the *Bismarck*, wishing him success in the continuing, hard fight. The ship's crew were, when possible, constantly kept informed of the situation. The information was passed to the crew's action stations by loudspeakers and the internal telephone network as often as possible. The signals received by the ship were read to the crew. After 01:13, Group West sent another message: tugs had been made ready at the harbour to help the *Bismarck* reach the haven even if she ran out of fuel or suffered machinery trouble. Also, three Focke Wulf 200 'Condor' aircraft were reported nearby and three groups of bombers were said to be taking off between 05:00 and 06:00. Half-an-hour later, Group West radioed the ship again, this time informing them about the deployment of the tanker *Ermland* from La Pallice scheduled for 05:00 to aid the *Bismarck* in reaching port. Six minutes later, Lütjens received a message from Adolf Hitler himself. In its second part, the Führer thanked the brave crew of the battleship for the fulfilment of their duty and their fight for the fatherland. At 02:17, Lütjens sent a message to Admiral Raeder in which he recommended Korvettenkapitän Schneider for the Iron Cross for the sinking of the *Hood*. An hour later, he received the confirmation of the award of this decoration to Schneider by Adolf Hitler himself.

In the meantime, the Luftwaffe had been preparing aircraft for frequent weather patrols. They were expected to be supplying the current cloudbase every two hours. Group West was also informing the ship to send out a signal at quarter-past and quarter-to every hour – it was to be of a five-minute duration on the frequency of 443Hz to be picked up by the bombers. On the morning of 27 May, Admiral Lütjens had no illusions about the fate of his ship. He knew that there was no chance to save her. He decided to save her war diary and film of the battle with the *Hood* by sending them to France via seaplane. From interviews with the survivors of the battleship we know about an attempt to launch a seaplane between 05:00 and 06:00. The first Arado had to be dumped overboard because of its extensive damage. Another one was unable to take off, either, after it was placed on the catapult. The hydraulic gear was bent and the device could not be properly operated. The damage came from the splinters of the shell that had hit the ship during the battle in the Denmark Strait. Besides, the *Bismarck* had a considerable list to port so that the port secondary battery turret dipped in the water as the ship rolled.

At 05:42, Group West informed the ship that three bomber groups had taken off from French airfields at 05:30. According to estimates, the aircraft should be arriving at the battleship's location about 09:00. The report was received on the ship at 06:08. Shortly after that, the weather changed – the wind was stronger and blowing from a different direction. It was then that an interesting event took place as described by the surviving German sailors and mentioned in the *Bismarck*'s reconstructed war diary. On sighting the *King George V*, the heavy cruisers and the escorting destroyers, action stations was sounded. Her opponent was the first to open fire, and the *Bismarck* responded with main and secondary battery salvoes. After a while, both sides were conducting a regular naval battle which lasted for about half an hour and resulted in the *Bismarck* receiving hits. All of these struck her amidships and in the forecastle. One bad hit was taken on the magazine of the starboard No. 3 turret of the secondary battery. The turret burst into flames and had to be abandoned by the crew. Another interesting thing was the submerged afterdeck, which prevented 'Dora' turret from being trained. These events are unfortunately not confirmed by British sources.

It being impossible to repair the catapult and save the ship's diary by air, Admiral Lütjens sought another option. He radioed Group West at 07:10 requesting that a U-boat arrive to take the diary and other important documents. Less than an hour later, Lütjens was informed that *U-556*, which was closest to his ship, would come to take the documents. The submarine was commanded by Korvettenkapitän H. Wohlfarth; however, he was unable to retrieve the *Bismarck*'s documents owing to lack of fuel. About 06:30, Wohlfarth sighted *U-74* under the command of Kapitänleutnant F. Kentrat and ordered him to make contact with the *Bismarck*, giving him her current bearing.

The Final Battle

Before sunrise, at 07:08, the *Bismarck* unexpectedly increased her speed to 12 knots. Captain Lindemann ordered the engines to be stopped and after a while restarted. He intended to take advantage of the wind and waves to alter the disagreeable course which was inevitably taking the ship toward the British. Despite this manoeuvre, he was unable to control her this way, and the ship continued in a northerly direction. After breakfast, the *Bismarck* crew began to prepare for the final battle. From time to time, the vessel entered squalls, which hid her from the enemy.

Between 06:00 and 07:00, Admiral Tovey received several reports from the destroyer *Maori* which provided information to determine the current position of the German battleship. Low in the water, the latter was sailing on a course of 330 degrees at a speed of 10 knots. The north-eastern horizon was clear, and visibility from 07:22, after the sun rose, was 22–24km (12–13 nautical miles) – almost ideal conditions for long-range gunnery. The only obstacles were the heavy seas and quite strong wind. Therefore Admiral Tovey wanted to position his ships in line with the wind so that his guns should be delivering a more accurate fire and be able to make corrections more quickly. He was coming from the north-west, and after 07:37 he altered course to 80 degrees, wanting to contact the enemy as soon as possible. At that time, the *Bismarck* was 39km (21 miles) away from him. The nearby *Rodney* was ordered to set a distance of six cables between herself and the flagship – this allowed safe firing by both battleships. At 07:53, the cruiser *Norfolk* signalled *King George V* that contact with the *Bismarck* had been made. The cruiser's commander, Captain A.J.L. Phillips, informed Tovey that the German battleship was steering 130 degrees and was 30km (16 nautical miles) away. The captain well remembered the engagement in the Denmark Strait and kept the *Norfolk* at a safe distance, waiting for the battleships to arrive. Soon the battleships, steering 110 degrees, spotted the *Norfolk*'s masts on the horizon. She was to take position on the north-eastern flank and join the battle upon receiving the order. The *King George V* was still too far to the north, and the admiral had the course changed to a southerly one. From the west came the heavy cruiser *Dorsetshire*. She had been escorting a convoy in the north on the day before, and after the receipt of the Catalina signal, the commander, Captain B.C.S. Martin, altered course, heading for the *Bismarck*. When he unexpectedly arrived at the battlefield, Tovey's ships mistook him for the *Prinz Eugen* at first. However, an exchange of identification signals removed any doubts.

The British battleships were approaching the *Bismarck* on a course of 110 degrees. The *King George V* was in the lead, whereas the *Rodney* sailed behind, on the port side of the flagship. The

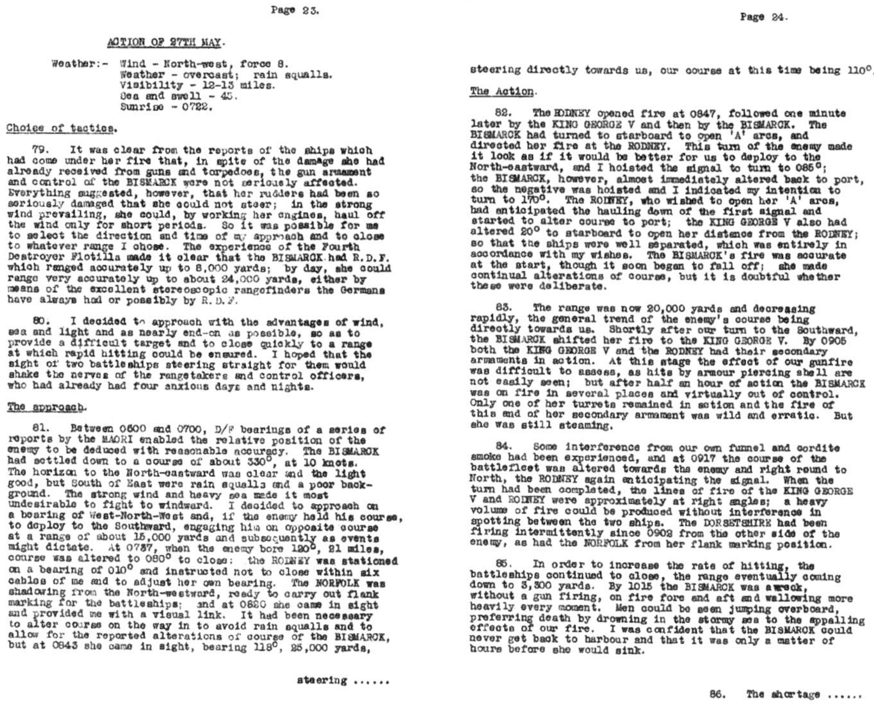

Page 23.

ACTION OF 27TH MAY.

Weather:- Wind - North-west, force 8.
Weather - overcast; rain squalls.
Visibility - 12-13 miles.
Sea and swell - 45.
Sunrise - 0722.

Choice of tactics.

79. It was clear from the reports of the ships which had come under her fire that, in spite of the damage she had already received from guns and torpedoes, the gun armament and control of the BISMARCK were not seriously affected. Everything suggested, however, that her rudders had been so seriously damaged that she could not steer; in the strong wind prevailing, she could, by working her engines, haul off the wind only for short periods. So it was possible for me to select the direction and time of my approach and to close to whatever range I chose. The experience of the Fourth Destroyer Flotilla made it clear that the BISMARCK had R.D.F. which ranged accurately up to 8,000 yards; by day, she could range very accurately up to about 24,000 yards, either by means of the excellent stereoscopic rangefinders the Germans have always had or possibly by R.D.F.

80. I decided to approach with the advantages of wind, sea and light and as nearly end-on as possible, so as to provide a difficult target and to close quickly to a range at which rapid hitting could be ensured. I hoped that the sight of two battleships steering straight for them would shake the nerves of the rangetakers and control officers, who had already had four anxious days and nights.

The approach.

81. Between 0600 and 0700, D/F bearings of a series of reports by the MAORI enabled the relative position of the enemy to be deduced with reasonable accuracy. The BISMARCK had settled down to a course of about 330°, at 10 knots. The horizon to the North-eastward was clear and the light good, but South of East were rain squalls and a poor background. The strong wind and heavy sea made it most undesirable to fight to windward. I decided to approach on a bearing of West-North-West and, if the enemy held his course, to deploy to the Southward, engaging him on opposite course at a range of about 15,000 yards and subsequently as events might dictate. At 0737, when the enemy bore 120°, 21 miles, course was altered to 080° to close: the RODNEY was stationed on a bearing of 010° and instructed not to close within six cables of me and to adjust her own bearing. The NORFOLK was shadowing from the North-westward, ready to carry out flank marking for the battleships; and at 0820 she came in sight and provided me with a visual link. It had been necessary to alter course on the way in to avoid rain squalls and to allow for the reported alterations of course of the BISMARCK, but at 0843 she came in sight, bearing 118°, 25,000 yards,

steering ......

Page 24.

steering directly towards us, our course at this time being 110°.

The Action.

82. The RODNEY opened fire at 0847, followed one minute later by the KING GEORGE V and then by the BISMARCK. The BISMARCK had turned to starboard to open 'A' arcs, and directed her fire at the RODNEY. This turn of the enemy made it look as if it would be better for us to deploy to the North-eastward, and I hoisted the signal to turn to 085°; the BISMARCK, however, almost immediately altered back to port, so the negative was hoisted and I indicated my intention to turn to 170°. The RODNEY, who wished to open her 'A' arcs, had anticipated the hauling down of the first signal and started to alter course to port; the KING GEORGE V also had altered 20° to starboard to open her distance from the RODNEY; so that the ships were well separated, which was entirely in accordance with my wishes. The BISMARCK's fire was accurate at the start, though it soon began to fall off; she made continual alterations of course, but it is doubtful whether these were deliberate.

83. The range was now 20,000 yards and decreasing rapidly, the general trend of the enemy's course being directly towards us. Shortly after our turn to the Southward, the BISMARCK shifted her fire to the KING GEORGE V. By 0905 both the KING GEORGE V and the RODNEY had their secondary armaments in action. At this stage the effect of our gunfire was difficult to assess, as hits by armour piercing shell are not easily seen; but after half an hour of action the BISMARCK was on fire in several places and virtually out of control. Only one of her turrets remained in action and the fire of this and of her secondary armament was wild and erratic. But she was still steaming.

84. Some interference from our own funnel and cordite smoke had been experienced, and at 0917 the course of the battlefleet was altered towards the enemy and right round to North, the RODNEY again anticipating the signal. When the turn had been completed, the lines of fire of the KING GEORGE V and RODNEY were approximately at right angles; a heavy volume of fire could be produced without interference in spotting between the two ships. The DORSETSHIRE had been firing intermittently since 0902 from the other side of the enemy, as had the NORFOLK from her flank marking position.

85. In order to increase the rate of hitting, the battleships continued to close, the range eventually coming down to 3,300 yards. By 1015 the BISMARCK was a wreck, without a gun firing, on fire fore and aft and wallowing more heavily every moment. Men could be seen jumping overboard, preferring death by drowning in the stormy sea to the appalling effects of our fire. I was confident that the BISMARCK could never get back to harbour and that it was only a matter of hours before she would sink.

86. The shortage ......

Admiral Tovey's report about the battle with the Bismarck, *27 May 1941.*

Via A. Jarski

wake of the British battleship was contaminated with a film of fuel oil. The pursuit of the *Bismarck* and sailing at the maximum speed of 20–21 knots over the past few days had resulted in serious vibration, which had affected the hull riveting and the sealing of fuel tanks. At 08:43, the *Bismarck* was sighted from the flagship at 7 degrees to port. She was 23km (12.3 nautical miles) away with a slight list to port and sailing straight in their direction. None of the British warships was in a good position to effectively engage the German opponent at the time. The *King George V* switched on her Type 284 radar, which indicated a distance of about 22,951m (25,100) yards from the target, decreasing every moment. The *Rodney* prepared to open fire.

The British battleships were sighted from the *Bismarck* when some 24,000m (26,250 yards) away, and battle stations were sounded. Up in the foretop, Korvettenkapitän Schneider was giving orders in a calm voice. The *Rodney* was his first target, leading the British formation. He reported the main and secondary batteries ready and requested permission to open fire. However, the first shells in this battle were fired by the British at 08:47. First, the *Rodney* delivered a salvo at the *Bismarck* from 'A' and 'B' turrets, and a minute later the *King George V* joined in. The range between the ships had already decreased to 20,000m (22,000 yards). The British shells took one minute to cover the distance separating them from German target. They fell some distance short of the ship. Two minutes after the first British salvo, the *Bismarck* returned fire from the forward 380mm turrets. The aft turrets could not bear. Schneider carefully observed the fall of shot: the first salvo appeared too short, whereas the second went over the target. The opponent was only straddled with the third salvo, fired at 08:53. However, there were no direct hits scored. Only one shell fell close to the *Rodney*, about 20m (21 yards) from her, close to the bridge. There were no casualties, only splinters piercing the bridge in three places and the plating above the armour belt. The next two salvoes from the *Bismarck* were short again. The initial accuracy of the *Bismarck*'s fire was quite good but, as her course was far from steady, it was very difficult to observe the fall of shot, not to mention making corrections.

On the British side, the *Rodney* fired two salvoes at 08:47. Their fall was not seen from the battleship but the cruiser *Norfolk*, positioned close to the German vessel, confirmed that the *Bismarck* had been hit by salvoes. At 08:50, though, the main gun director on the *Rodney* indicated a range of 2,286m (2,500 yards) over the actual range. This caused all the shells fired at the *Bismarck* to fall short of the target. For the next few minutes, the *Rodney* had to fire over the target until the correct settings were restored. At 08:59, the British ship fired the eighteenth salvo from 'B' turret, this one being successful. Two direct hits could be seen: the first one forward, and the second in the main superstructure.

Tovey had the flagship's course gradually altered to southerly so as to be able to employ her entire main armament. At 08:53, he ordered the *Rodney* to make a simultaneous 85 degrees turn in order to take a more favourable position to continue the fight with the *Bismarck*. However, the *Rodney* was already about to fire from 'A' turret and could not carry out the manoeuvre. Both battleships sailed on divergent courses for a while. Having fired two salvoes, the ship checked fire from 'A' turret, turned to starboard, and set a more easterly course. 'X' turret was turned slightly and it soon opened fire. It delivered three salvoes as the battleship turned, but they proved inaccurate and fell short of the *Bismarck*. In the meantime the *King George V* fired the first salvo, which could not be observed with accuracy, but radar showed it to fall short. At 08:53, the flagship fired another salvo, this time straddling the target and this was the first hit scored by *King George V*. After a slight correction, subsequent salvoes were fired according to radar readings. At 08:54, the heavy cruiser *Norfolk*, to starboard of the *Bismarck*, opened

Page 25.

86. The shortage of oil fuel in the KING GEORGE V and the RODNEY had become acute. It was not merely a matter of having sufficient oil to reach one of our harbours: I had to consider the possibility of damage to fuel tanks by a near miss from a bomb or a hit by a torpedo; this might easily result in the ship being stopped in an area where U-boats were known to be concentrating, and where I had been warned to expect heavy air attack. Further gunfire would do little to hasten the BISMARCK's end. I therefore decided to break off the action with the KING GEORGE V and the RODNEY, and I instructed any ships still with torpedoes to use them on the BISMARCK. The DORSETSHIRE anticipated my order and torpedoed the BISMARCK at close range on both sides: she sank at 1037 in position 48°09'N. 16°07'W. Although her sinking had been seen from the after Director Control Tower in the KING GEORGE V, the fact did not become known to me until 1100 and I informed the Flag Officer Commanding, Force 'H', that I could not sink the BISMARCK with gunfire: this signal (1045/27th May), which was perhaps unfortunately phrased, was addressed only to him and was intended to ensure that he should take any steps which might help to hasten her sinking: when intercepted by others, it may have caused some misunderstanding.

87. The BISMARCK had put up a most gallant fight against impossible odds, worthy of the old days of the Imperial German Navy, and she went down with her colours still flying. The DORESETSHIRE picked up four officers, including the Third Gunnery Officer, and 75 ratings; the MAORI picked up 24 ratings; but at 1140 the DORSETSHIRE sighted a suspicious object, which might have been a U-boat, and ships were compelled to abandon the work of rescue. Some of the remaining survivors may have been rescued by the Spanish cruiser CANARIAS.

88. From the information available, it appears that the BISMARCK suffered three hits by gunfire on 24th May, one hit by aircraft torpedo on 25th May and two on 26th May, two hits by destroyer torpedoes early on 27th May, one by the RODNEY's torpedo, and the subsequent heavy pounding by gunfire. At the end of this she was in a sinking condition, and the final torpedoes from the DORSETSHIRE only hastened her end. A few casualties and slight damage from splinters were incurred in the SHEFFIELD and the destroyers of the Fourth Destroyer Flotilla during the night of 26th/27th May; there were no casualties or damage to any of our ships during the subsequent day action.

89. In the KING GEORGE V W/T transmission on power on certain wave lengths interfered with reception on R.D.F. For this reason I was unable during the action to keep the Admiralty fully informed of its progress, especially in view of the fact that I had been warned to expect heavy attack by enemy aircraft, and I did not wish to risk being fixed by D/F. The BISMARCK's sinking was reported as soon as it was known and a description of the engagement was deferred until it was practicable to transmit a long signal by wireless. This limitation applies in some degree to all ships and will have to be borne in mind in the future.

Return of the Fleet ......

Page 26.

Return of the Fleet.

90. The KING GEORGE V and the RODNEY with the COSSACK, SIKH and ZULU, proceeded to the Northward. The DORSETSHIRE and the MAORI rejoined at 1230, and the screen was augmented by the JUPITER during the afternoon. Nine further destroyers had joined by 1600 the following day. Several signals were received on 28th May, indicating that air attacks on the fleet were impending, but only four enemy aircraft appeared. One of these bombed the screen without effect, while another jettisoned its solitary bomb on being attacked by a Blenheim fighter. The MASHONA and the TARTAR, 100 miles to the Southward, were heavily attacked, the MASHONA being sunk at noon, with the loss of one officer and 45 ratings: the TARTAR shot down one of the attacking aircraft. The PIORUN underwent six attacks by aircraft on her way back to Plymouth; all were driven off by gunfire.

91. The RODNEY, screened by the MAORI, SIKH and COLUMBIA (Lt.Cdr. Somerville W. Davis), was detached to the Clyde at 1700; the DORSETSHIRE was detached to the Tyne at 2316; the KING GEORGE V was delayed by fog, but eventually anchored in Loch Ewe at 1230 on 29th May. The GALATEA (Rear-Admiral Commanding, Second Cruiser Squadron), AURORA and PRINCE OF WALES arrived at Hvalfiord on 27th May, as did the VICTORIOUS: the EDINBURGH (Commodore Commanding, Eighteenth Cruiser Squadron) arrived at Londonderry on 28th May and the NORFOLK (Rear-Admiral Commanding, First Cruiser Squadron) at the Clyde on 29th May: Force 'H' returned to Gibraltar.

Conduct of officers and men.

92. Although it was no more than I expected, the co-operation, skill and understanding displayed by all forces during this prolonged chase gave me the utmost satisfaction. Flag and Commanding Officers of detached units invariably took the action I would have wished, before or without receiving instructions from me. The conduct of all officers and men of the Fleet which I have the honour to command was in accordance with the traditions of the Service. Force 'H' was handled with conspicuous skill throughout the operation by Vice-Admiral Sir James F. Somerville, K.C.B., D.S.O., and contributed a vital share in its successful conclusion.

Supply of information and disposition of forces.

93. The accuracy of the enemy information supplied by the Admiralty and the speed with which it was passed were remarkable, and the balance struck between information and instructions passed to the forces out of visual touch with

me was ....

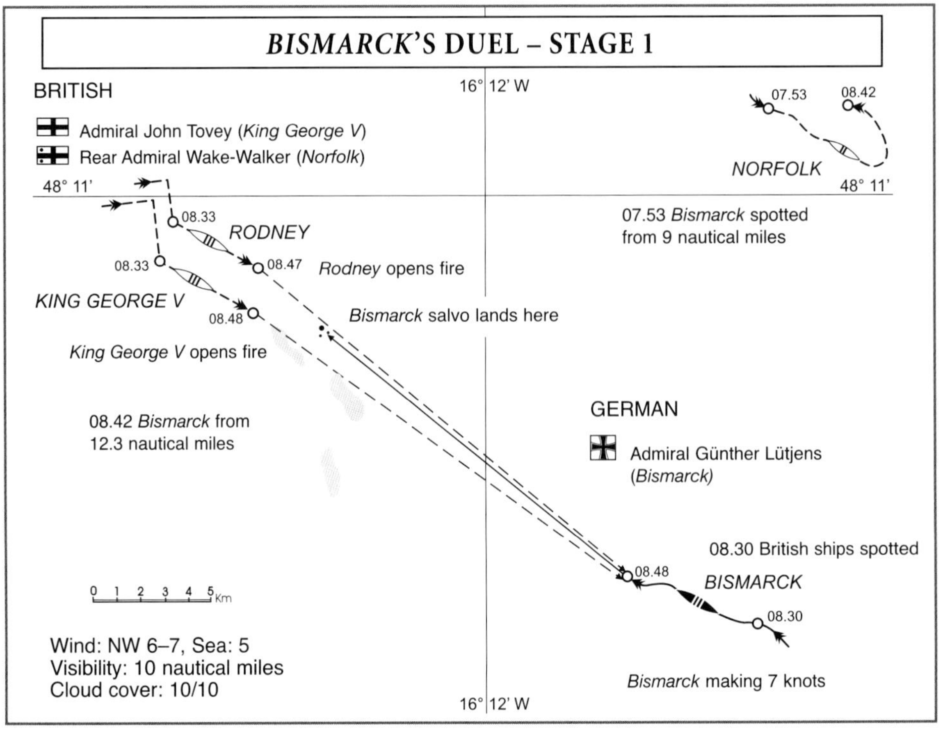
BISMARCK'S DUEL – STAGE 1
BRITISH
Admiral John Tovey (King George V)
Rear Admiral Wake-Walker (Norfolk)
16° 12' W
48° 11'
07.53
08.42
NORFOLK
48° 11'
08.33
RODNEY
08.33
08.47
Rodney opens fire
07.53 Bismarck spotted from 9 nautical miles
KING GEORGE V
08.48
Bismarck salvo lands here
King George V opens fire
08.42 Bismarck from 12.3 nautical miles
GERMAN
Admiral Günther Lütjens (Bismarck)
08.30 British ships spotted
08.48
BISMARCK
08.30
0 1 2 3 4 5 Km
Wind: NW 6–7, Sea: 5
Visibility: 10 nautical miles
Cloud cover: 10/10
Bismarck making 7 knots
16° 12' W

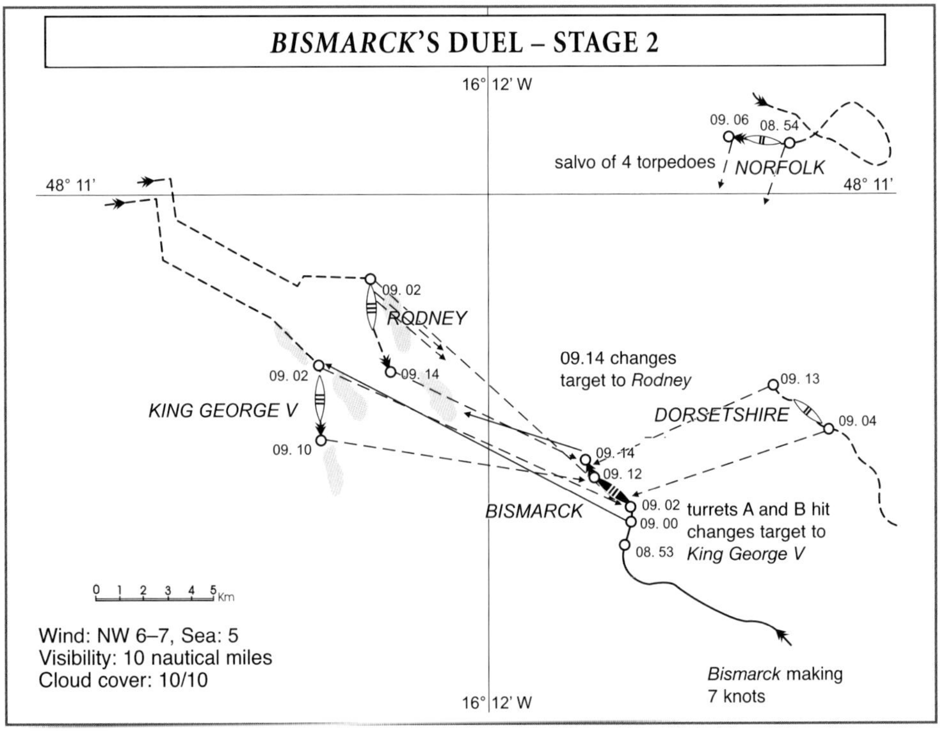
BISMARCK'S DUEL – STAGE 2
16° 12' W
09. 06
08. 54
salvo of 4 torpedoes
NORFOLK
48° 11'
48° 11'
09. 02
RODNEY
09.14 changes target to Rodney
09. 02
09. 14
09. 13
KING GEORGE V
DORSETSHIRE
09. 04
09. 10
09. 14
09. 12
BISMARCK
09. 02
turrets A and B hit
09. 00
changes target to King George V
08. 53
0 1 2 3 4 5 Km
Wind: NW 6–7, Sea: 5
Visibility: 10 nautical miles
Cloud cover: 10/10
Bismarck making 7 knots
16° 12' W

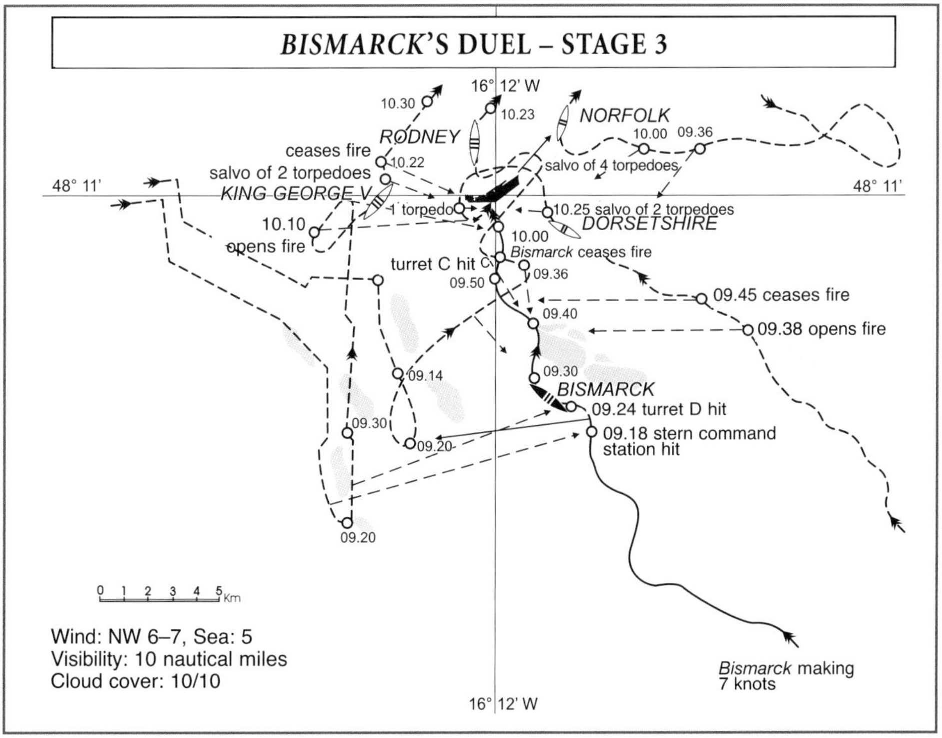

fire. A few minutes later, when the range had decreased, the secondary battery on the *Rodney* opened fire at 09:02, scoring a hit forward. Two minutes later, the heavy cruiser *Dorsetshire* joined in at a range of 18,000m (19,685 yards). Now, the *Bismarck* was under fire from virtually every direction.

In the meantime, the *Bismarck*'s gunnery officers – Schneider and Albrecht – concentrated on engaging the *Rodney*, which was ahead of them on the port quarter. They decided not to split their fire between different targets but deal with one opponent first, and then another, just like they had fought and sunk the *Hood*. They chose the *Rodney* because she had heavier armament and her hits were more devastating than those of the *King George V*. Despite the accurate enemy fire and hits on the *Bismarck*, the gunnery officers kept directing their fire coolly. Everything proceeded as if this was just an ordinary practice shoot.

Gradually and inevitably, the *Bismarck*'s upper deck was being reduced to scrap. The shorter the range, the more frequent were the explosions of hits she received. They were growing louder and louder. By this time, no less than five British shells had come through the upper deck and exploded on the main deck. One hit Section I, another blew up at the 'tweendeck with a blinding flash. Nitrogen was escaping from fractured bottles and equipment, entering through broken hatches into the damage control centre in Section III. Fragments of the third shell hit the ventilators on the main deck, putting them out of action at once and filling the area with smoke. Emergency lighting came on immediately. The fourth and fifth hits that the *Bismarck* received struck at Section IV, where they mainly damaged passageways and communication channels. The hits resulted in fires, with black pungent smoke coming out of the various compartments. The smoke and gases were spreading into all the adjacent compartments. At about 09:00, the *Bismarck* took hits on her forward turrets, the fire control post and the foremast. A few minutes later, a heavy-calibre projectile went through the superstructure, damaged the catapult, pierced the deck, and exploded in a 105mm ammunition magazine.

Tall pillars of water astern of the Bismarck *mark the fall of a salvo of 16in shells from the* Rodney.

Via IWM

The explosion of the shell and of the ammunition it set off killed all the men in the area.

At 09:02, the *Bismarck* had 'Anton' and 'Bruno' turrets put out of action, costing her half of her fighting capability. Korvettenkapitän Albrecht notified the main fire control position about an evacuation of the forward control position due to smoke and fumes. It was not an easy thing to do, as all the telephone lines were down because of short circuits or power failures. Further communication was carried out by runners. At the same time, the main battery fire control was moved to the aft fire control position, under the fourth gunnery officer, Kapitänleutnant Müllenheim-Rechberg. It was more or less then, at 09:02, that Kapitänleutnant Gerhard Junack below decks was ordered to prepare the ship for scuttling. He was working in the centre turbine room (Section VIII), where he supervised the execution of the manoeuvres ordered by the helm. A large amount of water and pungent smoke entered the compartment through ventilation shafts, and the men were forced to put on their gas masks. This was the last order they heard in this room because contact with them was lost completely after that. Explosive charges were prepared and placed around the cold-air outlet. Junack sent one of the petty officers for further orders. Time passed but the sailor did not return. Junack could not wait any longer and decided to fulfil his orders. He opened all the watertight hatches in the machinery room and shaft tunnels, and then ordered the entire crew to leave the compartment and assemble on the main deck. Together with the first mechanic, he set the fuses for a nine-minute delay. He was the last to leave the turbine room. When still struggling through the damaged areas of the ship, he heard a loud blast in the machinery room.

At 09:02, both British battleships made a 180 degrees turn and set a new southerly course. This made fire control on the *Rodney* more difficult because view from the spotting top was repeatedly obscured by the smoke coming from the main guns and the funnel. At 09:08, the *Norfolk* reported to the flagship: 'Fore main battery guns on *Bismarck* pointing very high. Probably out of action.' Meanwhile, the *Rodney* had altered course 40 degrees to port in order to prevent the smoke from hindering fire control.

After he took over the command of the aft main battery, Kapitänleutnant Müllenheim-Rechberg scanned the horizon with the gun director. The visibility and observation conditions were very good and permitted him to quickly straddle the enemy, even if they were moving at high speed. Since the *Rodney* was at a dead angle, the first target was the *King George V*. Upon computation of target data at 09:10, four salvoes were fired at the target. Two of them appeared to be over, whereas the other two were too short. At 09:13, as the guns were being redirected, the aft fire control position was smashed by an enemy shell. The gun director shook, as the heavy shell must have passed nearby, somewhere above its position. Everything in its path was wrecked, all the equipment being reduced to scrap. The loss of this fire position meant the end of centralized fire control on the battleship. An attempt to restore telephone connection with both computation rooms failed. After a short discussion, the officers decided that the two remaining turrets should maintain fire independently. The aft turrets 'Cäsar' and 'Dora' selected targets individually, aiming their guns according to their own rangefinders. Still, their fire grew more and more sporadic with every passing minute.

It was almost 09:15 when the task of installing explosive charges to scuttle the battleship ordered by Fregattenkapitän Oels and Kapitänleutnant Jahreis was finished. The first officer at the fore bridge informed all stations on the ship that the scuttling procedure had been completed. He also passed word to the damage control centre regarding the initiation of the appropriate procedures. In the rear of it was Obermaschinist W. Schmidt, who heard the sinking order issued by Oels to all stations. The pumps under his control, still functioning despite the damage that the ship had sustained, were now stopped. Slowly and steadily, water flooded all the compartments of the ship. In the boiler rooms, the still-working boilers blew up on contact with the cold water. The evacuation of the lower compartments within the armoured citadel was difficult because all the hatches were sealed. The upper deck could only be reached by passageways in the narrow ammunition elevators. The explosions of the charges caused an enormous amount of water to rush into the battleship's hull. She was slowly sinking.

At 09:15, both British battleships were noticed to turn by 180 degrees. After this manoeuvre, both 'A' and 'B' turrets of *King George V* maintained their fire, whereas 'Y' turret was still being prepared. A minute later, after she fired her fortieth salvo which straddled the target, the *Rodney* turned away. After the turn, her main battery resumed firing and the secondary battery joined in. Both British vessels now found it more difficult to spot the fall of shot. The *Bismarck* was

Via IWM

The Rodney *firing at the* Bismarck. *The picture was taken from the* King George V *during the last stage of the battle.*

A burning Bismarck *still afloat. This photograph was taken from one of the British warships during the final stage of the battle. The* Bismarck *sank shortly after.*

Via IWM

ever more obscured by fires and black smoke from the superstructure and the funnel. The wind carried the thick clouds of smoke straight in their direction. However, the *King George V* had her radar switched on, and this allowed making corrections to her shooting. At 09:16, the *Rodney* launched six torpedoes at the *Bismarck* at a range of about 10,000m (11,000 yards), but none of them managed to hit the target. At the same time, about 09:26, twelve Swordfishes were on stand-by aboard the *Ark Royal* some distance from the action, waiting to attack the *Bismarck*. However, owing to a high risk of their being hit during the exchange of fire between the ships, they were retained on board.

The four British warships – two battleships and two heavy cruisers – kept shelling the German battleship at close range. For the next several minutes, the *King George V* fired from 'A' and 'B' turrets but only three of her salvoes straddled the target, and a single hit was observed. The *Rodney*, which sailed beside her, had a somewhat better position than the flagship. Although the wind, blowing from the port bow, obliged her to allow for it when directing fire, it at least did not cause the battleship to roll. This allowed for very accurate gunfire. A little later, the *Rodney* made a turn to a new course of 21 degrees. A moment later, at 09:26, she turned once again, now steering 37 degrees. This alteration affected her gunnery for the worse – rolling increased and made maintaining accuracy more difficult.

At 09:21 *Bismarck*'s 'Dora' turret was put out of action when its right barrel was destroyed by a shell. Two more shells had been fired from the left gun when the commander of the turret was warned that it had burst into flames. The entire turret crew were immediately evacuated, while the commander, Bootsmannsmaat F. Helms, carried the news to the aft damage control centre. Pump No. 2 was engaged at once to flood the ammunition magazine below the turret; later, a shell exploded in there. After 09:27, one of the *Bismarck*'s fore turrets unexpectedly fired one last salvo. It was then that ammunition was finished. Damage to the turret had been quickly repaired, and they were able to continue shooting, and it was only lack of ammunition that caused the guns to fall silent. The same soon happened to 'Cäsar' turret directed by Leutnant zur See G. Brückner. The turret fired its last salvo at 09:31. Thereafter, the *Bismarck*'s main guns would not fire again.

On the British side, the target disappeared from the *Rodney*'s gun directors at 09:28 and could not be precisely located until 09:45. At 09:36, the ship made another, 180 degrees turn to port, to cross the path of the German battleship about 2,740–3,650m (3,000–4,000 yards) ahead of her. Passing her, the British observed an explosion at about 09:40 in 'Bruno' turret. At 09:42, the *Rodney* made one more turn, and after three more minutes, she opened fire from her main battery, firing four salvoes at the enemy. Direct hits were noticed during this barrage. At 09:49, the *Rodney* again turned 180 degrees. It was then that the gun director malfunctioned. This problem was not repairable, and fire control had to be moved to the secondary battery director. At 09:52, the *Rodney* fired a nine-gun broadside at the *Bismarck*, of which five or six shells were seen to hit. At 10:03, the *Rodney* altered her course by 190 degrees to starboard in order to close in on the enemy to avoid wasting ammunition. She continued firing at the *Bismarck* from about 3,650m (4,000 yards). Two minutes later, the guns were made ready to deliver the last twelve salvoes. They were all fired between 10:08 and 10:14, with hits observed again. After this, the *Rodney* held her fire and headed north to join the *King George V*. During the 45-minute battle, the British ships fired 2,157 shells of various calibres at the *Bismarck* (according to British sources), only a small proportion of which hit the target.

All the *Bismarck*'s main turrets and directors had been destroyed, putting her out of any further combat. The damage done by the scuttling charges was causing her to increasingly list to port as she went down. The ship was filled with choking smoke and fumes, forcing her surviving crew to wear gas masks. The crew were soon ordered to abandon ship. Her forecastle was heavily damaged and on fire. The main funnel had received a few hits but was still standing. From the aft conning tower to the mainmast was wreathed in pungent white smoke, which was blowing towards the bow and hiding everything like thick morning mist. Burned and battered, 'Cäsar' turret stood with the gun projecting to port and raised high toward the bow. Bright red flames and dark smoke bursting out from the superstructure shrouded the wreckage as it rocked on the stormy ocean.

Seeing no further action on the German side and due to the difficult fuel situation, Tovey ordered the cease-fire at 10:15. The *Rodney* and *King George V* set a new course of 27 degrees, which took them north, towards their home base, and increased speed to 19 knots. As Admiral Tovey's force departed, he notified the nearby Somerville that he was unable to sink the *Bismarck* with his own guns. Somerville was instructed to find out which vessel of those in the area was still carrying any torpedoes. This one was to be dispatched to put an end to the *Bismarck*. At 10:22, Admiral Somerville contacted the cruiser *Dorsetshire*, instructing her to launch torpedoes at the still-floating wreckage of the German battleship. Two minutes later, the commander of the cruiser, Captain Martin, ordered his men to launch two torpedoes from

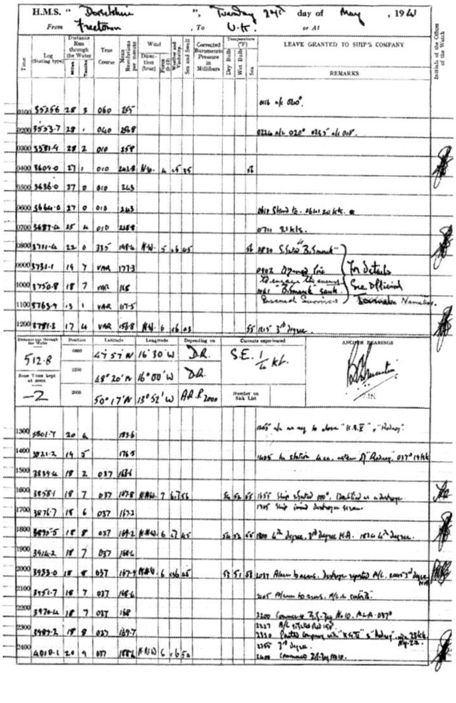
H.M.S. "Dorsetshire", Tuesday 27th day of May, 1941
From Freetown, To U.K.
LEAVE GRANTED TO SHIP'S COMPANY
REMARKS

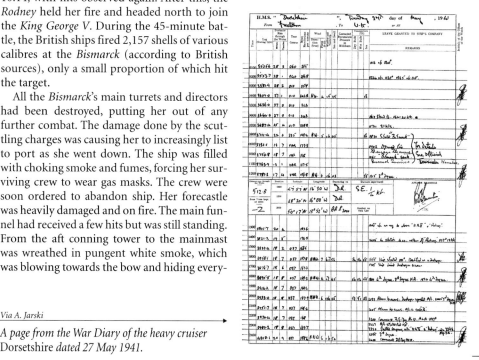

Via A. Jarski

A page from the War Diary of the heavy cruiser Dorsetshire *dated 27 May 1941.*

a range of 3,000m (3,280 yards). The *Bismarck* was hit on the starboard side below the bridge. Since she was still afloat, the British cruiser steamed to the other, port side, and at 10:36 launched another torpedo from a range of 2,200m (2,400 yards).

The sinking

At about 10:00, the first sailors began to assemble near the aft conning tower. They were mostly the crews of the already inactive stations reaching the stern in small groups. At that moment, it was

Via IWM

Survivors of the Bismarck *alongside the* Dorsetshire.

Crewmembers of the cruiser Sheffield *indicating splinter hits on the gun director.*

Via IWM

the safest place on the ship. Some of the men reached there through the narrow emergency door mounted at the aft auxiliary fire control position. The sight of the damage to this area of the ship was terrifying. Where anti-aircraft guns, searchlights and superstructure had once stood, there was now nothing but a pile of scrap. There was no trace of all that used to be there before. Most of the missing equipment had been blasted away by the explosions of heavy shells. The white haze above the ship topped the fires raging below. The assembling sailors waited at 'Dora' turret until the right moment to jump over the side. Some of them could not decide when that was. Kapitänleutnant Müllenheim-Rechberg came up to them and said that they should wait until the last moment – the ship was sinking slowly, and after leaving her they would anyway have to wait for a long time in the cold waters of the Atlantic Ocean before they were picked up. The *Bismarck* was increasingly listing to one side. The heavy waves were sweeping over her upper deck. The Kapitänleutnant saw that the British battleships were departing, apparently without any intention of rescuing survivors. However, he hoped that one of the light vessels would soon arrive and rescue them.

Within a short time, a few hundred men had assembled around the aft turrets to prepare to jump over the side. The ship was still sinking, the sea gradually taking possession of the stern. It could also be felt that the *Bismarck* was gradually turning over onto the port side. The starboard side was already projecting high out of the water. Strangely, this side had not sustained any damage. The Kapitänleutnant soon ordered the men to inflate their lifejackets and then he jumped over the side along with all the rest of them. As they jumped, the bilge keels appeared out of the water. It was now necessary to swim away as soon as possible to a safe distance from the sinking ship – she could suck him and the other surviving sailors down with her. Müllenheim-Rechberg took a last look at the overturned battleship. The stern was going under, while the bow projected out of the water. An ever-increasing area of the starboard side could be seen. When the survivors swam near the bow, they saw the commander of the *Bismarck*, Kapitän zur See Lindemann, standing there. With him, by 'Anton' turret, was his adjutant. When the ship had considerably increased her list, he signalled for the sailors to quickly swim away from the submerging ship. The commander and his adjutant were trying to reach the flagstaff. Lindemann climbed up the railing on the right side of the stem before the ship turned over completely. He was recognizable by his distinctive white cap. As the battleship sank, the commander saluted her.

The burial at sea of three Bismarck *sailors aboard the cruiser* Sheffield.

Via IWM

The survivors found themselves in the stormy Atlantic, in water of about 13 degreesC. They looked for British vessels that could rescue them but failed to see any nearby. Their situation was changing quickly. Until now, they had kept in small groups – now, frozen and weak, thrust about by the force of the waves, they were separated from one another, scattered over a large area. After an hour of floating in the water, they saw the cruiser *Dorsetshire* steaming in their direction. At 10:56, her crew threw them ropes and rescue nets, and began to collect them from the water. However, this was not an easy task. Apart from the rough water, the oil from the wreckage of the battleship had spread over a vast area, thus making things very difficult. The survivors, who were soaked with it, had serious problems holding onto the ropes. Only few of the sailors managed it. Those lucky men who got on board quickly disappeared below. There they were provided with new, dry clothes. Those who were particularly weak were placed in berths, whereas the wounded were taken to the ship's infirmary to receive first aid. The crew of the *Dorsetshire* did their utmost to rescue as many Germans as they possibly could. While doing so, the *Dorsetshire* sighted a suspicious object that could have been a U-boat. The rescue operation was immediately interrupted (it was 11:46). The cruiser rapidly accelerated in order to get away from the danger zone as quickly as possible. The rescue of the remaining survivors was passed to the destroyer *Maori*. The rescued sailors were assembled at the officers' mess of the *Dorsetshire*, where they were given hot tea. After that, they were divided into two groups – officers, and petty officers and ratings. In total, the *Dorsetshire* took on board four of the former and eighty-one of the latter. The nearby destroyer *Maori* picked up a further twenty-five survivors.

Searching for survivors

On the morning of 26 May, Kapitänleutnant Kentrat, the commander of *U-74*, received an order to provide support for the *Bismarck*. Other U-boats operating in the same waters also received the same instructions. He was told to collect detailed information about the *Bismarck*'s position and situation, and inform his superiors about the results. In the evening, his U-boat had arrived at the narrow operational area of the battleship. About 19:50, he sighted enemy warships passing nearby. These were Somerville's Force H. Forty minutes later, he notified headquarters about the presence of a battleship and an aircraft carrier sailing at high speed. He had to submerge again before midnight because destroyers came his way. Fortunately for him, they were not interested in the U-boat because their objective was the *Bismarck*. From midnight to 04:00 the next day, he saw gunfire on the horizon. He tried to come closer to the *Bismarck*, but the increasing wind and stormy seas made this difficult. About 04:30, he noticed that a heavy cruiser or perhaps a battleship was visible behind the German battleship, some 10,000m (10,950 yards) farther away. The U-boat commander turned but lost sight of the object owing to the low visibility.

About two hours later he made visual contact with Kapitänleutnant Wohlfarth's *U-556*, and requested him to take over the mission of making contact with the *Bismarck*. The operation was interrupted at 07:30, when the British cruiser and the destroyers unexpectedly appeared out of the squall, heading straight at him. The U-boat was about 5,000m (5,465 yards) from them and had to dive at once. After 09:00, the commander of *U-74* heard a powerful explosion, and another one shortly after the first. When his ship surfaced after approximately twenty minutes, he saw nothing. At first he thought that it might have been a Luftwaffe attack scheduled for this hour. Later, he came to the conclusion that it could have been the last battle of the *Bismarck*. At noon, *U-74* was instructed by the commander of the U-boat forces that the boat should begin a search for survivors from the battleship. After about seven hours of patrolling these waters, *U-74* spotted three men in a small dinghy. The crew found it difficult to extract the men from the water due to high waves, but after many attempts they finally succeeded. Soon, the boat was joined by *U-48* and *U-73*. The three submarines formed a line abreast and continued the search for *Bismarck* survivors. Apart from oil slick and wreckage, they did not see anybody. The U-boats did not end their search until midnight of 28 May. *U-74* turned back and headed for the base at Lorient. There, the three survivors were expected and were immediately taken to the Group West headquarters in Paris to be questioned.

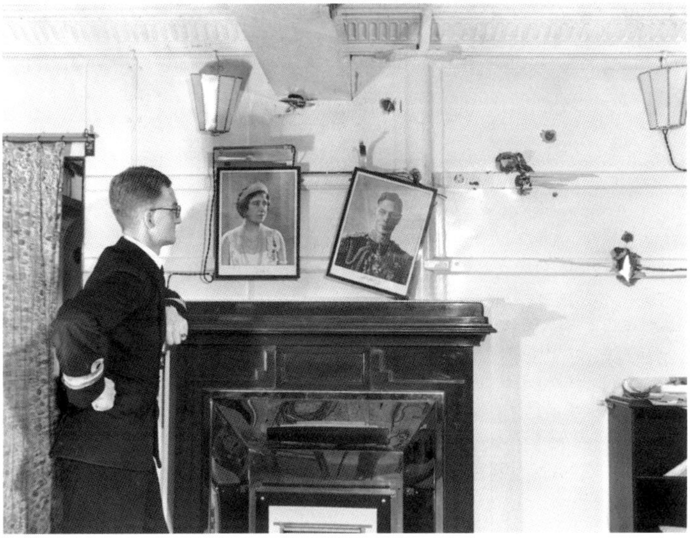

Via IWM

Splinter holes on the Sheffield.

The rescued crewmen of the Bismarck *at a British POW camp.*

Via IWM

While *U-74* had been searching for survivors, another ship joined the rescue operation on 27 May in an area to the south of the submarine. It was the German weather patrol ship *Sachsenwald*, commanded by Kapitänleutnant Schütte. About 02:00 in the morning, the ship was radioed with an order to immediately sail to the *Bismarck*'s location. She increased speed at once and headed for the area in question to the north-east. At about 06:00, she was instructed to stop. Between 11:00 and 12:00, German aircraft were spotted, and soon, at 14:00, the ship received an order to move to another location. In the meantime, the weather had worsened. At 20:10, a British Bristol Blenheim aircraft was sighted and immediately fired at. The *Sachsenwald* spent the entire morning of 28 May unsuccessfully searching for any survivors. In the afternoon, at 13:00, oil slicks were observed on the surface, and the ship turned slightly to the north. The lookouts soon spotted a German gas mask floating on the water. A minute later, they saw countless bodies in life vests, empty life vests, and pieces of wreckage. The *Sachsenwald* searched the area carefully, but no one was found alive. When darkness fell, about 22:30, they saw three red flares in the sky. The ship steamed in that direction at once, scanning the sea surface with infrared devices. Fifteen minutes later she picked up two survivors on a raft. The rescued sailors said that there was another raft nearby with more survivors from the *Bismarck*. They claimed that it might be some way from the ship, having probably been driven farther away from them by the strong wind. The ship continued the search until 01:00 on the night of 30 May, encountering the Spanish cruiser *Canarias*. Both ships exchanged identification signals and continued their search, but these were unsuccessful. The *Sachsenwald* turned back for France, and entered the Gironde on 1 June and sailed on to Le Verdon. On completion of the voyage, both survivors were taken to Paris to report to Group West. The *Canarias*, which continued her search, picked up two bodies (on 30 May), which were identified. Next day, about 10:00, the two sailors were given a burial at sea with full military honours.[9]

[9] *Before the first combat operation of the* Bismarck, *an additional 156 men came on board in mid-May, of whom sixty-five were Admiral Lütjens' staff, and ninety comprised the three prize crews. Departing Gotenhafen on 18 May 1941, the* Bismarck *had 2,221 men aboard, of whom only 115 survived.*

The Home Fleet Returns

Before the *Bismarck* sank, London anxiously awaited the final result of the several days' hunt by almost the entire Home Fleet for the German battleship. On 27 May at 11:00, Winston Churchill informed the House of Commons, meeting at Church House, about the engagement between the British warships and the *Bismarck*. At that moment, he did not yet know the outcome but was convinced that the sinking of the enemy was just a matter of minutes away. A moment later, just as he sat down, he was given a note with the most recent information about the *Bismarck*. He requested permission to speak, and when granted it, he rose and announced to the House that the *Bismarck* had just been sunk.

The battleships *King George V* and *Rodney*, and the destroyers *Cossack*, *Zulu* and *Sikh* were heading north for their bases. At 12:30, they were joined by the cruiser *Dorsetshire* and the destroyer *Maori*. During the day, nine other destroyers joined the group. On the following day, the admiral received several radio messages about the attacks made on the British warships. As the destroyers *Mashona* and *Tartar* were escorting the *Rodney* headed for Londonderry, they were attacked by a formation of German bombers. Despite the accurate anti-aircraft fire from both the destroyers, the *Mashona* took a hit on a boiler and rapidly rolled over. She began to sink, and the crew had to immediately abandon her. The British survivors were rescued by the crew of the destroyer *Tartar*, which also managed to shoot down one of the enemy aircraft.

One of the survivors from the *Bismarck* died aboard the *Dorsetshire* from the wounds he had received: Maschinengefreiter Gerhard Lüttich had suffered severe burns during the battle, and although doctors tried hard to save him, they failed. Next day, he was given a burial in the depths of the Atlantic in the presence of the assembled British and German sailors, in accordance with naval tradition. After a four-day voyage, the *Dorsetshire* brought the *Bismarck* survivors to Newcastle on 30 May. The *Maori*, which sailed separately with a small party of survivors, put in at the Clyde.

That was not the end of duty for the British crews, exhausted as they were after the long pursuit of the *Bismarck*. Most of them reached their bases between 27 and 29 May. They refuelled there and at once set off again, back to the convoys they had earlier abandoned. For many sailors, the joy of having sunk such an opponent as the *Bismarck* made up for the sleepless nights, extreme tension and uncertainty awaiting the final outcome of the chase.

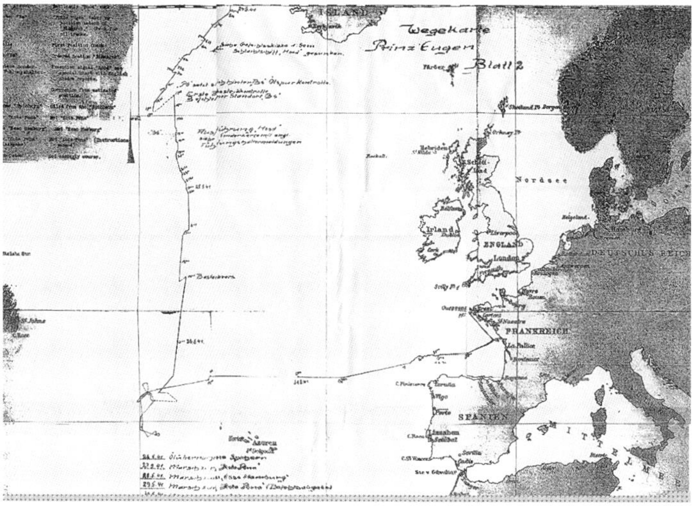

Original map from the heavy cruiser Prinz Eugen *war diary showing the entire course of events of Operation* Rheinübung. *Note* Prinz Eugen*'s route after leaving* Bismarck.

From J. Rico collection

Photo by Lagemann, via S. Breyer

A photograph of the Prinz Eugen *taken after she detached from the* Bismarck. *The cruiser is still bearing remnants of the striped camouflage on gun barrels, whereas her turret tops are painted yellow as an identification sign for German aircraft.*

A lone Prinz Eugen *sailing on a southerly course. The top surfaces of the main battery turrets are painted yellow for identification by aircraft. The swastika on the bow deck has been painted out, which may be an indication that the ship is operating within the range of British patrols and American reconnaissance.*

Photo by Lagemann, via M. Skwiot

British damage

For many years after the war, the British remained silent about the damage sustained by their ships in the battle against the *Bismarck*. The most severe was that suffered by the *Rodney*. Even though she did not receive any direct hits from the *Bismarck*, German shells exploding near her showered her with splinters. There were three small holes on the *Rodney*'s bridge. One penetrated the deck into the searchlight control room. Also, a 150mm shell went through the senior petty officers' mess. Another splinter bounced off to hit the gun director compartment, causing slight damage. As a result of these hits, the telephone lines in the superstructure were cut, which made further communication between the platforms impossible. This damage, however, was not as serious as that caused by the blast of the ship's own main battery! The upper deck around the towers and bulkheads was distorted in various ways. The longitudinals and pillars at the deck level were bent and ripped off like the deck itself. Also, all the ventilation shafts were damaged, with large sections being torn to pieces. The wooden panels in this area were all ripped off the deck. Most deck stringers were either broken or distorted.

The *Rodney* launched a few torpedoes at the *Bismarck* during the battle, an action without precedent in the Second World War. The British, of course, claim to have scored one torpedo hit on the *Bismarck*, but it is difficult to verify the truth of this claim. Most interesting of all, however, were the other things that were happening. The vibrations caused by the

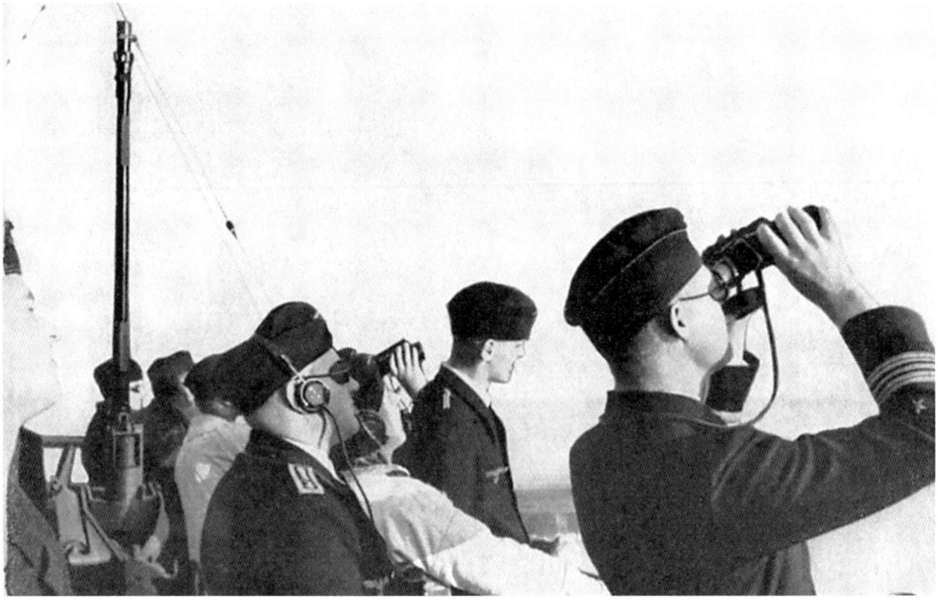

The cruiser's Second Gunnery Officer on duty on the foretop of the Prinz Eugen.

Photo by Lagemann, via AJ-Press

British ship's own main battery when firing and the nearby explosions of German shells caused rivets in the fresh-water tanks above the torpedo compartments to be displaced. The water leaking out of the tanks was slowly but consistently flooding the torpedoes. To make things worse, all the lamps that were installed in this area of the ship had been destroyed, and portable ones were needed. Owing to lack of time to search for them, torches had to be used instead. As if this was not enough, the sluice in the starboard torpedo compartment jammed twice. It was got working again after much effort but it would not stop causing problems and jammed for a third time, this time permanently. Therefore, the port torpedo tubes had to be used. In the meantime, the upper deck had been warped under the pressure of gun blast. These deformations were gradually transferred down through the bracing and brackets. As a result, the torpedo traverse mechanism collapsed by an inch. The two torpedoes that were still in the battleship were stored in the starboard compartment, and they needed to be transported across to the port side to be launched, for which this mechanism was used. The procedure had to be given up because it could not be completed owing to the mechanism's failure.

Finally, it is noteworthy that the hunt for the *Bismarck* and the *Rodney*'s steaming at the full speed of 20–21 knots over the last few days caused vibrations which loosened the riveted joints in the hull and unsealed the fuel tanks, the leaking fuel oil leaving a trail in the ship's wake. The broadside salvoes, vibrations and gas pressure were constantly increasing the damage to the hull. As a result, the defects and design flaws of the *Rodney* were revealed, which fact was not mentioned by the British for many years after the event.

The *Prinz Eugen* alone

On 24 May 1941, at 18:14, the *Prinz Eugen* had successfully executed Operation *Hood* – separating from the *Bismarck* – on the second attempt, and shook off her British pursuers. The lone *Prinz Eugen* accelerated to 31 knots and assumed her new course. Owing to the low fuel supply, this now being 1,350cu m (45 per cent of

The machinery crew of the Prinz Eugen *resting on the deck at leisure. Sitting on the left is the cruiser's anti-aircraft battery commander.*

Photo by Lagemann, via AJ-Press

capacity), the ship had to refuel in the next few hours. Two tankers, the *Lothringen* and the *Belchen*, were nearest. It was, however, difficult to find their exact bearings. Continuing on the same course, the cruiser launched a seaplane whose task was to search the area for the German tankers. The flight ended without the expected results – while patrolling, the seaplane only

Photo by Busch, via AJ-Press

The admiral's bridge on the Prinz Eugen *– the officer in sunglasses is the First Gunnery Officer.*

The cruiser's Navigation Officer finding the current position using a sextant.

Photo by Busch, via AJ-Press

sighted a lone American ship. In the evening, the commander of the *Prinz Eugen*, Kapitän zur See Brinkmann, radioed Group West, informing them of the cruiser's critical fuel situation. They replied saying that he should steer toward the tanker *Esso Hamburg*. Two hours later, the cruiser received another radio message containing the bearings of the tanker *Spichern* in Square BD 78. For the rest of the evening of 24 May, the cruiser continued her voyage south. The weather in the Atlantic began to grow worse. The wind became more forceful, and waves swept over the fore conning tower, reaching even as high as the admiral's bridge. Patches of fog appeared in places, visibility slowly decreasing. In the morning, refuelling became the most vital issue for the heavy cruiser. From intercepted radio messages, the situation of the nearby *Bismarck* was already known.

On 25 May, at about 02:11, Group West passed instructions to the *Prinz Eugen* about her rendezvous with the tanker *Spichern* that day and with the *Esso Hamburg* on the 26th. The *Prinz Eugen* was steering on a southerly course to reach the given bearings. Radio interception carried on the entire day but nothing happened until evening. An air raid alert was issued at 19:41 but this turned out to be a false alarm. On the morning of 26 May, the cruiser's

From Prinz Eugen *archive*

At the Prinz Eugen*'s AA artillery battle station.*

The Prinz Eugen *after the war.*

Via IWM

hydrophones picked up the sound of an unidentified vessel, which slowly appeared on the horizon. At 06:20, this was identified as the tanker *Spichern*. After less than two hours, refuelling started. A total of 480cu m was pumped into the cruiser, comprising turbine oil, aircraft fuel, and supplies of boiler, drinking and general-purpose water. The procedure was finished in the late evening, at 22:00. Her tanks now being full, the *Prinz Eugen* was able to resume operations against British shipping along the HX convoy routes, to the west of the 35th Parallel. The ship was instructed to go to that area, where the patrol vessels *Kota Pennang* and *Gonzeheim* were already operating.

On 27 May, Brinkmann decided to alter course, heading straight for the southern area of

Via IWM

The Prinz Eugen *being escorted by the* Dorsetshire. *The German heavy cruiser survived the war and finished her career at the Bikini Atoll A-bomb tests.*

operations. While *en route* there, the *Prinz Eugen* received a message from the *Bismarck* about a torpedo hit in the morning. When she was sunk, most of the British ships were in the north, headed for home. The cruiser shortly received a worrying message from Group West – it was sent from an Italian submarine and informed them about five battleships steaming south-west at a very high speed. The current bearings of the British warships indicated that they were off the Azores, and Brinkmann thought they were deployed in search of his cruiser. Therefore he changed his route, turning more to the north. This decision was not the best one, however, as he could be quickly found there by the British and American Catalina flying boats. Although war had not been officially declared, the Americans were informally helping the British in reconnaissance and searching for German U-boats in the Atlantic. Going east, the *Prinz Eugen* was located by an American Coast Guard vessel, the USS *Spencer*. Brinkmann knew that his course would be forwarded to the British and that their heavy warships would arrive there. With this in view, he decided to move further to the south and attack ships along the Lisbon–New York route, depending on supplies from the *Breme* and the *Ermland*. In the afternoon, the cruiser intercepted a message about the sinking of the *Bismarck*. This news had a very depressing effect on her men.

At 22:50, there was trouble in the engine room. High-pressure steam escaped from the main pipeline between No. 1 and No. 2 port boiler rooms. As a result, the port turbine could not work at full power, whereas the starboard one had a limited capacity. The propulsion unit was suffering from vibrations caused by a propeller after it was damaged by a piece of floating ice during the passage of the Denmark Strait. This was not the end of the trouble. More defects were discovered, and they were sufficient for the interruption of the operation. The critical issue appeared when the port turbine stopped following a failure of the bearing in the low-pressure side turbine. The cruiser's maximum speed dropped to 28 knots, and it seemed that it might drop even lower later on. Such bad news from the engine rooms caused the commander's decision to advise Group West on 31 May that the operation be suspended and the ship recalled to Brest. He also requested the 5th Destroyer Flotilla to provide escort while he was heading for Brest. His mission was over.

Appendix

DAMAGE TO THE *BISMARCK*

24 May 1941 (all port)

1. 14in shell hit (from the *Prince of Wales*) around compartments XXI–XXIII.
2. 14in shell hit (from the *Prince of Wales*) in one of the boats.
3. 14in shell hit (from the *Prince of Wales*) – underwater, around compartments XIII–XIV.
4. Aerial torpedo hit (Swordfish from the *Victorious*) – starboard.

26 May 1941 (Two aerial torpedo hits by Swordfish from the *Ark Royal*)

5. Around engine room – compartments VIII and IX
6. Near the rudders.

27 May 1941

No	Time	Calibre	Description
7.	08:59	16in	Shell fired at a range of 18,300m (20,000 yards), caused fires on the fore deck near 'Anton' and 'Bruno' turrets, knocking them out (afterwards only one salvo was fired from them, at 09:27 from 'Anton' turret).
8.	08:59	8in	Shell hit the forward fire control position, devastating it.
9.	09:00–05	?	Shell hit below the catapult platform and exploded among 105mm shells.
10.	09:00–15	8in	Shell hit the starboard forward 150mm gun turret. The explosion jammed the hatch, trapping the crew inside.

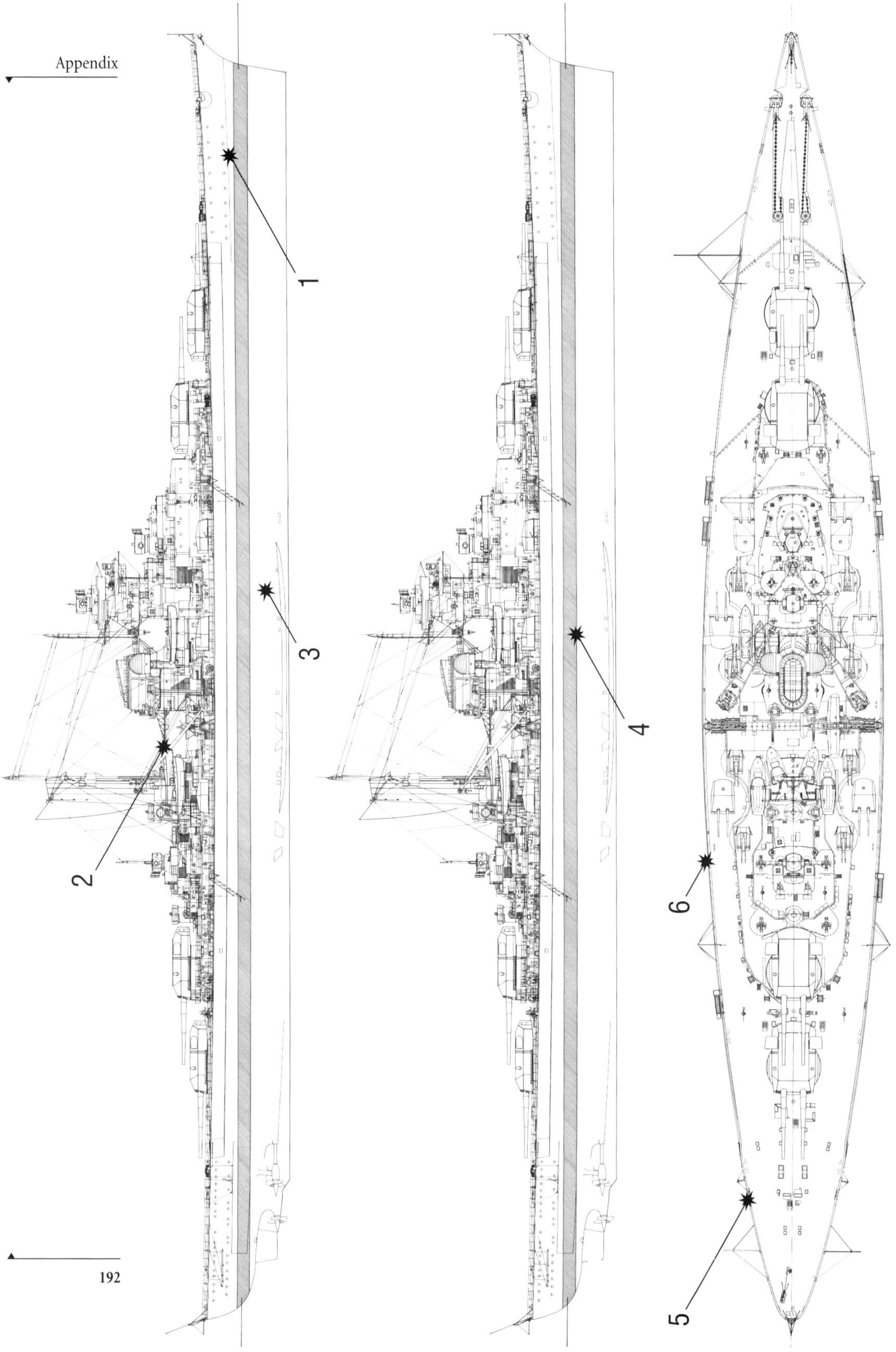
1
2
3
4
5
6

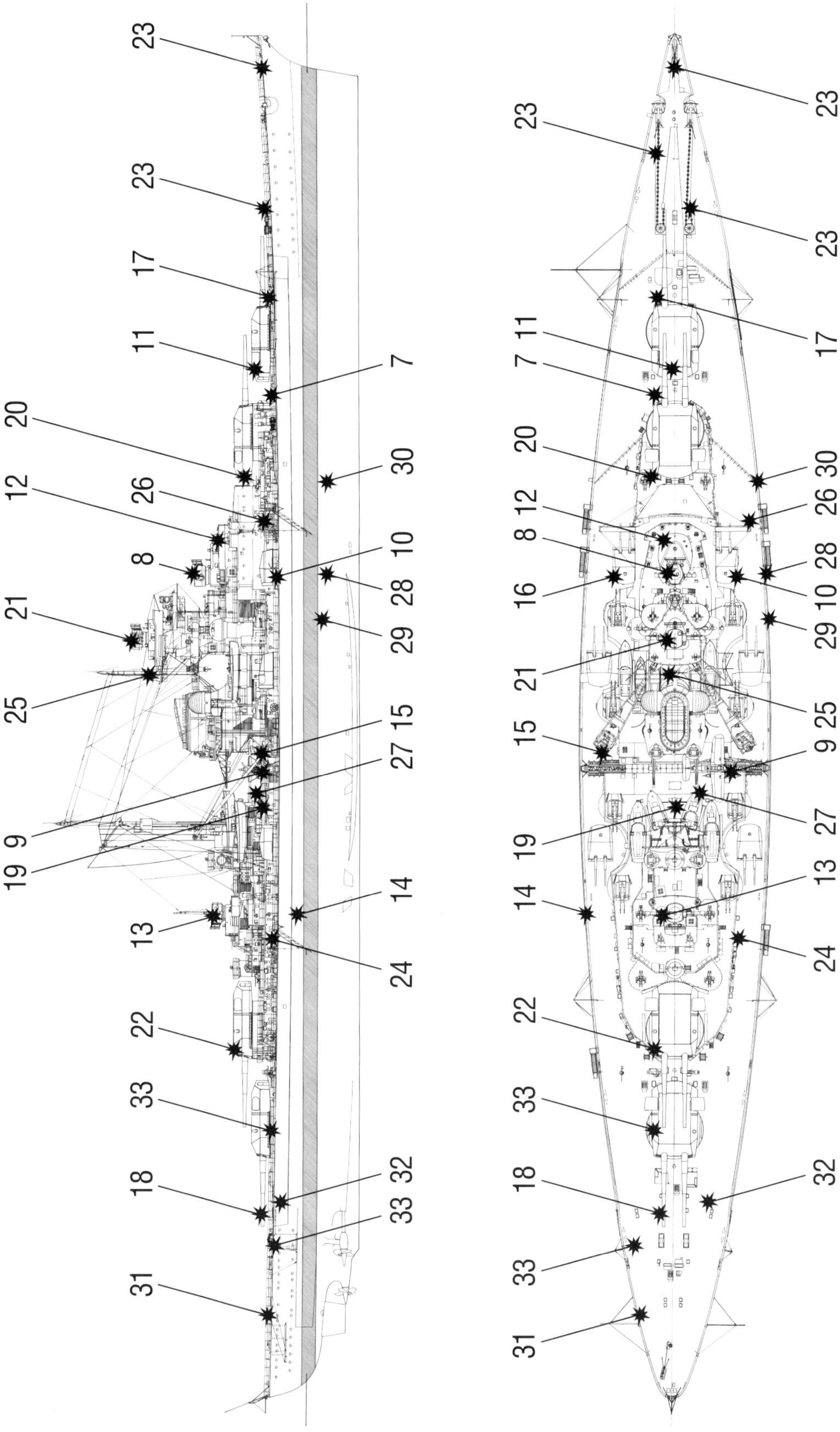
23
23
17
11
7
20
30
12
26
8
10
28
21
29
25
15
27
9
19
14
13
24
22
33
32
18
33
31
23
23
23
17
11
7
20
30
12
26
8
28
16
10
29
21
25
15
9
27
19
13
14
24
22
33
18
32
33
31

No	Time	Calibre	Description
11.	09:02	16in	Shell hit 'Anton' turret. Fragments damaged 'Bruno' turret and killed almost all personnel on the exposed part of the bridge.
12.	09:12	14in or 16in	Shell destroyed the bridge and forward conning tower.
13.	09:13	14in	Shell hit the aft range finder arm and blew off the optical equipment.
14.	?	14in or 16in	Shell (or shells) hit the portside forward power plant, starting a fire in the transformer.
15.	?	14in or 16in	Shell hit the main deck (level 01) portside, setting off the ready-use ammunition stored there.
16.	?	14, 16 and 8in	Shells hit the port forward 150mm turret and its magazine, causing an internal explosion which shattered the roof plate. Splinters and armour fragments damaged nearby superstructure.
17.	09:27	14in	A salvo (observed from the *Norfolk*), fired at a range between 7,300 to 10,000m (8,000 to 11,000 yards). hit near 'Anton' turret. The turret suffered hydraulic failure and the gun barrels fell to downmost position.
18.	09:31	?	Left gun barrel of 'Dora' turret was blown off. The right gun managed to fire two more rounds. Smoke and flames forced the crew to evacuate the turret.
19.	09:30–35	16in?	Shell, probably 16in, fired from 3,700m (4,050 yards) hit the armoured deck and penetrated into the port engine room.
20.	09:40	16in	Shell (or shells), fired from 6,900–7,400m (7,550–8,100 yards) caused a massive explosion behind 'Bruno' turret, blowing off most of the upper armour plates covering the bridge. A big hole in the barbette and a small fire in the turret was observed.
21.	009:30–35	16in	A probable hit on the foretop fire control position caused it to fall to port.
22.	09:21	14in	Shell hit the front plate of 'Cäsar' turret. It failed to penetrate, but the concussion damaged the elevation mechanism of the left gun. Splinters penetrated the deck and started a series of fires, which were quickly extinguished.
23.	?	?	A series of hits on the bow. One, probably a 16in shell, opened up the deck and started a fire in the living quarters below. Other shells blew off the stem and all the bow anchors.
24.	?	?	Three shells hit near the aft conning tower and blew great holes in the upper deck.
25.	09:50–10:00	?	A hit brought down the foremast.
26.	?	?	Shell destroyed the radio room in compartment XV.
27.	?	?	Shell hit the hangar. The plane was burned (compartment X or XI).
28.	?	?	Two or three shells killed the personnel in the radio room in compartment XV.
29.	10:00–05	16in	Shell exploded in the forward canteen, killing around 200 men who were there.

No	*Time*	*Calibre*	*Description*
30.	?	16in	Shell penetrated the armoured belt below the waterline between 'Bruno' turret and the bridge. The hit was reported by a junior officer from the *Bismarck*, who was rescued. At that time the *Rodney* was firing at a range of just 2,500m (2,750 yards).
31.	10:11	16in	Shell hit compartments I and II, causing structural damage to the stern, which fell off around fifteen minutes later.
32.	?	?	Shell hit compartment IV, destroying the ventilation system of the aft part of the main deck.
33.	09:50–10.00	16in	Two shells hit compartment IV. Escape routes were damaged. One shell penetrated the port rear quarter of the barbette of 'Dora' turret. Prompt flooding of the magazine prevented further explosion of 380mm ammunition.

Note: The hits are described according to observations made from the ships firing on the *Bismarck* and accounts of the surviving crewmembers of the German battleship. The accounts were often contradictory. There could have been more hits, especially in the final stages of the engagement.

Based on: Koop, Schmolke, *Bismarck*.
W. H. Garzke, R. O. Dulin, *Battleships. Axis and Neutral Battleships in World War II.*

Index

German ranks abbreviated thus:
Kapitän zur See – KS; Fregattenkapitän – FK; Korvettenkapitän – KK; Kapitänleutnant – KL; Oberleutnant Zur See – OL; Leutnant zur See – Ltn.

Bibliography

Basic source documents regarding Operation *Rheinübung*:

1. Kriegstagebuch *Bismarck* (*Bismarck* war diary),
   Bundesarchiv/Militärarchiv, RM 92/5100.
2. Kriegstagebuch *Prinz Eugen* (*Prinz Eugen* war diary),
   Bundesarchiv/Militärarchiv, RM 92/5220.
3. Kriegstagebuch Marinegruppenkommando Nord, Marinegruppenkommando West (documents of German Group 'Nord' HQ and Group 'West' HQ), from Bundesarchiv/Militararchiv, Naval Historical Centre and authors' collections.

Books:

1. Burkard von Müllenheim-Rechberg: *Battleship* Bismarck, *a Survivor's Story.*
   Naval Institute Press, Annapolis 1990.
2. W. Garzke, R. Dulin: *Battleships – Axis and Neutral Battleships in World War II.*
   Naval Institute Press, Annapolis 1985.
3. W. Garzke, R. Dulin: *Battleships – Allied Battleships in World War II.*
   Naval Institute Press, Annapolis 1990.
4. R. Ballard: *The Discovery of the* Bismarck.
   Madison Press Books 1990.
5. S. Breyer, G. Koop: *Schlachtschiff* Bismarck. *Eine technikgeschichtliche Dokumentation.*
   Bechtermünz Verlag, Augsburg 1997.
6. J. Brennecke: *Schlachtschiff* Bismarck.
   Herford 1960.
7. M. Whitley: *German Capital Ships.*
   Arms & Armour Press 1990.

We also used many other publications and magazines, which due to their quantity were omitted here.